CONTENTS

HOW TO PLAY — 4

Game Basics	6
Winning Tactics	26
Equipment	36

WALKTHROUGH — 40

Introduction	42
Level 1	44
Level 2	62
Level 3	76
Level 4	88
Level 5	102
Level 6	116
Level 7	130
Level 8	142

EXTRAS — 144

Secrets: Croft Manor	146
Secrets: Rewards	155
Secrets: Unlockables	164
Secrets: Cast	171
Previous Adventures	174
Behind the Scenes	180

INDEX — 193

Index Tab

The index tab on the right-hand margin of each double-page spread is a navigational tool designed to help you find your way around the guide. The upper index lists chapters, while the lower indexes display the different sections of the chapter you are currently reading.

Using the Foldout

The back cover foldout features both an explanation of the symbols that appear on maps throughout the guide, plus details on basic button commands for the PlayStation 2, Xbox 360, Xbox and PC versions of Tomb Raider Legend.

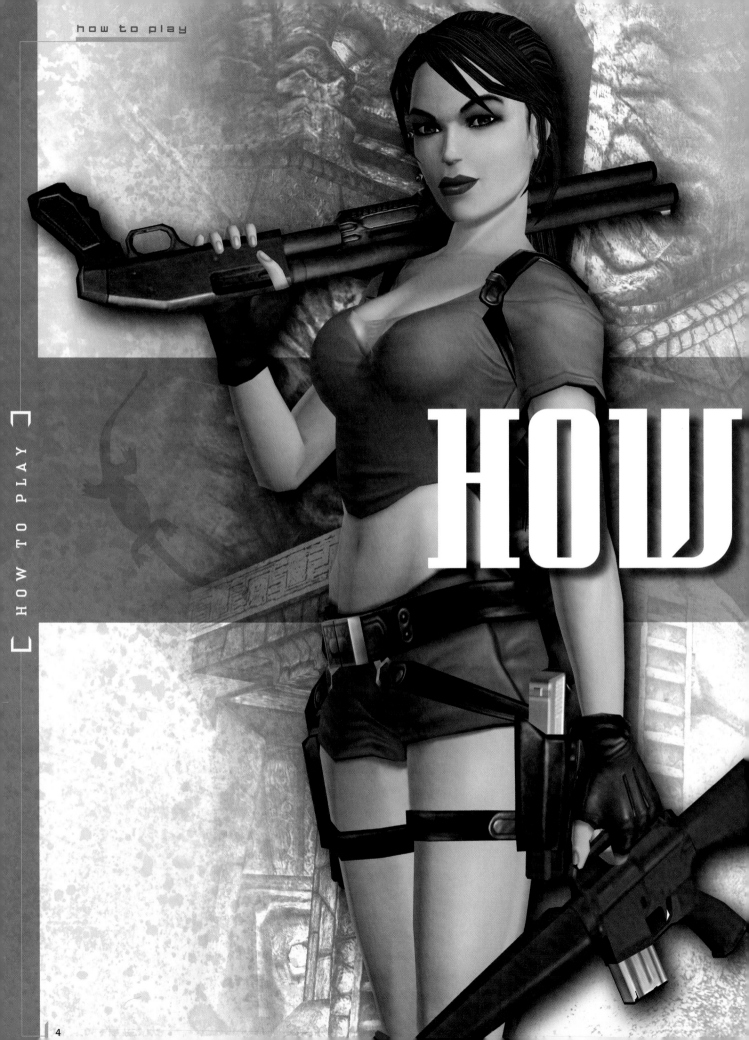

HOW

1st CHAPTER

TO PLAY

This chapter has been designed to introduce you to everything you'll need to know in order to play Tomb Raider Legend. It has been arranged in a manner that will enable you to choose the level of assistance you require. If you simply want to study how to control Lara, the Game Basics section will suit your needs without revealing any spoilers. If, on the other hand, you want to maximize your chances of success, you should read the Winning Tactics section as well. The final part of this chapter covers the equipment, weapons and vehicles Lara can use during her adventure.

GAME BASICS

This section deals with the fundamental mechanics of Tomb Raider Legend. It will help you to get up and running (and, moreover, leaping, diving and climbing) by covering all essential gameplay functions, commands and features.

FIRST STEPS

USING MENUS

Menu navigation is easy. Move the cursor and make your selection with ✛ or ⓛ, then confirm with ⓧ or (START). To cancel or return to a previous screen or menu, press ⓪. These commands are universal, and apply to all menus.

HOW TO START A GAME

The first time you load Tomb Raider Legend there are two ways to begin play. You can select Start Game on the Main Menu, or choose Load and then New Game (Fig. 1). Both methods are functionally identical. If Tomb Raider Legend recognizes a previous save file, Start Game will be replaced by the Resume Game option. This enables you to immediately restart your last saved game.

[0 1]

CHOOSING A DIFFICULTY LEVEL

When you choose the Start Game option for the first time, you are given three options to adjust, including the difficulty level (Fig. 2). Depending on your past gaming experience and expectations, be sure to choose the level that will best suit you. You can also choose to change the difficulty level after successfully completing each stage. Please consult the table below for a detailed description on how the difficulty levels affect the gameplay.

If you have the requisite hardware, you can also activate the Widescreen and Progressive Scan Mode options here.

[0 2]

Parameter	Difficulty level	Influence		
Level of enemy accuracy when shooting at Lara	Explorer – Easy	Ineffective ◄	40%	► Effective
	Adventurer – Medium		80%	
	Tomb Raider – Hard		100%	
Health lost when hit by an enemy or environmental hazard	Explorer – Easy	Less damage ◄	39%	► More damage
	Adventurer – Medium		77%	
	Tomb Raider – Hard		100%	
Frequency of health packs dropped by enemies	Explorer – Easy	Less ◄	38%	► More
	Adventurer – Medium		28%	
	Tomb Raider – Hard		20%	
Window of opportunity for saving grab after an inaccurate jump	Explorer – Easy	Less ◄	2 sec.	► More
	Adventurer – Medium		1.5 sec.	
	Tomb Raider – Hard		1 sec.	

HOW TO SAVE

Once play begins, you can save your position at any time via the Pause menu. To do so, press (START) and select the Save option (Fig. 3). Complete the process by choosing a save file slot, and then press ⊗. If you select a slot that already contains a file, remember that you will overwrite that file, replacing it permanently with the new save data. You will, however, be asked for confirmation before this takes place.

No matter when or where you save your game, Lara's death will lead to you resuming the adventure from the last activated checkpoint.

HOW TO LOAD

Select Resume Game at the Main Menu to load your most recent save file. To load a specific save file, select Load, and then Load Game (Fig. 4). If you have more than one save file available, choose the one you want to use and confirm with ⊗. Once you have completed a level, you can chose to load it from its starting point by selecting Load Level. This feature is also accessible during the game via the Pause menu: press (START) to reach it. Please turn to page 10 for more information.

[0 3]

[0 4]

HOW TO PLAY

WALKTHROUGH

EXTRAS

GAME BASICS

WINNING TACTICS

EQUIPMENT

FIRST STEPS

BUTTON CONFIGURATION

THE MAIN MENU

ONSCREEN DISPLAY

CONTROLLING LARA

SUPER ACTIONS

USING THE CAMERA

THE PAUSE MENU

THE PDA MENU

BUTTON CONFIGURATION

PS2 controller

SELECT START

DIRECTIONAL BUTTONS ✛

LEFT ANALOG STICK/ⓛ BUTTON Ⓛ

RIGHT ANALOG STICK/ⓡ BUTTON Ⓡ

SONY PlayStation ANALOG

L2 R2

L1 L3 R3 R1

Command	In menus	Normal gameplay	Vehicles
✛	Move cursor	✛: change weapon ✛: use Health Pack ✛: turn Personal Light Source on/off ✛: draw/put away binoculars	- ✛: use Health Pack - -
Ⓛ	Move cursor	Move Lara	Steer
Ⓡ	-	Move camera; tap to move lock-on between targets	Move camera
⊗	Confirm	Jump; activate Magnetic Grapple during jump (if grapple point is near); dive	Accelerate
△	Cancel	Kick, grab/release objects; pull Magnetic Grapple; move at a faster rate; shoot destructible objects	-
▢	-	Use Magnetic Grapple	Brake/reverse
○	Cancel	Crouch/roll; surface	-
L1	-	Combat Lock	Raise fork (forklift only)
L2	-	Reset camera (moves view to behind Lara's back)	Lower fork (forklift only)
R1	-	Fire weapon	Raise fork (forklift only)
R2	-	Throw grenade, throw flare	Lower fork (forklift only)
R3	-	Activate/deactivate Manual Aim mode	-
START	Confirm	Display Pause menu	Display Pause menu
SELECT	-	Display PDA menu	-

Xbox 360 controller

BACK	◀	
LEFT THUMBSTICK/ Ⓛ BUTTON	Ⓛ	
START	▶	
DIRECTIONAL PAD	✛	
RIGHT THUMBSTICK/ Ⓡ BUTTON	Ⓡ	

LB · LT · ⓧ · RT · RB · Y · B · A · X

Command	In menus	Normal gameplay	Vehicles
✛	Move cursor	✛: change weapon ✛: use Health Pack ✛: turn Personal Light Source on/off ✛: draw/put away binoculars	- ✛: use Health Pack - -
Ⓛ	Move cursor	Move Lara	Steer
Ⓡ	-	Move camera; tap to move lock-on between targets	Move camera
Ⓐ	Confirm	Jump; activate Magnetic Grapple during jump (if grapple point is near); dive	Accelerate
Ⓨ	Cancel	Kick, grab/release objects; pull Magnetic Grapple; move at a faster rate; shoot destructible objects	-
Ⓧ	-	Use Magnetic Grapple	Brake/reverse
Ⓑ	Cancel	Crouch/roll; surface	-
LT	-	Combat Lock	Raise fork (forklift only)
LB	-	Reset camera (moves view to behind Lara's back)	Lower fork (forklift only)
RT	-	Fire weapon	Raise fork (forklift only)
RB	-	Throw grenade, throw flare	Lower fork (forklift only)
Ⓡ	-	Activate/deactivate Manual Aim mode	-
▶	Confirm	Display Pause menu	Display Pause menu
◀	-	Display PDA menu	-
ⓧ	Display Xbox 360 Dashboard	Display Xbox 360 Dashboard	Display Xbox 360 Dashboard

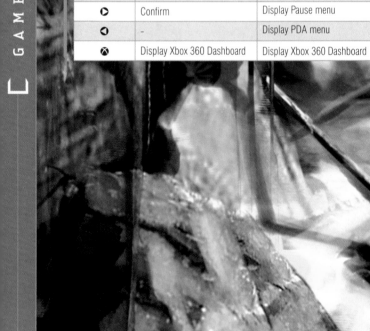

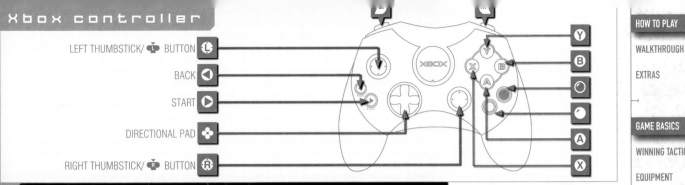

Xbox controller

LEFT THUMBSTICK/ 🅛 BUTTON 🅛

BACK ◀

START ▶

DIRECTIONAL PAD ✜

RIGHT THUMBSTICK/ 🅡 BUTTON 🅡

HOW TO PLAY

WALKTHROUGH

EXTRAS

GAME BASICS

WINNING TACTICS

EQUIPMENT

FIRST STEPS

BUTTON
CONFIGURATION

THE MAIN MENU

ONSCREEN
DISPLAY

CONTROLLING
LARA

SUPER ACTIONS

USING THE
CAMERA

THE PAUSE MENU

THE PDA MENU

Command	In menus	Normal gameplay	Vehicles
✜	Move cursor	✜: change weapon ✜: use Health Pack ✜: turn Personal Light Source on/off ✜: draw/put away binoculars	- ✜: use Health Pack - -
🅛	Move cursor	Move Lara	Steer
🅡	-	Move camera; tap to move lock-on between targets	Move camera
Ⓐ	Confirm	Jump; activate Magnetic Grapple during jump (if grapple point is near); dive	Accelerate
Ⓨ	Cancel	Kick, grab/release objects; pull Magnetic Grapple; move at a faster rate; shoot destructible objects	-
Ⓧ	-	Use Magnetic Grapple	Brake/reverse
Ⓑ	Cancel	Crouch/roll; surface	-
LT	-	Combat Lock	Raise fork (forklift only)
◯	-	Reset camera (moves view to behind Lara's back)	Lower fork (forklift only)
RT	-	Fire weapon	Raise fork (forklift only)
●	-	Throw grenade, throw flare	Lower fork (forklift only)
🅡	-	Activate/deactivate Manual Aim mode	-
▶	Confirm	Display Pause menu	Display Pause menu
◀	-	Display PDA menu	-

PC controller

Command	In menus	Normal gameplay	Vehicles
✜	Move cursor	✜: change weapon ✜: use Health Pack ✜: turn Personal Light Source on/off ✜: draw/put away binoculars	- ✜: use Health Pack - -
🅛	Move cursor	Move Lara	Steer
🅡	-	Move camera; tap to move lock-on between targets	Move camera
Jump button	Confirm	Jump; activate Magnetic Grapple during jump (if grapple point is near); dive	Accelerate
Kick button	Cancel	Kick, grab/release objects; pull Magnetic Grapple; move at a faster rate; shoot destructible objects	-
Grapple button	-	Use Magnetic Grapple	Brake/reverse
Crouch button	Cancel	Crouch/roll; surface	-
Weapon button	-	Combat Lock	Raise fork (forklift only)
Reset camera button	-	Reset camera (moves view to behind Lara's back)	Lower fork (forklift only)
Fire button	-	Fire weapon	Raise fork (forklift only)
Grenade button	-	Throw grenade, throw flare	Lower fork (forklift only)
Manual Aim button	-	Activate/deactivate Manual Aim mode	-
Start button	Confirm	Display Pause menu	Display Pause menu
PDA button	-	Display PDA menu	-

BUTTON COMMANDS ON OTHER FORMATS

We use PlayStation 2 controller symbols to represent button commands and combinations throughout this guide. If you are playing Tomb Raider Legend on Xbox, Xbox 360 or PC, don't worry: while there are obvious differences between the controllers used with each format, translating PS2 button commands to suit your Xbox, Xbox 360 or PC joypad is easy – as the table on the right demonstrates.

For your convenience, this table also appears on the back cover foldout for easy reference. You'll find that the translation of button commands becomes second nature in next to no time. We have tried to limit the use of button symbols in the Walkthrough and Extras chapters to instances when they are absolutely necessary. If you take the time to learn the various moves you can achieve with your controller – as listed from page 14 onward – you will soon find that performing each action as required (or prompted) becomes entirely instinctive.

PS2	Xbox	Xbox 360	PC
✕	Ⓐ	Ⓐ	Jump button
□	✕	✕	Grapple button
◎	Ⓑ	Ⓑ	Crouch button
△	Ⓨ	Ⓨ	Kick button
L1	LT	LT	Weapon button
R1	RT	RT	Fire button
L2	◐	LB	Reset camera button
R2	●	RB	Grenade button
R3	Ř	Ř	Manual Aim button
START	◐	◐	Start button
SELECT	◖	◖	PDA button

[05]

THE MAIN MENU

START GAME/RESUME GAME

This option (Fig. 5) is the equivalent of a "quick start" feature. It enables you to resume your game directly from where you last saved it – the corresponding details appear to the right of the menu – or start from the beginning of the adventure when you play for the first time.

LOAD

Use this menu to start a new game from the beginning (New Game), load a file that you have previously saved (Load Game – Fig. 6) or play a level that you have unlocked in one of your save files (Load Level).

[06]

CROFT MANOR

This option is unlocked once you complete the first level of Tomb Raider Legend and save your progress. It offers access to Lara's home (Fig. 7), where you can enjoy a virtual "scavenger hunt" as you explore its rooms in search of 27 Rewards. A comprehensive walkthrough of this level, including instructions on how to play and useful tips for independent-minded treasure hunters, can be found in the Extras chapter.

[07]

OPTIONS

You can configure various elements of Tomb Raider Legend via the Options menu (Fig. 8). Any changes you make with ✛ must be confirmed with ⊗, or they will not be implemented. Please note that certain options are only available on specific platforms.

[0 8]

SOUND: ENABLES YOU TO…

- Adjust the volume of the music (between 0 and 100).
- Adjust the volume of sound effects (between 0 and 100).
- Adjust the volume of speech (between 0 and 100).

DISPLAY: ENABLES YOU TO…

- Turn subtitles on or off.
- Position the screen vertically.
- Position the screen horizontally.
- Turn the Widescreen option on or off.
- Activate/disable the Progressive Scan display mode.

CAMERA: ENABLES YOU TO…

- Invert the X-axis, which means you have to tilt 🕹 left to move the camera to the right, and right to move it to the left.
- Invert the Y-axis, which means you have to tilt 🕹 up to move the camera downwards, and down to move it upwards.
- Invert the X-axis in Manual Aim mode and while using the binoculars.
- Invert the Y-axis in Manual Aim mode and while using the binoculars.

CONTROL: ENABLES YOU TO…

- Choose a controller configuration: the default setup, or one of three alternatives.
- Choose from one of three "Combat" modes. With "Standard", you hold L1 to draw Lara's weapon, and release the button to put it away. She will automatically target the nearest enemy in the direction that she is facing, and the camera will follow that assailant until the lock-on is lost. With "Advanced Hold", the same button discipline applies, but camera control is manual, and Lara will specifically target the enemy nearest the centre of the screen. "Advanced Toggle" is the same as "Advanced Hold" with one key difference: rather than holding L1, you tap it once to place Lara in a state of combat readiness, and press it again to put her weapons away.
- Turn the vibration function on or off.

CALIBRATION/PICTURE: ENABLES YOU TO…

- Adjust the brightness within a range running from 0 to 100.
- Adjust the contrast within a range running from 0 to 100.

HOW TO PLAY

WALKTHROUGH

EXTRAS

GAME BASICS

WINNING TACTICS

EQUIPMENT

FIRST STEPS

BUTTON CONFIGURATION

THE MAIN MENU

ONSCREEN DISPLAY

CONTROLLING LARA

SUPER ACTIONS

USING THE CAMERA

THE PAUSE MENU

THE PDA MENU

EXTRAS

The Extras menu (Fig. 9) enables you to view and interact with all the bonuses you have unlocked in a specific save file. A complete list of all Rewards featured in Tomb Raider Legend – and how to unlock them – can be found in the Extras chapter. However, bear in mind that you could spoil a number of surprises if you rush to read it now. We recommend that you consult the Extras chapter as and when required during play – but this is, of course, entirely at your discretion.

[09]

USING THE PAUSE MENU

During play, you can access the Pause menu by pressing START at any time. The basic options – Return to Game, Options, Save, Load and Quit – are fairly self-explanatory, or are covered earlier in this chapter. However, an additional option – Skip Cinematic – appears during cutscenes. Use this to resume play immediately when required.

ONSCREEN DISPLAY

HOW TO PLAY

WALKTHROUGH

EXTRAS

GAME BASICS

WINNING TACTICS

EQUIPMENT

FIRST STEPS

BUTTON
CONFIGURATION

THE MAIN MENU

ONSCREEN
DISPLAY

CONTROLLING
LARA

SUPER ACTIONS

USING THE
CAMERA

THE PAUSE MENU

THE PDA MENU

1 LIFE GAUGE – The life gauge represents Lara's health. If it is ever completely depleted, the game will be over and you will be sent back to the last activated checkpoint. There are a number of ways that Lara's life gauge can be reduced partially or entirely, such as plummeting from great heights, falling afoul of traps, or being attacked by enemies.

2 CURRENT WEAPON – The weapon you select is the one Lara will use during fights. Lara can carry one extra weapon in addition to her standard pistols. You can switch between them by pressing ✛. Refer to page 19 for more information.

3 CURRENT AMMUNITION – This number shows the amount of shots remaining in Lara's current weapon. Whenever it reaches 0, Lara automatically reloads (but only if she has a magazine in reserve). This takes time, which can make her extremely vulnerable during combat encounters. Lara also reloads whenever she puts her weapon away.

4 TOTAL AMMUNITION – The number shows the remaining stock of bullets of Lara's current weapon, excluding those currently loaded in the weapon's magazine. If this figure is at 0, remember that the bullets loaded in the weapon are the last ones you can count on. Handily, Lara carries an infinite supply of ammo for her default pistols.

5 GRENADES – The number of grenades Lara is carrying, up to a maximum of 4. See page 39 for further details.

6 EQUIPMENT – Most of the time, Lara has four different items of equipment at her disposal. Their icons appear in the corresponding position to the direction that must be pressed on ✛ to use them: ✛ for Health Packs, ✛ for the Personal Light Source, ✛ to change weapons, and ✛ for the binoculars.

7 HEALTH PACKS – This number shows how many Health Packs you have in stock. Lara can carry a maximum of three at any time. If Lara's health is dangerously low, the Health Pack icon will flash to indicate that it's a good idea to use one immediately. Refer to page 38 to learn more.

8 PLS POWER GAUGE – Every time you activate the Personal Light Source, its power gauge will steadily decrease. Once it is completely empty, the device will automatically turn itself off – which means you must wait a few seconds for its power source to recharge. Turn to page 37 for more information.

9 TARGETING CURSOR – The targeting cursor highlights the enemy that Lara currently has in her sights. Any shot you take will be in the direction of that assailant. There are a few different types of targeting cursor, and each one relates different information that will help you during combat. Please turn to page 30 for more information.

10 DESTRUCTIBLE OBJECTS – Press Ⓐ when you see the Ⓐ symbol (or, for other formats, equivalent button icon) highlighting an object or piece of scenery to make Lara automatically aim and shoot at it. Refer to page 19 for further information.

CONTROLLING LARA

BASIC MOVES

RUNNING
🄛

Make Lara run by tilting 🄛 firmly in the required direction. This is the standard pace at which you will move for much of the game, so take time to become accustomed to directing Lara at this speed. Running is vital throughout Tomb Raider Legend: as well as getting from A to B, you'll need to run to reach distant ledges while leaping, to dodge traps or boulders and, of course, to avoid gunfire.

WALKING
🄛

Whenever you encounter something that you know (or simply suspect) should be approached with a degree of care and caution, you can make Lara walk or creep by tilting 🄛 gently in the required direction. This is, for example, an ideal way to check what lies below when you reach a cliff.

JUMPING
🄛 + ⊗

Press ⊗ to make a vertical jump; press ⊗ with 🄛 held to make Lara jump in a specific direction, with her speed of movement determining the distance traveled. While running on a flat surface, tap ⊗ to hop, and double-tap ⊗ to perform a jump and somersault. It's a rather more advanced technique – and one that serves no specific purpose – but if you begin rapidly tapping ⊗ just before Lara lands after a somersault, she can perform up to three eye-catching forward flips followed by a final double flip.

MOVE CAMERA
Ⓡ

More often than not, the trick to solving puzzles and finding the exit to a room is observation. By using Ⓡ, you can move the camera around, above and under Lara, which enables you to scan each location from almost every angle.

RESET CAMERA
L2

Every time you wish to reset the camera – that is, move it back to the direction Lara is facing – simply press L2. This can be very useful when lining Lara up for a long-range leap.

USE PERSONAL LIGHT SOURCE
✛

To activate the Personal Light Source, simply press ✛. You can deactivate the PLS by repeating the button press.

TOMB RAIDER
LEGEND

HOW TO PLAY

WALKTHROUGH

EXTRAS

GAME BASICS

WINNING TACTICS

EQUIPMENT

FIRST STEPS

BUTTON
CONFIGURATION

THE MAIN MENU

ONSCREEN
DISPLAY

CONTROLLING
LARA

SUPER ACTIONS

USING THE
CAMERA

THE PAUSE MENU

THE PDA MENU

PICK UP ITEMS △ (HOLD)

You can pick up any item you find – such as a Reward, or a secondary weapon – by holding △ while standing above it. Lara automatically collects health packs, grenades and ammunition for her current weapon, up to the maximum total allowed for each.

CROUCH ◎ (HOLD), THEN L TO MOVE

As soon as you press ◎ Lara crouches. If you then tilt L, she will walk in a crouched position. This not only enables you to walk through very low passages, but also to take cover behind small obstacles during combat encounters.

ROLL & SOMERSAULTS L + ◎

Press ◎ while running to perform a roll; hold the button to end it in a crouched position. If you press ◎ at the midpoint of the roll, Lara will use her hands to spring to her feet in a different way. If you're a fan of athletic exhibitionism, rapidly tap ◎ to make Lara perform a sequence of up to three forward flips followed by an outstanding double somersault. Once Lara begins to perform this sequence, you can alternate between ◎ and ⊗ to access the two different types of forward flip. If you string a number of these together, Lara's assistants may pass comment...

USE A HEALTH PACK ✚

Press ✚ to use a Health Pack. As each one fills Lara's health gauge by approximately 50%, be careful to not use one by mistake when she is only mildly injured. The Health Pack you waste at the beginning of a level could be the very item that, later, you desperately need to reach its conclusion…

SAVING GRAB △

There are times when you will jump towards a ledge or horizontal bar and find that Lara will catch it with one arm and hang precariously. A △ icon will appear: press that button immediately to make Lara establish a more secure grip.

DISPLAY PAUSE MENU (START)

At any point during a game, you can call up the Pause menu by pressing (START). The options available in this menu are described on page 12.

DISPLAY PDA MENU (SELECT)

Check your PDA whenever you need guidance by pressing (SELECT). In the PDA menu, you will find regularly updated information on your objectives, general data, and details regarding your equipment. Please turn to page 26 to learn more about the use of this device.

<table>
<tr><td>

EXPRESSIONS OF IMPATIENCE

NO COMMANDS

</td><td>

If you leave the controller alone for a while, you will soon notice Lara fixing her ponytail, stretching, and basically wondering what the heck you're doing. You can't be eager to raid tombs **and** patient, you know…

</td><td>

</td></tr>
</table>

MOVING OBJECTS

<table>
<tr><td>

KICK OBJECTS

△

</td><td>

If a small object is bothering you, you can try to kick it away with △.

</td><td>

</td></tr>
<tr><td>

GRAB OBJECTS

△

</td><td>

Every time you encounter a moveable object, such as a boulder or a crate, you can make Lara take hold of it by pressing △ while standing directly next to it. Press the button a second time to instruct Lara to release her grip.

</td><td>

</td></tr>
<tr><td>

MOVE OBJECTS

L

</td><td>

Once you have grabbed an object, you can rotate it by pressing L left or right. If you move the stick forwards or backwards, Lara will either push or pull the object.

</td><td>

</td></tr>
</table>

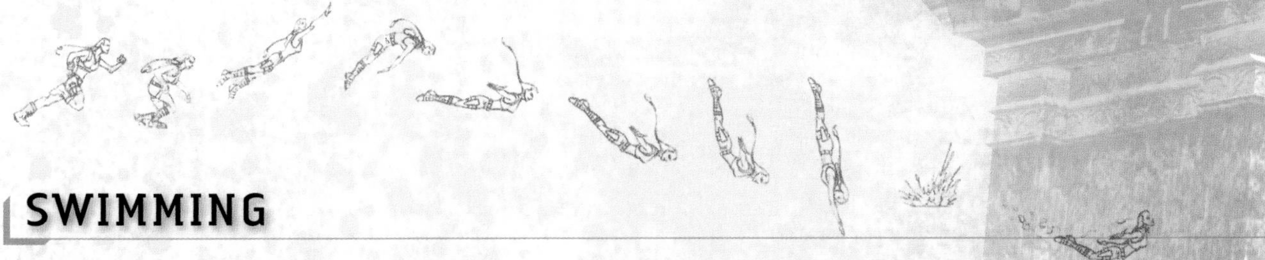

SWIMMING

<table>
<tr><td>

SWAN DIVE

L

FORWARDS

+ ⊗,

THEN ◎

</td><td>

If you want to make a graceful dive into a pool of water, run towards a ledge, and then quickly press ⊗ followed immediately by ◎. There must be practically no delay between the two presses: they need to be almost simultaneous. If you succeed, Lara will perform a beautiful swan dive. Note that you can also perform this move on dry land – Lara will conclude her dive with a deft forward roll.

</td><td>

</td></tr>
</table>

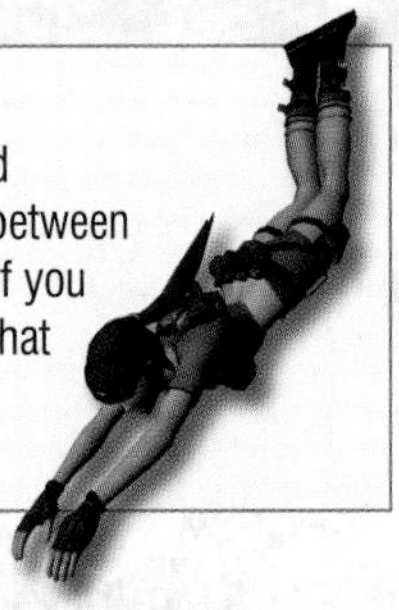

GAME BASICS

SWIM

L

Swimming is as easy as running around: just tilt L and Lara will swim in that direction. You can increase the speed of her strokes by pressing △ repeatedly.

DIVE

◎

(HOLD)

If you want to swim deeper, hold ◎. You can use L at the same time to swim in a direction while diving. An oxygen meter appears above Lara's life gauge once she plunges into the depths. If this is exhausted completely, Lara's health will begin to drop at an alarming rate. For this reason, you should always ensure that her oxygen reserves are sufficient for a quick and painless return to the surface.

SURFACE

✕

(HOLD)

Conversely, when you need to surface, hold ✕ and, if necessary, tilt L at the same time in a chosen direction. Lara swims as fast when she dives as when she surfaces. When you embark on a long swim through a deep underwater section, pay attention to your oxygen gauge. When it reaches its midpoint, you should either be at least halfway towards your destination, or swimming back to the most immediate opportunity to grab a lungful of air.

EXIT WATER

L

To exit water, simply swim against a ledge, a suitable floating object, or any accessible platform with L. Lara will automatically climb onto it.

GRAPPLE MOVES

USE MAGNETIC GRAPPLE

□

To use the Magnetic Grapple, simply press □. As a rule, Lara will automatically aim at any object that the grapple can be attached to – providing there is such a thing within range, of course. When the Magnetic Grapple is attached to something, you can move around freely within the range of the cord. Press □ again to detach the grapple.

PULL MAGNETIC GRAPPLE

△

Once your grapple is attached to an object, you can pull it back by holding or repeatedly pressing △. This could make the object in question move towards Lara, or even fall down.

HOW TO PLAY

WALKTHROUGH

EXTRAS

GAME BASICS

WINNING TACTICS

EQUIPMENT

FIRST STEPS

BUTTON CONFIGURATION

THE MAIN MENU

ONSCREEN DISPLAY

CONTROLLING LARA

SUPER ACTIONS

USING THE CAMERA

THE PAUSE MENU

THE PDA MENU

MANUAL GRAPPLING

R3 + ☐

When you switch to Manual Aim by pressing R3, the first-person view enables you to observe your surroundings. If you move the gray reticle over an object and observe that it turns blue, this means that you have found an object that can be used with the Magnetic Grapple. Press ☐ to fire it.

GRAPPLE SWING

⊗ TO MAKE INITIAL JUMP, THEN ⊗ AGAIN TO FIRE MAGNETIC GRAPPLE

When you need to swing across a gap with the Magnetic Grapple, use ⊗ to leap into the air, and then immediately press ⊗ again to attach the device. Lara will begin swinging as if hanging from a rope. Note that a grapple point "indicator" appears when Lara can use the Magnetic Grapple in this fashion. The presence of this visual cue guarantees that Lara can safely attempt a grapple swing.

EXTEND/ RETRACT & CLIMB GRAPPLE CORD

△ + L↑ OR L↓

Lara can extend (or reduce) the length of her grapple cord while swinging. Hold △, then press up or down on L to climb or descend. It's rarely necessary to do so, however. More often than not, the default length of the grapple cord is more than sufficient for the task at hand – usually, swinging from A to C, avoiding untimely death at B on the way – so adjusting it can lead to complications.

COMBAT

COMBAT LOCK

L1

(HOLD)

With the default "Standard Lock Mode" activated in the Control menu, holding L1 will make Lara draw her weapon and automatically target the nearest enemy. To put the weapon away, simply release L1. While Lara is in this state of combat readiness, the game camera will track an enemy until the lock-on is broken (which happens when they are killed, or Lara holsters her pistols). The "Advanced Hold" option is identical in terms of execution, but Lara will be more particular in her choice of target: you must control the camera manually, with Lara aiming for the enemy nearest the centre of the screen. Finally, the "Advanced Toggle" option works in the same way as the "Advanced Hold" option, but L1 works instead as an on/off switch: tap it once to draw Lara's weapons, and again to put them away.

FIRE AND LOCK-ON

R1

Press R1 to open fire. Lara will automatically draw her weapon if you are not holding L1; when you release R1, she will put her weapon away.

SWITCH TARGET

Ⓡ

When you face multiple enemies while using the "Standard Lock Mode" option, you can switch your current target by tapping Ⓡ in their general direction. Use this function when you need to dispatch a specific opponent before you turn your attention to his associates – such as a soldier wielding a powerful shotgun, for example.

HOW TO PLAY

WALKTHROUGH

EXTRAS

GAME BASICS

WINNING TACTICS

EQUIPMENT

FIRST STEPS

BUTTON
CONFIGURATION

THE MAIN MENU

ONSCREEN
DISPLAY

CONTROLLING
LARA

SUPER ACTIONS

USING THE
CAMERA

THE PAUSE MENU

THE PDA MENU

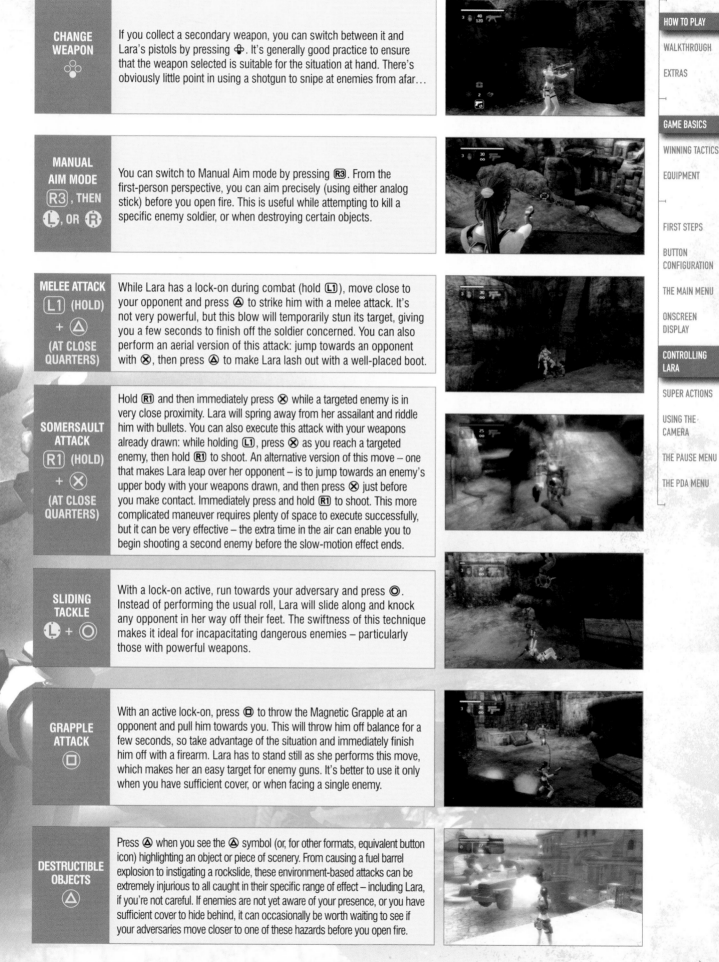

CHANGE WEAPON ⊕

If you collect a secondary weapon, you can switch between it and Lara's pistols by pressing ⊕. It's generally good practice to ensure that the weapon selected is suitable for the situation at hand. There's obviously little point in using a shotgun to snipe at enemies from afar…

MANUAL AIM MODE R3 , THEN L, OR R

You can switch to Manual Aim mode by pressing R3. From the first-person perspective, you can aim precisely (using either analog stick) before you open fire. This is useful while attempting to kill a specific enemy soldier, or when destroying certain objects.

MELEE ATTACK L1 (HOLD) + △ (AT CLOSE QUARTERS)

While Lara has a lock-on during combat (hold L1), move close to your opponent and press △ to strike him with a melee attack. It's not very powerful, but this blow will temporarily stun its target, giving you a few seconds to finish off the soldier concerned. You can also perform an aerial version of this attack: jump towards an opponent with ✕, then press △ to make Lara lash out with a well-placed boot.

SOMERSAULT ATTACK R1 (HOLD) + ✕ (AT CLOSE QUARTERS)

Hold R1 and then immediately press ✕ while a targeted enemy is in very close proximity. Lara will spring away from her assailant and riddle him with bullets. You can also execute this attack with your weapons already drawn: while holding L1, press ✕ as you reach a targeted enemy, then hold R1 to shoot. An alternative version of this move – one that makes Lara leap over her opponent – is to jump towards an enemy's upper body with your weapons drawn, and then press ✕ just before you make contact. Immediately press and hold R1 to shoot. This more complicated maneuver requires plenty of space to execute successfully, but it can be very effective – the extra time in the air can enable you to begin shooting a second enemy before the slow-motion effect ends.

SLIDING TACKLE L + ◯

With a lock-on active, run towards your adversary and press ◯. Instead of performing the usual roll, Lara will slide along and knock any opponent in her way off their feet. The swiftness of this technique makes it ideal for incapacitating dangerous enemies – particularly those with powerful weapons.

GRAPPLE ATTACK ▢

With an active lock-on, press ▢ to throw the Magnetic Grapple at an opponent and pull him towards you. This will throw him off balance for a few seconds, so take advantage of the situation and immediately finish him off with a firearm. Lara has to stand still as she performs this move, which makes her an easy target for enemy guns. It's better to use it only when you have sufficient cover, or when facing a single enemy.

DESTRUCTIBLE OBJECTS △

Press △ when you see the △ symbol (or, for other formats, equivalent button icon) highlighting an object or piece of scenery. From causing a fuel barrel explosion to instigating a rockslide, these environment-based attacks can be extremely injurious to all caught in their specific range of effect – including Lara, if you're not careful. If enemies are not yet aware of your presence, or you have sufficient cover to hide behind, it can occasionally be worth waiting to see if your adversaries move closer to one of these hazards before you open fire.

GAME BASICS

THROW GRENADES
(R2)

Face a chosen direction with (L) (or aim manually with (R3)), and then press (R2) to throw a grenade. The longer you hold the button, the further the grenade will be thrown. If you have an active lock-on, the grenade will automatically be directed at the targeted enemy. The power and blast radius of grenades make them the perfect weapon for dealing with groups of enemies.

DODGING
(L) + (X)
OR (O)

When Lara has a weapon drawn, run in a direction with (L) and press (X) to jump, or (O) to perform an evasive roll. Lara can jump forward, left and right, and perform backflips while she has a weapon at the ready; she can also fire at enemies as she flies through the air. She cannot shoot while rolling, but it's a quicker and more effective way to dodge or dive behind cover.

USING BINOCULARS

LOOK AROUND WITH THE BINOCULARS
, (L)
OR (R)

Activate the binoculars by pressing and then look around using either analog stick. This first-person view is an ideal way to observe your surroundings. You can switch back to the normal view by pressing (X), (□), (O) or again. You cannot use the binoculars while Lara has a weapon drawn.

ZOOM IN/OUT
(R1) / (L1)

Once you have activated the binoculars, you can zoom in with (R1) or out with (L1). Take advantage of this feature to closely study your environment: it can be invaluable while solving puzzles, planning a route, or searching for hidden Rewards.

ACTIVATE/ DEACTIVATE R.A.D. MODE
(△)

When you activate R.A.D. Mode while using the binoculars, Lara will make observations when you point the central reticle at objects of interest. These comments can act as helpful clues: she may identify something as being part of a mechanism required to solve a puzzle, for example, or remark that a particular object will explode if shot.The four icons displayed in R.A.D. Mode reveal the nature of environmental objects in the following ways:

Explosive object   Mechanism   Moveable object   Fragile object

HANGING FROM LEDGES

GRABBING A LEDGE
○ (OPTIONAL) + L
OR L + ✕

To drop over and grab a ledge at Lara's feet, simply walk steadily (or crouch walk) towards it. To grab a ledge that is opposite a gap or a precipice, run and jump in its direction. If your angle of approach isn't quite accurate, you might need to also press △ to help Lara gain a firm grip after she lands.

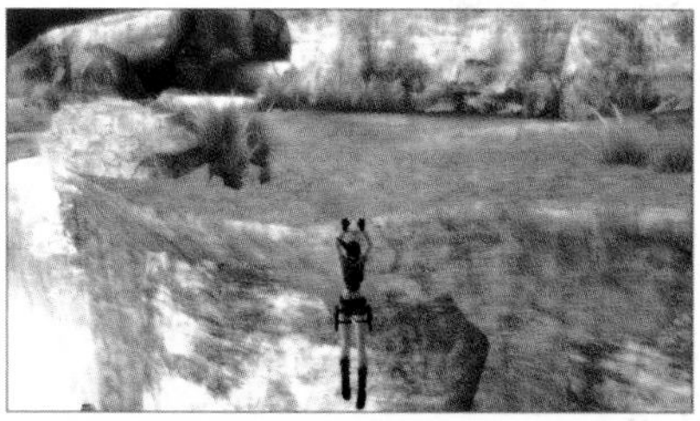

MOVING SIDEWAYS
L + △ (OPTIONAL)

While hanging from a ledge, use L to move sideways. If you press △ repeatedly, Lara will move at a faster rate.

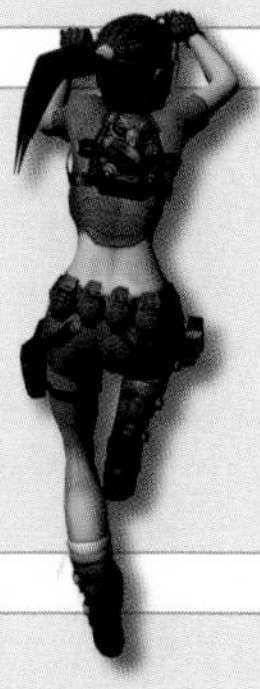

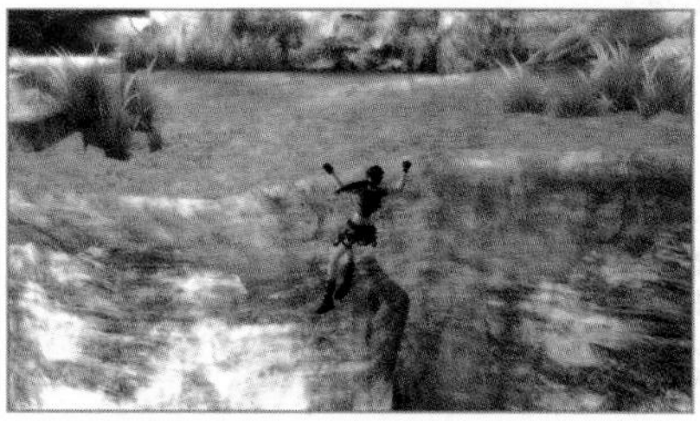

VERTICAL JUMP
✕

While hanging from a ledge, press ✕ to jump. If a ledge or an accessible platform is within reach, Lara will grab it.

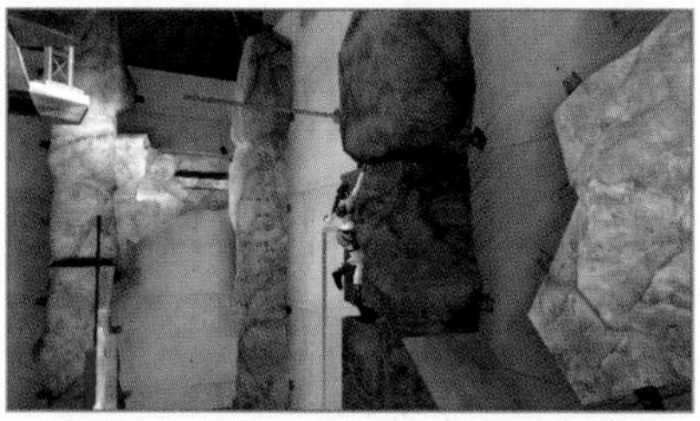

HANDSTAND
✕ (HOLD)

Hold ✕ while hanging from a ledge if you want Lara to climb up onto the platform with a graceful handstand.

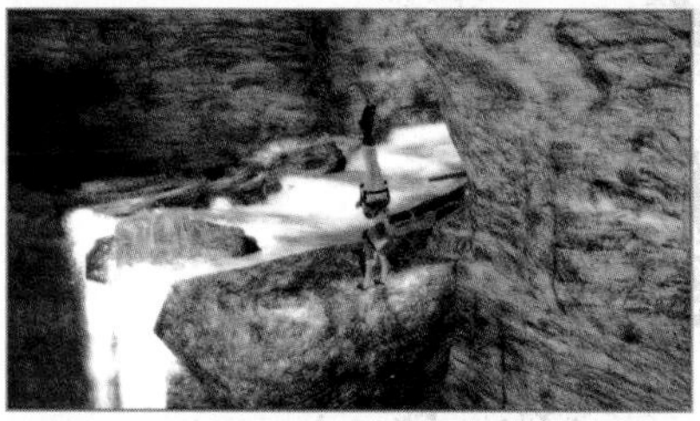

JUMP SIDEWAYS FROM LEDGE
L, THEN ✕

Move sideways until you reach the required end of a ledge and keep tilting L. Lara will let one arm go and look in the corresponding direction: this is a visual cue that indicates she's ready to make the required leap. Press ✕, and Lara will jump sideways.

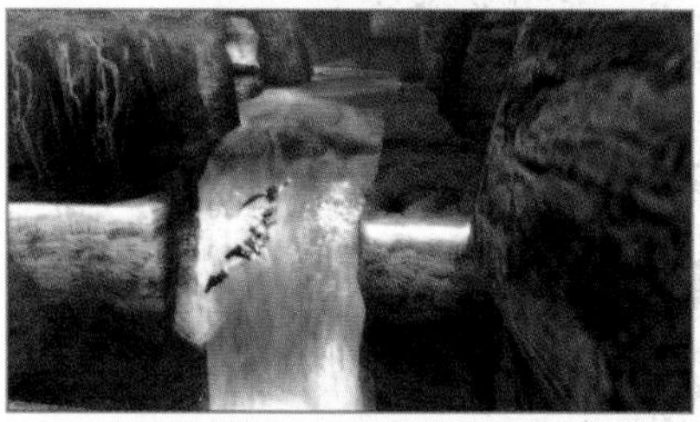

JUMP BACKWARDS FROM LEDGE
L + ✕ (HOLD)

Place Lara at the desired spot on a ledge, and then tilt L towards her back; again, she will let one arm go and look in that direction to indicate that she's ready to jump. Now press ✕ to make Lara spring away from the surface.

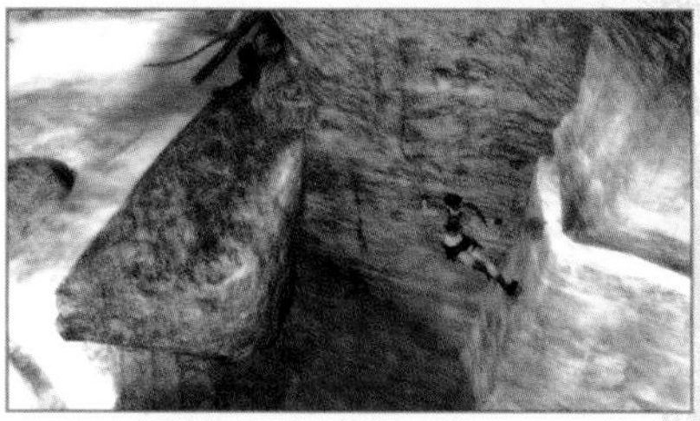

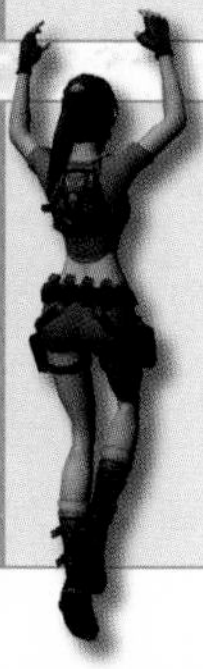

LET GO
○

While hanging from a ledge, press ○ to make Lara let go. Be sure that the drop is not too great, or that there's another platform or ledge directly below. Plummeting from great heights has an extremely adverse effect on Lara's general wellbeing…

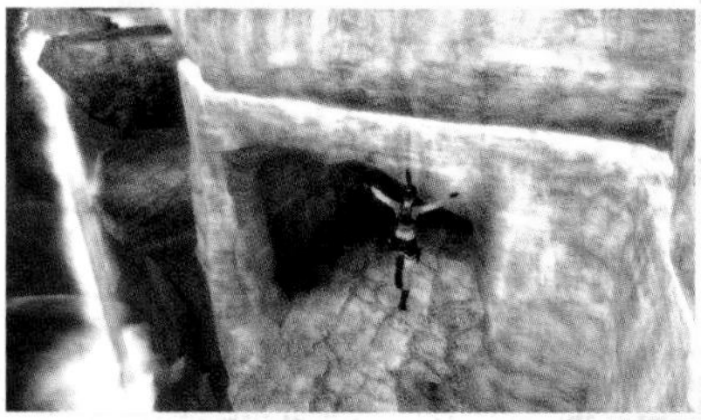

CLIMBING FIXED ROPES, POLES AND LADDERS

**CLIMB UP
OR DOWN**
L + △
(OPTIONAL)

While holding a fixed vertical element, such as a ladder, pole, vine or stationary rope, move L up or down to climb or descend. Pressing △ repeatedly will enable you to ascend at a faster rate.

JUMP
L (HOLD),
THEN ✕

While holding a fixed vertical element, move Lara to the required position, press L in the desired direction, then press ✕ to make her jump.

LET GO
◎

Press ◎ if you want Lara to let go of the pole, rope or ladder she is climbing. Again, it's just common sense to check that a safe landing awaits her before you do so…

SWINGING MOVES

**TURN
AROUND**
L

While swinging from a vine, rope or the Magnetic Grapple, tilt L sideways to change the direction that Lara faces.

SWING
L (HOLD),
✕ TO JUMP

Tilt and hold L towards the direction Lara is facing to make her swing on a hanging rope (or her Magnetic Grapple). From a stationary position, it may take a few moments for her to build up the necessary momentum. If you then press ✕ when she's at the peak of her swing, she will leap from the rope.

GAME BASICS

GAME BASICS

WINNING TACTICS

EQUIPMENT

FIRST STEPS

BUTTON CONFIGURATION

THE MAIN MENU

ONSCREEN DISPLAY

CONTROLLING LARA

SUPER ACTIONS

USING THE CAMERA

THE PAUSE MENU

THE PDA MENU

CLIMB UP OR DOWN
△ (HOLD) + L

Hold △ and simultaneously move L up or down for Lara to change her position on a rope. Use this feature whenever you want to reach a platform or ledge that is above or below Lara. Don't forget that the lower you are on a rope, the greater the swinging radius will be, and vice versa.

LET GO
◎

While holding a swinging rope, press ◎ to instruct Lara to let go.

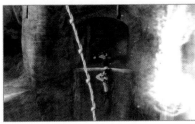

HORIZONTAL POLE MOVES

MOVE SIDEWAYS
L

While hanging from a horizontal pole, use L to make Lara move along it. This enables you to make positional adjustments that are sometimes necessary to reach certain ledges.

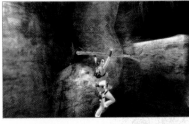

SWING
L (HOLD)

While holding a horizontal pole, tilt and hold L in the direction that Lara is facing. This will make her swing energetically around the pole. If you hold L in the opposite direction, Lara will stop, turn around, and swing that way instead.

JUMP
L (HOLD), THEN ✗

While swinging around a horizontal pole, press ✗ to make Lara jump forward.

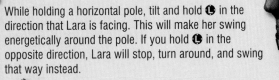

CHANGE DIRECTION/ FLIP MOVES
L + △

While swinging around a horizontal pole, use L to change the direction that Lara is swinging in and immediately press △ to make her perform stunning flips and turning moves.

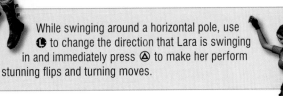

LET GO
◎

While hanging from a horizontal pole, press ◎ if you want Lara to let go.

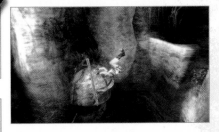

VEHICLE CONTROLS

USE VEHICLE △	To get behind the controls of a vehicle, simply press △.	
ACCELERATE ⊗	To accelerate while using a vehicle, hold ⊗.	
BRAKE / REVERSE □	To brake or reverse while using a vehicle, hold □.	
STEER	While using a vehicle, tilt 🕹 to steer.	
MOVE FORK UP OR DOWN (FORKLIFT ONLY) L1/R1 L2/R2	While driving a forklift, you can move its fork up or down by pressing L1/R1 or L2/R2.	

GAME BASICS

TOMB RAIDER LEGEND

HOW TO PLAY

WALKTHROUGH

EXTRAS

GAME BASICS

WINNING TACTICS

EQUIPMENT

FIRST STEPS

BUTTON
CONFIGURATION

THE MAIN MENU

ONSCREEN
DISPLAY

CONTROLLING
LARA

SUPER ACTIONS

USING THE
CAMERA

THE PAUSE MENU

THE PDA MENU

SUPER ACTIONS

At certain points during Lara's adventure, you will encounter "Super Actions": dramatic interactive cutscenes where your ability to press specific buttons on cue will determine whether Lara lives or dies during these dangerous moments. In these tense, high-pressure cinematic interludes, you must immediately press the controller button that corresponds with an onscreen icon as it appears (Fig. 10). If you succeed, you will advance. If you fail, Lara will die and you will be returned to the last checkpoint passed. (More often than not, though, that will fall just prior to the interactive cutscene.)

You can beat these sections with pure reactions, but it's worth noting that the buttons you need to press always correspond to the action Lara needs to perform: ⊗ to jump, ◎ to roll, ▢ to throw the grapple, ▲ to safely grab a ledge, or even 🄻 to move in a specific direction. No matter which button you need to use, you should always try to press it as soon as the icon appears.

Interactive cutscenes usually consist of two or three button presses in total. They are generally rather short, but you can never be sure when they will occur. For that reason, don't be too quick to release your grip on your controller when you see the beginning of a cinematic sequence. You may be called into action sooner than you think…

[1 0]

USING THE CAMERA

For much of your time spent playing Tomb Raider Legend, you will not need to worry about the game camera: it is designed to automatically follow Lara's footsteps and offer you the best, most practical view of the action.

However, in certain instances – for example, when you turn around suddenly, or when you want to observe your surroundings – you will need to adjust or take full control of the camera. To do so, you can use three different commands. The first, accessed with 🄻2, simply resets the camera to make it face the direction in which Lara is looking. This can be extremely useful in many situations, not least when you are a little disorientated. The second is to take full control of the camera's movements with 🄡, which enables you to peruse your surroundings and look for new routes or hidden Rewards (Fig. 11). Finally, you can also look around from a

first-person perspective by using the Manual Aim mode: press 🄡3 to activate or disable it.

THE PAUSE MENU

You can access the Pause menu (Fig. 12) at any time during the game by pressing (START). This screen provides access to the following options.

RETURN TO GAME: As its name suggests, this option enables you to leave the Pause menu and resume play.

OPTIONS: Select this to reach the main Options menu. Turn to page 11 for more details.

SAVE: Use this to save your progress (up to the last checkpoint activated) at any point during the adventure. Be sure to take full advantage of this feature: it's not simply something you use when you're ready to take a break. If you're trying to collect everything, it can sometimes be worth making an alternative save point to return to if you later discover that you've missed something important.

LOAD: If you've missed a crucial secret, or simply want to replay from your last save, use this option to load the required file.

QUIT: If you select Quit, you will be asked to confirm your decision before you are returned to the Main Menu. Any progress made since your last save will be lost.

SKIP CINEMATIC: Only available when a cutscene is being played, this enables you to jump straight back into the action.

[1 2]

THE PDA MENU

You can open the PDA menu (Fig. 13) with **SELECT**. Using it, you can find out all you need to know about your mission status and equipment.

OBJECTIVES: Select this option to view a mission summary for the current level, and to study the objectives you need to achieve in order to complete it.

DATA: This menu enables you to browse useful information on unlocked missions and Croft Manor, including Rewards collected, the time taken to complete them, and whether or not each stage has been completed in Time Trial mode.

GEAR: Open this page to read information on the equipment Lara has to hand. If you want to, say, check when your next pistols upgrade is due (see Extras chapter for more information), or learn more about the Magnetic Grapple, this is the place to go to.

Weapons/Gear/Items	Magnetic Grapple
Dual Pistols	
---	A portable grappling device that replaces the standard hook with a superstrong electromagnet that can be turned on and off remotely from the base unit. 25ft of 300lb test microfilament wire connect the two pieces.
Grenades	
Magnetic Grapple	
Health Pack	
Binoculars	
PLS	

Back

[13]

WINNING TACTICS

Now that we've covered the basics, it's time to examine how to put that knowledge into practice: making the most of Lara's moves, anticipating enemy tactics, and spotting solutions to puzzles and traps.

LARA'S BEHAVIOR

There are a few fundamental things you should know about controlling Lara and interacting with the environments she encounters. If you master them quickly enough, you will find that you instinctively have the right reaction to suit the situation at hand.

MULTITASKING

[01]

One of the first things you will need to understand about controlling Lara is that you often need to perform more than one action at a time. Jump without running, and you won't even cross the first small gap you encounter; advance without checking your surroundings with the camera, and you could fall victim to the most elementary trap or enemy ambush.

Remember: Lara is enormously versatile, and is capable of some quite astounding athletic feats. Given the challenges she faces throughout her adventure, you need to learn how to skillfully make use of all her abilities – and often in quick succession, if not simultaneously. If you cannot do this, you will find it increasingly hard to survive. To put it simply, you will almost always need

to perform at least two actions at a time: running and jumping, crouching and walking, swimming and surfacing, and so forth. In some instances, you will even need to execute three or four actions simultaneously. During combat, for example, you will find that you will often need to run, jump, fire and switch targets all at once in order to dodge enemy shots and eliminate the most dangerous opponents first (Fig. 1).

If you feel that you need practice to master the many moves you can perform in Tomb Raider Legend, take the time to carefully study the "Controlling Lara" section (see page 14 onwards). Now go and actually try each one out in the first level of the adventure.

TOMB RAIDER
LEGEND

HOW TO PLAY

WALKTHROUGH

EXTRAS

GAME BASICS

WINNING TACTICS

EQUIPMENT

LARA'S BEHAVIOR

ENEMY BEHAVIOR

TRAPS AND
PUZZLES

REWARDS AND
BONUSES

"MOVE OR DIE"

Every single time you enter combat, "Move or Die" is a mantra that should remain at the forefront of your mind throughout the battle. If Lara is static, she's a sitting duck; conversely, by remaining in motion, she becomes a hard target to track. It may seem like stating the oh-so-obvious, but it's easy to forget this at first. As soon as you see or hear that an enemy has noticed you, use 🕹 to keep moving, and jump or roll as required until you neutralize the threat (Fig. 2) or reach cover.

THINK CREATIVELY

As long as you are under no particular pressure, take the time to observe your surroundings. Watch for triggers and traps, and look for hidden Rewards, exits, or any other potentially accessible elements that don't immediately appear to be within reach. Every time you are stuck within a specific room, you will frequently find that you have simply failed to spot, for example, a rope or a small ledge that leads, in turn, to another step in your path through that area. Be patient, and always be sure to pay attention to tiny details.

Sometimes, there are obvious visual clues: there is usually a distinct animated sheen to grappling points, which is something that you should learn to recognize immediately (Fig. 3). You should also take notice when Lara turns her head: she has a tendency to look at points of interactivity or interest as she walks by. Conquering each environment-based puzzle is also a matter of making the best use of Lara's gear and abilities. If you notice a rope that is currently unavailable, or immobilized

by an object hanging from it, think logically: you could perhaps free it for use by manually aiming and firing at the base of the rope (Fig. 4). It's also important that you have a keen appreciation of Lara's limitations. If you think that the way forward is via a jump over a gap that seems too wide for Lara to leap, it probably **is** too far. Instead, take a good look at your surroundings with your binoculars. If you can see the exit from an area, try to imagine the journey from its conclusion and move backwards, rather than from the start. Reverse engineer the steps Lara needs to take to reach it, and you may find that you discover a missing link – such as a concealed ledge, or a movable object.

When you enter combat, don't panic: keep moving, of course, but take note of any destructible objects (such as explosive barrels) that are highlighted by a △ icon. If you time your attack well and press △ at the right moment, you can wreak havoc without expending needless effort or ammo.

[03]

[04]

LARA'S MOVES PER SURFACE

Knowing what you can do based on where Lara is in the environment will always help you to find solutions to puzzles and locate exits to rooms. The following table details the moves (excluding those particular to combat) that she can perform in specific situations, and the corresponding controller commands.

Surface	Relevant moves	Commands
Ground	Walk	Ⓛ
	Run	Ⓛ
	Vertical jump	ⓧ
	Directional jump	Ⓛ + ⓧ
	Roll	Ⓛ + Ⓞ
Ledge	Move sideways	Ⓛ (sideways)
	Pull up/jump up	ⓧ
	Drop down	Ⓞ
	Jump backwards	Ⓛ (backwards), ⓧ
	Jump sideways	Ⓛ (sideways), ⓧ
	Diagonal jump (if hit at a diagonal angle)	Ⓛ + ⓧ
Slope	Slide down	No button(s)
	Jump off	ⓧ
Swimming	Surface swim	Ⓛ
	Fast swim	Ⓛ + repeatedly tap △
	Dive	Ⓞ
	Surface	ⓧ
	Exit water	Ⓛ
Horizontal pole	Move along	Ⓛ (sideways)
	Drop down	Ⓞ
	Swing around	Ⓛ (forwards)
	Swing off	Ⓛ + ⓧ
	Flip moves	Ⓛ + △
Vertical pole	Climb up/down	Ⓛ (upwards/downwards)
	Rotate around	Ⓛ (sideways)
	Drop off	Ⓞ
	Jump off	ⓧ
Vertical pole (wall mounted)	Climb up/down	Ⓛ (upwards/downwards)
	Drop off	Ⓞ
	Jump off	ⓧ
	Jump laterally	Ⓛ (sideways) + ⓧ
Rope	Climb up/down	△ + Ⓛ (upwards/downwards)
	Drop off	Ⓞ
	Rotate around	Ⓛ (sideways)
	Swing	Ⓛ (forwards)
	Jump off (while swinging)	Ⓛ (forwards) + ⓧ
Ladder	Climb up/down	Ⓛ (upwards/downwards)
	Drop off	Ⓞ
	Jump off	ⓧ
	Jump laterally	Ⓛ (sideways) + ⓧ
	Reverse direction	Ⓛ (backwards)

UNDERSTANDING YOUR ENVIRONMENT

HOW TO PLAY

WALKTHROUGH

EXTRAS

GAME BASICS

WINNING TACTICS

EQUIPMENT

LARA'S BEHAVIOR

ENEMY BEHAVIOR

TRAPS AND PUZZLES

REWARDS AND BONUSES

Much as in real life, environments, objects and entities in Tomb Raider Legend adhere to certain obvious (and palpable) physical laws. Knowing how these mechanics work will help you enormously. There are many cause-and-effect puzzles that will be very difficult to solve unless you take this fact into account.

PHYSICS: All moveable objects in Tomb Raider Legend are governed by authentic physical mechanics. The most obvious of these are gravity and momentum. Therefore, every time a force – water current, an explosion, Lara pushing – is applied to a dynamic object, you can expect it to react accordingly. If an object is on a slope, for example, it will roll or slide down (Fig. 5). If Lara pushes a round boulder on a flat surface, it will roll and slowly come to a halt; if she pushes a crate, it will cease to move as soon as she stops pushing; if she swings on a rope or her grappling device, she will experience momentum. Look to real life for inspiration: think of what you might plausibly attempt if in Lara's shoes, and don't be afraid to experiment.

WATER, FIRE AND ELECTRICITY: You should also take things like fire, water and electricity into account when they are present in an area. For example, flowing water could be used to exert force to solve a puzzle. Electrified water (Fig. 6) and fire are harmful to any living creatures that come into contact with them – including Lara.

[0 5]

CHECKPOINTS

Whenever you reach a checkpoint (Fig. 7) you can rest assured that, even if Lara dies, you will resume the adventure at that position. After passing one, always feel free to try risky things that you would not normally attempt. From making a near-suicidal dash to engage multiple combatants with foolhardy close-quarters melee attacks, to jumping towards a ledge that seems slightly too far away to catch, it's a perfect opportunity to experiment. Worse case scenario, you will restart from a point recorded mere minutes beforehand. Knowing that there will be no backtracking or repetition after passing a checkpoint gives you license to be as adventurous as you please. Take advantage of this whenever you can.

[0 6]

CHECKPOINT...

[0 7]

TARGETING CURSORS

Targeting cursors appear whenever Lara enters combat (Fig. 8). Additionally, when you switch to Manual Aim mode, a circular reticle will appear at the centre of the screen (Fig. 9). Depending on the circumstances, the appearance of targeting cursors and the Manual Aim mode reticle may be modified. The following table explains how to interpret these changes.

[08]

[09]

Cursor/reticle	Lara's status	Meaning
○	Normal mode (free motion)	This red targeting cursor highlights an enemy within shooting range
○	Normal mode (free motion)	The gray targeting cursor highlights an enemy out of shooting range
✥	Normal mode, weapon drawn (lock-on)	This red targeting cursor highlights an enemy within shooting range when Lara has a lock-on
✥	Normal mode, weapon drawn (lock-on)	The gray targeting cursor highlights an enemy out of shooting range when Lara has a lock-on
＞	Normal mode (free motion)	This red targeting arrow indicates a highlighted enemy who is positioned off-screen, irrespective of shooting range
○	Manual Aim mode	In Manual Aim mode, the targeting cursor at the centre of the screen is colored gray if Lara is not aiming at an enemy
⊙	Manual Aim mode	In Manual Aim mode, the reticle at the centre of the screen is colored red if Lara is aiming at an enemy within shooting range
⊙	Manual Aim mode	In Manual Aim mode, the reticle at the centre of the screen is transparent if Lara is aiming at an enemy out of shooting range
⊙	Manual Aim mode	In Manual Aim mode, the reticle at the centre of the screen is colored light blue if Lara is aiming at an object that can be used with the Magnetic Grapple
⊗	Normal mode (free motion)	This grapple point indicator appears when Lara can use the Magnetic Grapple to swing across a gap. The presence of this visual cue guarantees that Lara can safely attempt a grapple swing

RAIDER
LEGEND

HOW TO PLAY

WALKTHROUGH

EXTRAS

GAME BASICS

WINNING TACTICS

EQUIPMENT

LARA'S BEHAVIOR

ENEMY BEHAVIOR

TRAPS AND
PUZZLES

REWARDS AND
BONUSES

ENEMY BEHAVIOR

If you learn to predict how your enemies are likely to behave in any given situation, Lara's chances of emerging from each combat encounter unscathed will increase. Study the following advice carefully, and you'll make short work of your opponents.

[10]

PRE-COMBAT BEHAVIOR

Until they notice something that makes them suspicious, or actively attack Lara, enemies tend to follow a set routine; for example, they may stand guard, or patrol a specific area. The element of surprise can work in your favor when you launch an assault. If you plan your attack carefully, you can eliminate an adversary before they have the opportunity to retaliate (Fig. 10).

In some instances, an enemy may catch a fleeting glimpse of Lara, and then move to investigate. Unless you're actively ready to fight, it's wise to find an alternative hiding spot before he arrives.

[11]

ENEMY MOVEMENT

Once enemies become aware of Lara's presence and open fire, they will begin to move freely within the battle zone. Try to anticipate their actions. If you notice a soldier sprinting in the direction of a turret, for example, try to find cover immediately (Fig. 11) or, ideally, kill him before he reaches his goal.

[12]

ENEMY TACTICS

Enemy soldiers often work together to eliminate Lara, and will adopt different tactics based on the opportunities presented by the environment and your behavior. It's important that you identify their strategies, and quickly formulate an appropriate plan of action.

CHARGE: Most of the time, your opponents will simply attempt to shoot Lara, and will run towards her in order to get a clear shot. Depending on the architecture of the area in which the combat takes place, they can either run directly towards you, or take a detour to reach your position by an alternative route. Try to keep track of all targets, and switch targets when appropriate to take down the closest (or most dangerous) assailants.

USING COVER: When you launch a surprise attack on an enemy, his instinctive reaction will sometimes be to dash for cover. This gives you a temporary advantage as you will be the only one firing. However, he will eventually retaliate, and he may have allies that will rush to his assistance. It's better to be prudent, and to ascertain how many soldiers are waiting for you before you open fire. In some cases, assailants will endeavor to perform flanking

moves, finding cover at either side of Lara's position before pinning her down in a crossfire. Remember that while enemies are behind cover they can neither target nor see Lara.

WORKING AS A TEAM: Enemies tend to regroup and support each other (Fig. 12) every time they detect Lara (visually or aurally), or hear a call for help from a comrade. As they tend to make a lot of noise by opening fire or communicating, listen carefully in order to locate them. Pay close attention to what they say, as it can reveal their intentions and enable you to prepare for an imminent attack.

Watch your opponents closely and find the right balance between offensive and defensive tactics. Be as mobile as you can be, diving from cover to cover, and remember that you can fire with abandon while using the default pistols (they have infinite ammunition). Desperate situations often call for more powerful weapons. If you are in a real predicament, don't hesitate to use a secondary firearm (if you have one), and be quick to use grenades to take out large groups or flush awkward enemies from cover.

USING THE ENVIRONMENT DURING COMBAT

When the ⍙ (or equivalent) icon appears next to an object or architectural feature, you can press that button to make Lara shoot it and instigate an event that can injure or kill nearby opponents. You will encounter many different types of environmental attacks in Tomb Raider Legend. These include crushing opponents by toppling a pillar (Fig. 13), initiating a rockslide, or detonating explosive objects. When you have the opportunity to do so – if you have yet to be detected, for example – try to wait until the optimum moment before you open fire. The more adversaries you can dispatch at once, the easier the resultant battle will be.

[13]

BOSS BATTLES

Boss battles are far more challenging than standard combat, as the enemies you face can endure much more damage before they die or surrender, and have far more deadly techniques at their disposal.

Every time you fight a boss, it's vital that you remain focused. Try to analyze your opponent's attack strategies and general behavior. You will soon find a way to avoid their assaults and identify their weaknesses. Keep moving, and experiment with the effects of your equipment (grenades, Magnetic Grapple) and the environment. If your foe appears to be immune to bullets, maybe you can harm him or her by using the surrounding scenery…

If you have a hard time defeating a specific boss, worry not: you will find detailed explanations and tactics in the Walkthrough chapter.

HOW TO PLAY

WALKTHROUGH

EXTRAS

GAME BASICS

WINNING TACTICS

EQUIPMENT

LARA'S BEHAVIOR

ENEMY BEHAVIOR

TRAPS AND
PUZZLES

REWARDS AND
BONUSES

TRAPS AND PUZZLES

You won't go very far in Tomb Raider Legend if you don't learn how to solve puzzles and dodge or disable traps. Although you will find yourself in many unique situations, you will soon realize that there are some general principles and tricks that are almost always helpful, whatever the nature of the problem you face.

USE MOVEABLE OBJECTS

The key to solving puzzles or avoiding traps is frequently the use of a moveable object. Pushing a box on top of a floor switch (Fig. 14), placing a crate between two closing walls, positioning an object in order to reach a high ledge… these are but three examples of solutions that you will use to help Lara progress through a level. No matter how perplexed you may be by a particular situation, try to be as methodical as possible. Consider the objects you have access to, and then think about (and actively experiment with) ways in which they can be used.

[14]

LOOK FOR TRIGGERS

Triggers can either activate a device that helps you to solve a puzzle, or unleash a trap. The most common types of triggers you will face are as follows:

- **PRESSURE PLATE/FLOOR SWITCH:** a simple switch that responds to weight or pressure. These can be activated if Lara stands on them, or if they are covered by moveable objects such as crates.

- **SWITCH/LEVER:** a device that Lara can interact with in order to set off a trap or open a door.

- **SCRIPTED TRIGGERS:** a trap or event occurs as soon as Lara reaches a specific part of a level.

- **FRAGILE ELEMENT:** a crumbling platform, weak ledge or a rope that can only support Lara's weight for a limited period of time.

- **LIGHT BEAM:** a beam of light triggers an event when activated or interrupted.

FORESEE THE CONSEQUENCES OF YOUR ACTIONS

Activating a trigger brings about immediate consequences, good or bad. The main types of events you can expect are:

- **PATH BLOCKED/REVEALED:** activating a trigger often opens a path or renders it inaccessible.

- **REWARD:** the trigger reveals an item that can be collected.

- **HARM ENEMIES:** some traps may harm or kill enemies (Fig. 15).

- **DAMAGE/DEATH:** the trap might have a harmful effect that might injure or even kill Lara outright – for example, being crushed by a boulder.

- **OPPORTUNITY:** some trap components may work to Lara's advantage, such as a spear jutting from a wall that provides a route to an otherwise inaccessible platform.

- **MOVEMENT:** impacts resulting from activated traps might change Lara's position – by throwing her backwards, for example.

- **DELAY/INCONVENIENCE:** some traps simply force Lara to wait, or take a more circuitous route to her destination.

[15]

LEARN TO "READ" CUES

Most of the time, the activation of a trigger is accompanied by a visual or aural cue. Paying attention to these clues and understanding the types of mechanisms involved will assist you in solving puzzles and avoiding traps.

- **OBVIOUS TRIGGER:** the trigger is plainly visible and stands out from nearby terrain, such as a floor switch or lever. In most instances, you can carefully observe your surroundings to deduce its effect. Will it open a door (Fig. 16), or cause spears to fire from a wall? Investigate carefully to find out.

- **MOTION:** there is sometimes a very obvious visual cue, with the camera moving to draw your attention to an event.

- **ENEMY INTERVENTION:** enemies might trigger a trap ahead of Lara, revealing its location.

- **WARNING SIGNS:** when an area is damaged with cracks, scratched, or is surrounded by human remains, it's likely that

a trap is hidden somewhere nearby – you are viewing damage and/or victims of past activations.

- **PARTICLE EFFECTS:** dust clouds falling from the ceiling or a ledge, water droplets, or other particle effects may indicate danger. Study the immediate area carefully before you continue.

[16]

FIND SOLUTIONS

Once you've identified a puzzle mechanism or a trap, you need to find a solution to either use it to your advantage, or pass by unscathed. In general, puzzle mechanisms will present a way forward or reveal a bonus item, whereas traps are better off deactivated or bypassed. The following tips will help.

- **HAVE A KEEN EYE FOR OBVIOUS SOLUTIONS:** think logically. If you can see a lever in a locked room, it can almost certainly be used to open a door or gate. Actually reaching that lever, however, may be a puzzle in itself…

- **USING DEVICES:** in instances where a puzzle involves machinery or devices (such as counterweights – Fig. 17 – or a waterwheel), Lara can probably interact with it in one way or another. A trial-and-error approach will help. If no obvious solution presents itself, take the time to explore the area, and look for a "cause" for the desired effect.

- **USE OF MOVEABLE OBJECTS:** if you can see a moveable object in the same room as a trap or puzzle, it's likely to be involved in the solution. Think creatively: moveable objects can be used in a variety of ways. Push a box ahead of you and it could trigger

a floor trap; place a crate between closing walls, and it could provide a wide enough path for Lara to move through.

- **USE OF EQUIPMENT:** Lara's equipment can be indispensable as you attempt to solve a puzzle or get past a trap. Brighten a dark corner with the Personal Light Source and you might find a hidden trigger; take out your grapple and you might be able to swing to a different location, or move a particular object.

- **AGILITY:** in order to survive many traps, you will generally need to demonstrate perfect control over Lara. Timing and reflexes are often of the essence.

- **PERCEPTION:** certain traps are easy to avoid, but hard to notice. When you encounter them, survival is a question of how adept you are at spotting clues that reveal their existence, and preparing for them in advance.

[17]

REWARDS AND BONUSES

Rewards are small items that you can collect throughout the adventure (Fig. 18). It is through the discovery and collection of both ancient and modern "artifacts" that you can unlock the game's many bonuses (see page 155 onwards for more information). Essentially, the more Rewards you discover, the more goodies you will find in the Extras menu.

Rewards are scattered throughout each level. If you explore each stage thoroughly, you will almost certainly find many of them. However, if you need guidance to retrieve some that are particularly well hidden or hard to reach, you will find the necessary help in the Walkthrough chapter. Identify the Reward you're looking for on the map, refer to the corresponding text paragraph, and simply follow the page and code references to reach the relevant section of the Extras chapter.

[18]

HOW TO PLAY

WALKTHROUGH

EXTRAS

GAME BASICS

WINNING TACTICS

EQUIPMENT

LARA'S BEHAVIOR

ENEMY BEHAVIOR

TRAPS AND PUZZLES

REWARDS AND BONUSES

EQUIPMENT

Lara can make use of many resources during her adventure. She has her default gear, of course, but she can also take various items dropped by enemies, and even use vehicles when the situation demands it.

GEAR

Lara carries the following items with her and can use them whenever they are needed. Do not underestimate how useful they can be.

Magnetic Grapple

This device consists of a magnetic grapple head that can attach itself to certain (visually distinct) surfaces, a lengthy cord, and internal mechanics hidden within a fashionable designer belt.

The Magnetic Grapple has a number of uses. Lara can use it to swing across gaps, manipulate scenery from afar, and move certain objects. Any device or item that can be used with the Magnetic Grapple has a distinctive animated "sheen" (Fig. 1). When you notice this, you'll know that you can attach your grapple to it by pressing ▣.

Lara can use the Magnetic Grapple while standing on the ground, in Manual Aim mode, and while flying through the air (but only if there is a grapple point within reach). To find out more about the use of this essential piece of equipment, turn to page 17.

[01]

TOMB RAIDER
LEGEND

HOW TO PLAY

WALKTHROUGH

EXTRAS

GAME BASICS

WINNING TACTICS

EQUIPMENT

GEAR

WEAPONS

Binoculars

The binoculars are a straightforward but highly useful piece of equipment. When you press ⊕, you enter the first-person binoculars view, which is ideal for observing Lara's surroundings in detail. The zoom feature enables you to magnify distant objects, which makes the binoculars essential for planning a path to a distant exit, scanning a room for potential solutions to a tricky puzzle, or reconnoitering a group of enemy soldiers (Fig. 2). You can also use the optional R.A.D. Mode to pick up useful clues. Refer to page 20 for more information.

Toggle R.A.D. Mode

[02]

Personal Light Source

Whenever you press ⊕, the Personal Light Source illuminates Lara's immediate vicinity (Fig. 3). However, it can only be used for a limited period of time before it automatically (though, thankfully, briefly) deactivates in order to recharge. Its current power level is displayed in the form of a yellow gauge situated at the bottom left-hand corner of the screen. Once this gauge is empty, the device will be turned off; you will notice the yellow bar is rapidly replenished when this happens. In emergency situations, remember that you don't need to wait until power is completely restored before you reactivate it.

[03]

Flares

At one point in Tomb Raider Legend, Lara is equipped with unlimited flares rather than the Personal Light Source. They are accessed in the same way, though: simply press R2. As they are thrown, and not carried, flares only illuminate the area that they land in (Fig. 4). They are approximately twice as bright as the Personal Light Source, and you can have two active at any one time.

Health Packs

An essential tool for the rough-and-rugged adventurer, the Health Pack enables Lara to treat her injuries immediately by filling approximately 50% of her life gauge. In dangerous situations, with her energy severely depleted, be ready to quickly press ✛ to heal her wounds. Slain enemies will sometimes drop a Health Pack as they expire, which you should always be sure to collect (Fig. 5). The Health Pack icon will flash when Lara's health gauge is dangerously low. See page 13 for further details.

[04]

[05]

WEAPONS

Dual Pistols

MAGAZINE SIZE:
15 (upgraded magazine size: 20)
MAX AMMUNITION: Infinite

Dual RGP Mach 5 pistols, counterbalanced to reduce recoil. This set includes custom high capacity magazines.

Advantages	Drawbacks
Infinite ammo	Deal little damage
Good rate of fire (especially if you hold R1)	Limited range
Decent accuracy	-

Shotgun

MAGAZINE SIZE: 5
MAX AMMUNITION: 20

Pump Action shotgun. Fires a wide spray of buckshot that can cause great damage at close range, with decreasing effectiveness based on distance from target.

Advantages	Drawbacks
Powerful	Frequent reloading necessary
-	Long reloading time
-	Very limited range

Submachine Gun

MAGAZINE SIZE: 40
MAX AMMUNITION: 120

MG415 submachine gun allows for single shots and full-automatic fire. Close range accuracy is above average for a weapon of this type.

Advantages	Drawbacks
Powerful, with a high rate of fire	Short range
Easy to wield	-
Fully automatic	-

EQUIPMENT

Assault Rifle

MAGAZINE SIZE: 30
MAX AMMUNITION: 120

The RC650 assault rifle fires 5.56mm rounds housed in a syntheric polymer magazine. This weapon sacrifices power and accuracy for range with sustained fire.

Advantages	Drawbacks
Long range	Not very powerful
High accuracy	Unwieldy for close quarters
Fully automatic	-

Grenade Launcher

MAGAZINE SIZE: 3
MAX AMMUNITION: 12

Multi-shot, military-grade grenade launcher. Fires 40mm fragmentation grenades with pinpoint accuracy.

Advantages	Drawbacks
Very powerful	Delay before grenade explosion
Ideal for killing concealed enemies	Not practical for indoor use
Very long range	Low accuracy
Good rate of fire	-

Grenades

MAX AMMUNITION: 4

Hugely damaging, the large blast radius of JW33 fragmentation grenades enables you to dispatch groups of enemies quickly or flush assailants from behind cover.

Advantages	Drawbacks
Powerful explosion	Lara is vulnerable as she throws them
Distracts enemies	Relatively easy for enemies to dodge
Can be used while behind cover	-

Granular TNT filler provides for a powerful, highly lethal blast radius. As they do not explode immediately, you can bounce them from walls or ceilings if required. They can also be used to destroy certain environmental objects. The power and distance of Lara's throw can be increased by holding R2 for a longer period. With an active lock-on, they are thrown at Lara's current target; at all other times, they will be hurled in the direction that she is currently facing. You can also manually aim grenades by using Manual Aim mode.

HOW TO PLAY

WALKTHROUGH

EXTRAS

GAME BASICS

WINNING TACTICS

EQUIPMENT

GEAR

WEAPONS

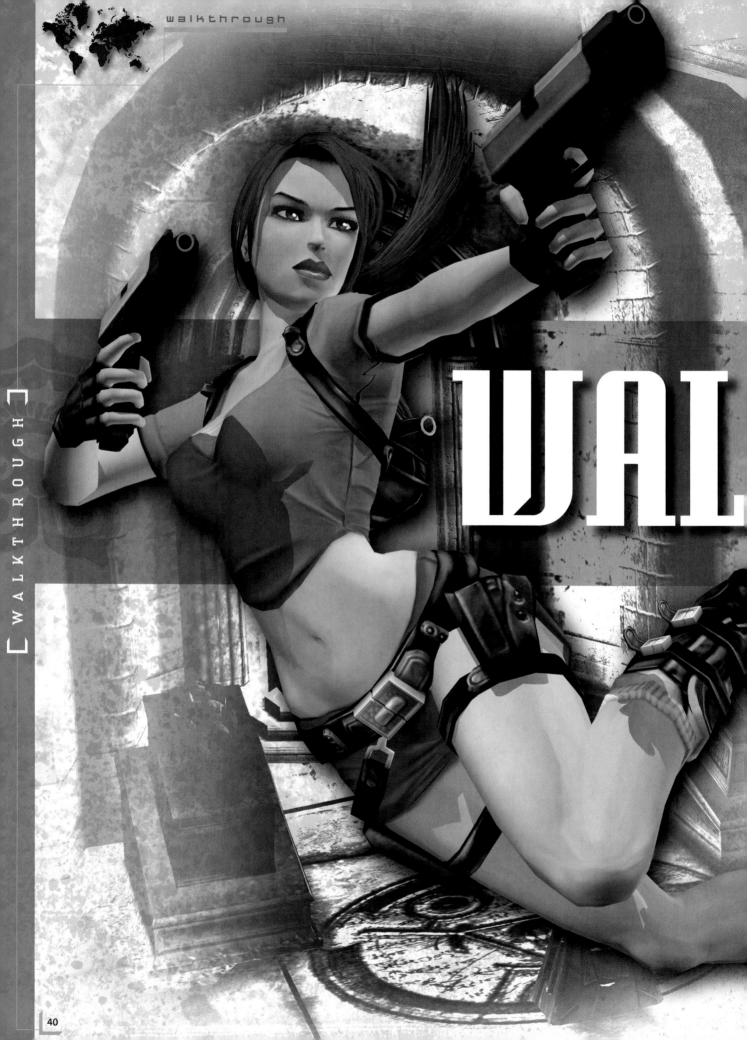

WALKTHROUGH

WAL

2nd CHAPTER

KTHROUGH

This chapter provides detailed instructions on how
to complete every level of Tomb Raider Legend. It
also features countless useful tips and techniques to
help you through tricky combat encounters, traps and
puzzles. To familiarize yourself with the structure of the
walkthrough – and to learn how to immediately obtain
the information you need at any given moment – we
suggest that you peruse the short introduction that
follows before you read any further.

INTRODUCTION

This walkthrough has been designed to assist players of all ability levels. How and when you use it is entirely your decision. It can be followed on a step by step basis, or be consulted for occasional reference if you prefer to solve Tomb Raider Legend's puzzles by yourself whenever possible.

Each mission walkthrough has the following structure:

- The first double-page spread features an annotated area map. If you require a very low level of assistance, this provides a bare minimum of clues to help you find your own way through the level. These maps reveal the general route you must take, but not how to get from A to B. If you want to simply refer to these maps for basic directions and ignore the main walkthrough text during your first playthrough, you can do just that.

- The double-page spreads that follow feature magnified sections of the current area map annotated in greater detail. These are accompanied by instructions that explain everything you need to know about Lara's progress through specific sections of each level. You will also find cross-references to the Secrets section of the Extras chapter, as well as tip boxes and "boss" battle tactics.

1 AREA MAPS

Each area map provides a succinct overview of the locale that Lara must explore. Displayed over two pages, these maps will enable you to acquire a better understanding of a level's structure. If you feel lost but do not want to consult the magnified map portions (or, indeed, the walkthrough text), try to reorient yourself by identifying distinctive architectural features. If you require further assistance, you can use the letter icons to jump to the specific point of the walkthrough that covers that area – no more, no less.

If you don't recognize a particular notation, open and refer to the back cover foldout: it features a legend that explains the meanings of the symbols used.

2 MISSION DATA

This table offers trivia for the current mission, such as the weather conditions, time of day, and Lara's current outfit.

3 DETAILED MAP SECTIONS

These magnified sections of the area maps are designed to help you find the way forward with a minimum of fuss. Presented at a scale that makes them easier to read, they feature continuous lines that represent the optimum route Lara can take. Each path is punctuated by letter icons – such as A, B, C and D – that correspond with a respective portion of the walkthrough text. As long as you know your approximate position on the map, you can immediately find the advice you need.

4 STEP BY STEP GUIDANCE

The walkthrough text that accompanies each magnified map section offers detailed directions and instructions. It is divided into bite-size pieces that are clearly marked with letters that correspond to positions on the map. Each piece of text explains what Lara has to do to travel from, for example, point B to point C.

You will notice that codes such as "(1-A)" and page references occasionally appear within the walkthrough text. These link to the Secrets section of the Extras chapter, where you will find instructions that explain how to collect the Gold, Silver or Bronze Rewards that Lara can find at that specific point of her journey. If you require assistance, simply use the references provided to jump to the relevant paragraph in the Secrets chapter.

5 SCREENSHOTS

The many screenshots featured throughout this chapter are designed to be used as visual points of reference, and frequently illustrate tips, tricks and tactics explained in the walkthrough text. Each screenshot is clearly marked with a number that corresponds to a "(Fig. X)" reference in a related sentence.

6 TIPS

These information boxes offer useful and pertinent advice, such as combat tactics, details on moves that Lara can perform, and how to interact with certain objects when you encounter them for the first time.

HOW TO PLAY

WALKTHROUGH

EXTRAS

INTRODUCTION

LEVEL 1
LEVEL 2
LEVEL 3
LEVEL 4
LEVEL 5
LEVEL 6
LEVEL 7
LEVEL 8

BOLIVIA - TIWANAKU

AREA MAP

LOCATION	TIWANAKU (BOLIVIA)
WEATHER	PARTLY CLOUDY
TERRAIN	ROCKY, TEMPLE INTERIOR
TIME	AFTERNOON
LARA'S OUTFIT	LEGEND

2 **3** **1** **4** **5** **6**

LEVEL 1: BOLIVIA - TIWANAKU A-B

MISSION DETAILS

A From the beginning of the level, run towards the ramp you can see directly to your right (1-A). Jump across the gap to reach the other side (Fig. 1). Walk over to the small pool at the base of the waterfall (1-B). Jump (or dive, if you prefer) into the pool. Swim to the opposite side and climb onto the small platform. Jump vertically to grab the ledge above and pull yourself up.

PRACTICE MAKES PERFECT

In these first few moments of the game, there are no enemies, time limits, traps or unseen dangers. For that reason, this is a good time to try out as many new moves as you can. Handstands, jumping, diving, kicking rocks around... these are just a few examples of the activities you can experiment with here. For a comprehensive list of all moves that Lara can perform (a number of which can be practiced here), turn to page 14.

B Walk over to the large rock blocking the path and grab it. Push it forward so that it falls down. Having cleared the way, jump to the opposite platform, doing so will activate the first checkpoint of the game. Turn to the right and jump onto the vertical vine. Climb up until you draw level with another vine to the right. Jump over to it, and then leap once again to reach the platform to the right and another checkpoint. Run forward and jump onto the rope hanging in front of you (1-C). Swing straight ahead and jump as soon as you have sufficient speed to land on the platform hidden behind the waterfall (Fig. 2). Don't worry if you miss the jump: you'll simply plunge abruptly but safely into the pool below. Retrace your steps to make another attempt.

FOLLOW HER EYES...

Every time Lara stands near certain points of interest, she will turn her head to look at them. This clue often indicates that you can somehow interact with the object in question. Whenever her gaze strays from the path ahead, always take the time to find out what is drawing her attention elsewhere.

BOLIVIA - TIWANAKU

AREA MAP

LOCATION	TIWANAKU (BOLIVIA)
WEATHER	PARTLY CLOUDY
TERRAIN	ROCKY, TEMPLE INTERIOR
TIME	AFTERNOON
LARA'S OUTFIT	LEGEND

LARA CROFT
TOMB RAIDER
LEGEND

HOW TO PLAY

WALKTHROUGH

EXTRAS

INTRODUCTION

LEVEL 1

LEVEL 2

LEVEL 3

LEVEL 4

LEVEL 5

LEVEL 6

LEVEL 7

LEVEL 8

AREA MAP

A – B

C – D

E

F – G

H

I – J

K

L – M

MISSION DETAILS

HOW TO PLAY

WALKTHROUGH

EXTRAS

INTRODUCTION

LEVEL 1

LEVEL 2

LEVEL 3

LEVEL 4

LEVEL 5

LEVEL 6

LEVEL 7

LEVEL 8

AREA MAP

A – B

C – D

E

F – G

H

I – J

K

L – M

A From the beginning of the level, run towards the ramp you can see directly to your right (**1-A**). Jump across the gap to reach the other side (Fig. 1). Walk over to the small pool at the base of the waterfall (**1-B**). Jump (or dive, if you prefer) into the pool. Swim to the opposite side and climb up onto the small platform. Jump vertically to grab the ledge above and pull yourself up.

PRACTICE MAKES PERFECT

In these first few moments of the game, there are no enemies, time limits, traps or unseen dangers. For that reason, this is a good time to try out as many new moves as you can. Handstands, jumping, diving, kicking rocks around… these are just a few examples of the activities you can experiment with here. For a comprehensive list of all moves that Lara can perform (a number of which can be practiced here), turn to page 14.

[01]

[02]

B Walk over to the large rock blocking the path and grab it. Push it forward so that it falls down. Having cleared the way, jump to the opposite platform; doing so will activate the first checkpoint of the game. Turn to the right and jump onto the vertical vine. Climb up until you draw level with another vine to the right. Jump over to it, and then leap once again to reach the platform to the right and another checkpoint. Run forward and jump onto the rope hanging in front of you (**1-C**). Swing straight ahead and jump as soon as you have sufficient speed to land on the platform hidden behind the waterfall (Fig. 2). Don't worry if you miss the jump: you'll simply plunge abruptly but safely into the pool below. Retrace your steps to make another attempt.

FOLLOW HER EYES…

Every time Lara stands near certain points of interest, she will turn her head to look at them. This clue often indicates that you can somehow interact with the object in question. Whenever her gaze strays from the path ahead, always take the time to find out what is drawing her attention elsewhere.

 47

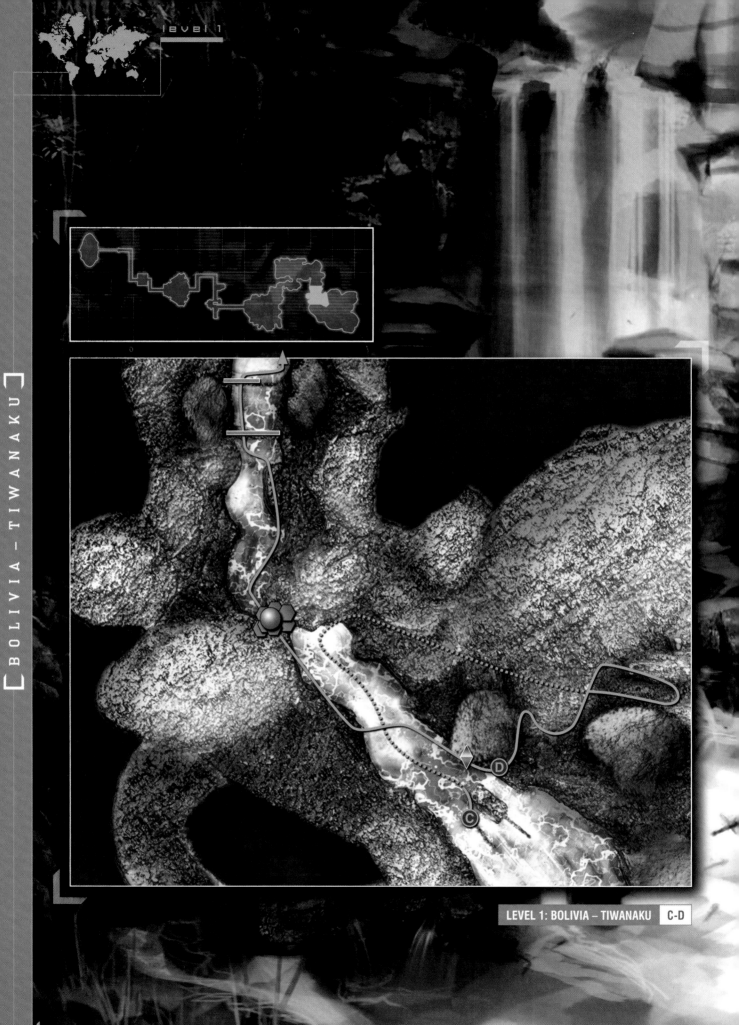

BOLIVIA – TIWANAKU

LEVEL 1: BOLIVIA – TIWANAKU C-D

C Activate your Personal Light Source and walk through the tunnel. As you return to the afternoon sunshine, jump over to the opposite platform. Approach the wall to your left and jump vertically to grab the horizontal ledge (Fig. 3). Move along it to the left until you can go no further, and then jump backwards to grab the ledge behind you. Now climb up to reach the top of the waterfall.

[0 3]

D You will trigger a checkpoint as you first wade into the stream. Note the boulder at the top of the slope. As you approach it, it will suddenly roll forward. Move Lara close to a wall in order to avoid it (Fig. 4). If you prefer, you can also use Manual Aim mode to shoot the debris holding the boulder in place from a position of safety at the bottom of the stream. Continue forward until you reach a small ramp on your right, just before a second waterfall. Use it to jump forward and grab the horizontal pole. Move across to the left side of the pole. Now swing on it and jump over to the second pole. Continue swinging, then jump again to grab the ledge to the left of the waterfall. Move to the right and then jump horizontally to reach the the opposite side.

[0 4]

JUMPING FROM HORIZONTAL POLES

When performing a jump while swinging around a horizontal pole, try to press the jump button just before Lara's feet reach their lowest point during her rotation. If you press the jump button at any other time, there's a greater chance that Lara's leap will be slightly inaccurate. This may mean that you will need to make an additional button press to help her gain a secure grip after she lands on a ledge or another vertical pole.

HOW TO PLAY
WALKTHROUGH
EXTRAS

INTRODUCTION
LEVEL 1
LEVEL 2
LEVEL 3
LEVEL 4
LEVEL 5
LEVEL 6
LEVEL 7
LEVEL 8

AREA MAP
A – B
C – D
E
F – G
H
I – J
K
L – M

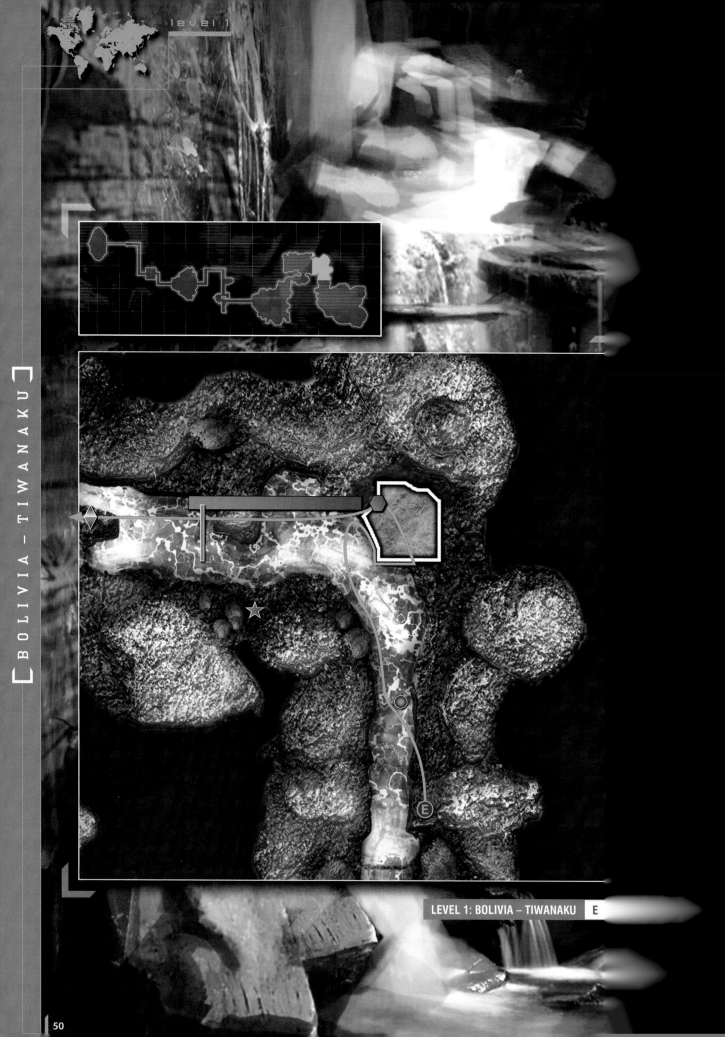

LEVEL 1: BOLIVIA – TIWANAKU   E

HOW TO PLAY

WALKTHROUGH

EXTRAS

INTRODUCTION

LEVEL 1

LEVEL 2

LEVEL 3

LEVEL 4

LEVEL 5

LEVEL 6

LEVEL 7

LEVEL 8

AREA MAP

A – B

C – D

E

F – G

H

I – J

K

L – M

E After the short cutscene, walk slowly towards the soldier, draw your guns and shoot him while his back is turned. If he drops a Health Pack, be sure to collect it (**1-D**). Walk out of the stream and onto the small dry area to your right, beneath the overhang of the raised platform, as the stream bends to the left. Jump up to grab the horizontal ledge above (Fig. 5), then move along to the right until you reach the end of it. Jump up twice to reach the platform above. Grab the big rock and push it forward over the edge. This changes the position of the tree trunk at the centre of the stream, moving a branch into position that can be used to scale the next waterfall. Drop back down into the river, run onto the rock next to the tree trunk, then jump onto the branch. Swing, and then leap: Lara will grab the ledge at the centre of the waterfall. Pull yourself up and run forward to reach a checkpoint.

SPOILS OF WAR

Whenever Lara defeats human adversaries they will, as a rule, drop their weapons, although this does not apply in this first level until you reach the temple exterior (described in paragraph "H"). They may also leave Health Packs behind. You won't find grenades in Bolivia, but these are dropped by mercenaries in the missions that follow. You should always take the time to collect required items once combat ends. Bear in mind that Lara can only carry one weapon in addition to her default pistols. Therefore, if you are carrying a submachine gun and pick up an assault rifle, she will drop the submachine gun.

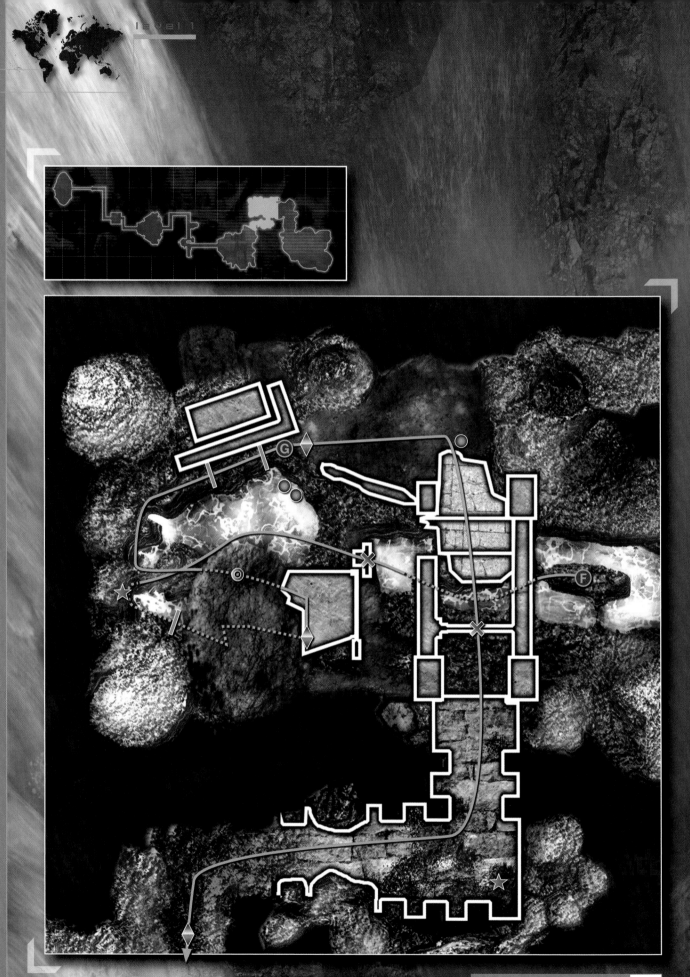

LEVEL 1: BOLIVIA – TIWANAKU   F-G

HOW TO PLAY

WALKTHROUGH

EXTRAS

INTRODUCTION

LEVEL 1

LEVEL 2

LEVEL 3

LEVEL 4

LEVEL 5

LEVEL 6

LEVEL 7

LEVEL 8

AREA MAP

A – B

C – D

E

F – G

H

I – J

K

L – M

 Throw your Magnetic Grapple at the shimmering circular object and then pull it to clear the way forward. As soon as you approach the opening, a cutscene will begin. Afterwards, you will find yourself standing behind two soldiers. Don't hesitate: draw your weapons and open fire, remembering to constantly move and dodge as you do so. With a checkpoint just behind you, this is a good time to practice different attacks and combat techniques. You can find a list of Lara's attacking moves on page 18.

Once the battle is over, walk onto the rock beneath the waterfall and jump up to grab the ledge above. Move quickly to the left: if you are too slow, the middle part of it will crumble, and Lara will fall into the water. This is no great hardship: just climb back up, then jump laterally across the gap to reach the far side of the ledge. Now jump backwards to the horizontal pole, swing around it, and jump towards the opposite ledge. Move along it towards the left, around the corner, and finally jump horizontally to reach yet another ledge. Jump up twice to reach the platform above. Turn around and jump towards the vine hanging from a tree branch. Now swing and jump over to the platform (Fig. 6) hidden behind the waterfall (1-E). Leap over to the horizontal pole that extends from the nearby wall. Swing around it and jump to the second pole; jump again to reach the destination platform and a checkpoint.

[0 6]

[0 7]

G As soon as you land, an enemy soldier will attack you. As the path leading to him is narrow, you have few dodging options. Instead, draw your weapon to automatically aim, run straight at him and perform a sliding tackle (see page 19 for details). This way you can not only avoid his attacks, but also disable him quickly. It's then easy to finish him off.

Run over to the broken bridge and stop as you reach the edge (Fig. 7). You now have to use the Magnetic Grapple to swing for the first time. Simply run forward, jump, and then repeat the button press immediately to attach the grapple. Once you have sufficient momentum, jump over to the platform on the other side (1-F). If you time this badly and fall, you can climb up again using the ruins of the broken bridge below. Continue along the passage until a cutscene is initiated.

BOLIVIA – TIWANAKU

HOW TO PLAY

WALKTHROUGH

EXTRAS

INTRODUCTION

LEVEL 1

LEVEL 2

LEVEL 3

LEVEL 4

LEVEL 5

LEVEL 6

LEVEL 7

LEVEL 8

AREA MAP

A – B

C – D

E

F – G

H

I – J

K

L – M

[0 8]

H After reaching the checkpoint, shoot the branches that are holding the boulders in position directly ahead of Lara. Once the rockslide begins, slide down the slope and open fire. Although these soldiers are often killed by the rolling boulders, you may need to finish one of them off at close quarters. Keep moving as you fight, and don't forget to pick up any Heath Packs they may leave behind (1-G). Two more soldiers await you around the corner once you arrive at the bottom of the slope, with another lying in wait at the top of the path to the left; this soldier drops a submachine gun that you can collect. Try to eliminate the first two before they drop down from the ledge that they appear on (Fig. 8) before you run up to face their comrade (1-H).

Once you have neutralized all immediate dangers, take the sloped path to the left until you reach a rope. Jump onto it, climb higher (approximately two or three meters should suffice), then swing and jump towards the platform ahead. At this point, you have two options. You can begin your attack on the enemies below in Manual Aim mode, or you can attempt an immediate (and direct) assault. As the combat practice is invaluable, we suggest you try the latter. Slide down the slope, draw your weapon, and shoot at the pillar – as it's an environmental hazard, this can be achieved by pressing the relevant button when an icon is displayed – so that it crushes any nearby soldiers as it falls. Kill any other enemies within firing range before you cross the stone bridge, then run over to the other side and finish off any remaining combatants; be sure to check behind the destructible wall to the right of the vehicle (1-I). You can now climb the temple steps. You will see a brief cutscene as you do so and, following that, a checkpoint.

SHOOTING FROM DISTANCE

You will soon find that Lara's ability to hit distant targets is rather limited while using the standard automatic aiming feature. To highlight this, the targeting cursor turns gray when you are too far away from an enemy, indicating that most of your bullets will miss. However, switch to Manual Aim mode, and you can shoot with greater accuracy over longer distances. This is generally only effective against stationary enemies, though: using Manual Aim to hit mobile opponents can be extremely difficult.

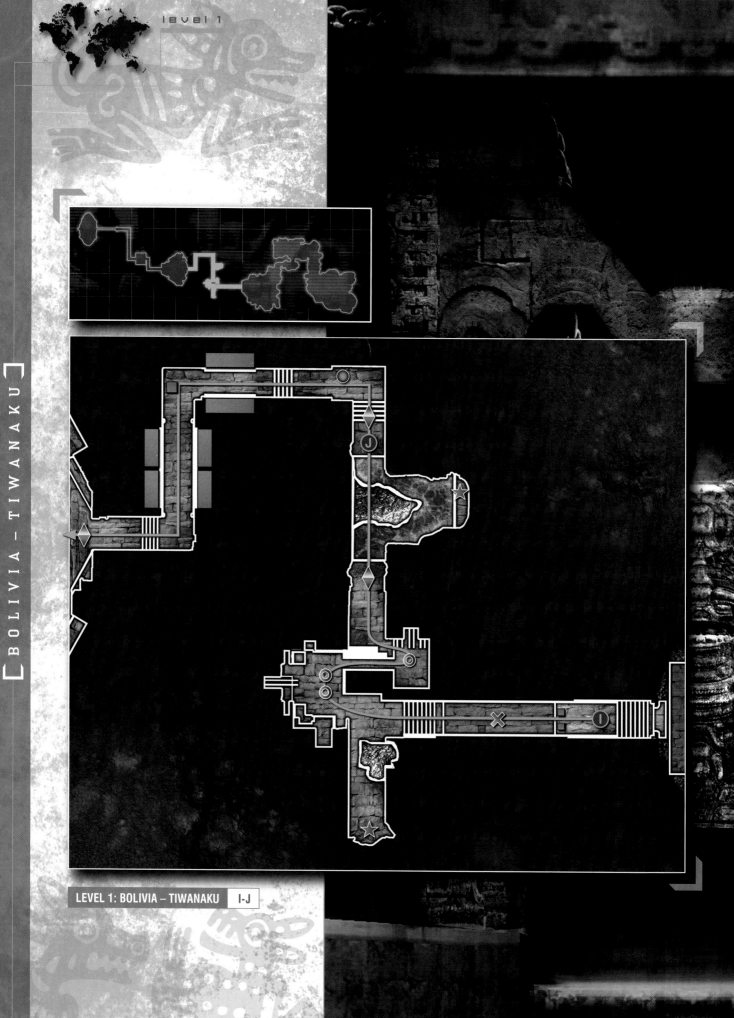

BOLIVIA — TIWANAKU

LEVEL 1: BOLIVIA — TIWANAKU I-J

HOW TO PLAY

WALKTHROUGH

EXTRAS

INTRODUCTION

LEVEL 1

LEVEL 2

LEVEL 3

LEVEL 4

LEVEL 5

LEVEL 6

LEVEL 7

LEVEL 8

[09]

I As you walk along the entrance corridor, kick one of the small stones forward to reveal a deadly floor trap. Approach the gap and attach the Magnetic Grapple to the shimmering metallic seal set in the ceiling (jump, then immediately press the button again), then swing and jump over to the opposite platform. Now climb the steps (**1-J**). Enter the room with two vertical chains. Climb as high as you can up the chain to the right; from there, jump to the second chain. Speed is of the essence here: move as quickly as you can to the top of it, and then jump back to the first chain. You should now be above the obstruction that previously blocked your climb, and can jump over to the opening (Fig. 9). As you enter the next room, jump onto the chain and slide down to reach the ground safely.

Continue forward until you reach a pool of water and a checkpoint (**1-K**). Dive in, swim to the right, then follow the passage around to the left and return to the surface. As long as you don't linger unnecessarily, you will not need to worry about Lara's oxygen gauge. As soon as you exit the water, you will reach a new checkpoint.

JUMPING FROM THE VERTICAL CHAINS

If you have trouble jumping from one vertical chain (or, indeed, rope or pole) to another, try manually aligning the camera so that both chains are on the same axis in your field of vision. This makes leaping between them much easier. Incidentally, bear in mind that Lara can jump both forward and backward while hanging on a chain.

J Prepare yourself: you now have to fight a wild jaguar. Try to catch it by surprise, then dodge it by jumping as you fire. Continue along the corridor. As you descend the second set of steps, watch out for the crushing wall trap (Fig. 10). Approach the walls as they close, dash between them as soon as they reopen, and be ready to roll when they close in again if necessary. Around the corner you face two successive wall traps, and even Lara isn't fast enough to run through both. Grab the nearby crate, and use it as a "shield" to advance through the first wall trap. While it is possible to use the crate to get through both traps in this manner, it's probably easier (and safer) to simply run through the second set of walls. Follow the path until you reach a checkpoint and, as the brief cutscene reveals, the first meaningful puzzle in Tomb Raider Legend.

[10]

MOVING CRATES

When you move crates around, remember that you need to press to the left to move right while pushing them, and vice versa. This does not apply when you drag them, however. It can be frustrating at first, but you'll soon get the hang of it. Handily, in this instance at least, the presence of crushing walls will help to focus your attention on perfecting the technique...

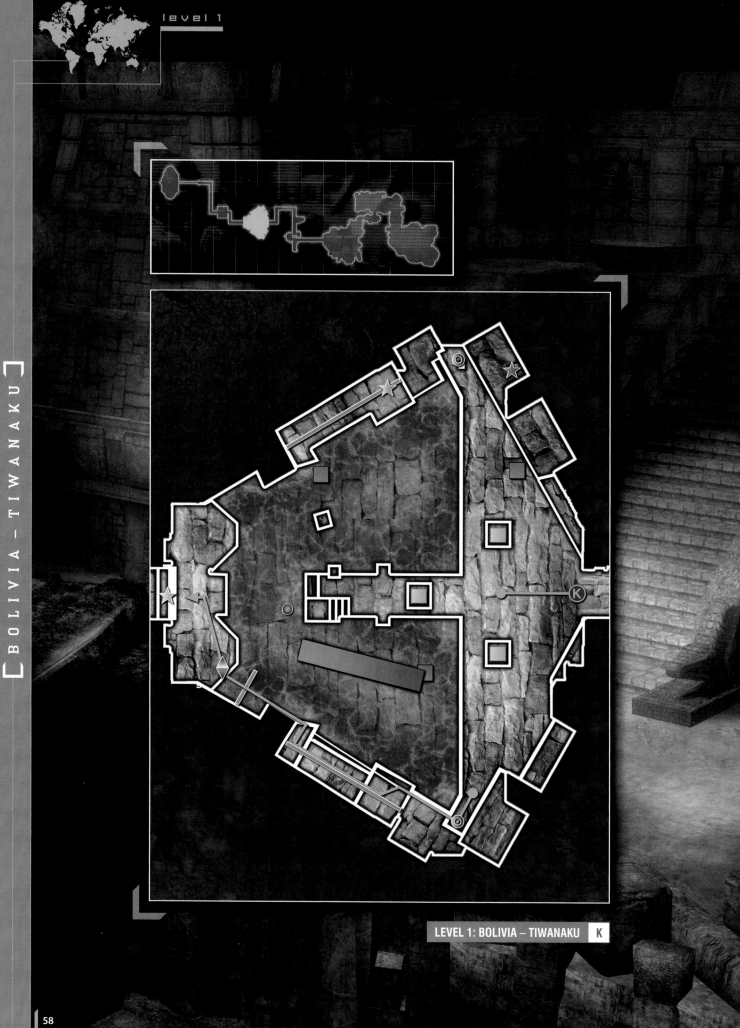

BOLIVIA – TIWANAKU

LEVEL 1: BOLIVIA – TIWANAKU   K

K To solve this puzzle and exit the room, you will need to use three crates. The first is to your right as you enter (**1-L**); the second and third are on the lower level of the room. Before you do anything else, run to the end of the central raised area and dispose of the jaguar lurking below. Do so from above, and you'll be safe from its claws – it's hardly sporting, but it's safer that way. Jump down, grab the crate beneath the teetering-log and pull it out. Now position the crate on the lower teetering-platform. Return to the upper level. Stand at the top of the small set of steps in the centre of the room and, from there, jump onto the upper teetering-platform. The force of Lara's impact will propel the crate onto the upper level. Now grab the crate on the other side of the room, move it into position on the teetering-platform, and then repeat the process described above.

You now have the required three crates on the upper level. Move two of them into position above the pair of adjacent floor switches, then move the third onto the central floor switch. The barrier blocking the exit will be lifted, but there's still a long way to go to reach it (**1-M**). Facing the exit, run to the left-hand corner of the room on the upper level. Climb the chain there and jump over to the narrow ledge (Fig. 11). Move along it, around the corner, and then jump up to the ledge above, before finally pulling yourself up onto the platform. Jump up to grab the chain, move along it until you're above the opposite platform, and then drop down. Walk over the edge of the platform: Lara will drop and hang from it. Drop down again to grab the ledge below. Move sideways along the ledge, jump across to reach the horizontal pole, swing around it, then jump to reach both the exit to the room and a checkpoint (**1-N**).

[11]

HOW TO PLAY

WALKTHROUGH

EXTRAS

INTRODUCTION

LEVEL 1

LEVEL 2

LEVEL 3

LEVEL 4

LEVEL 5

LEVEL 6

LEVEL 7

LEVEL 8

AREA MAP

A – B

C – D

E

F – G

H

I – J

K

L – M

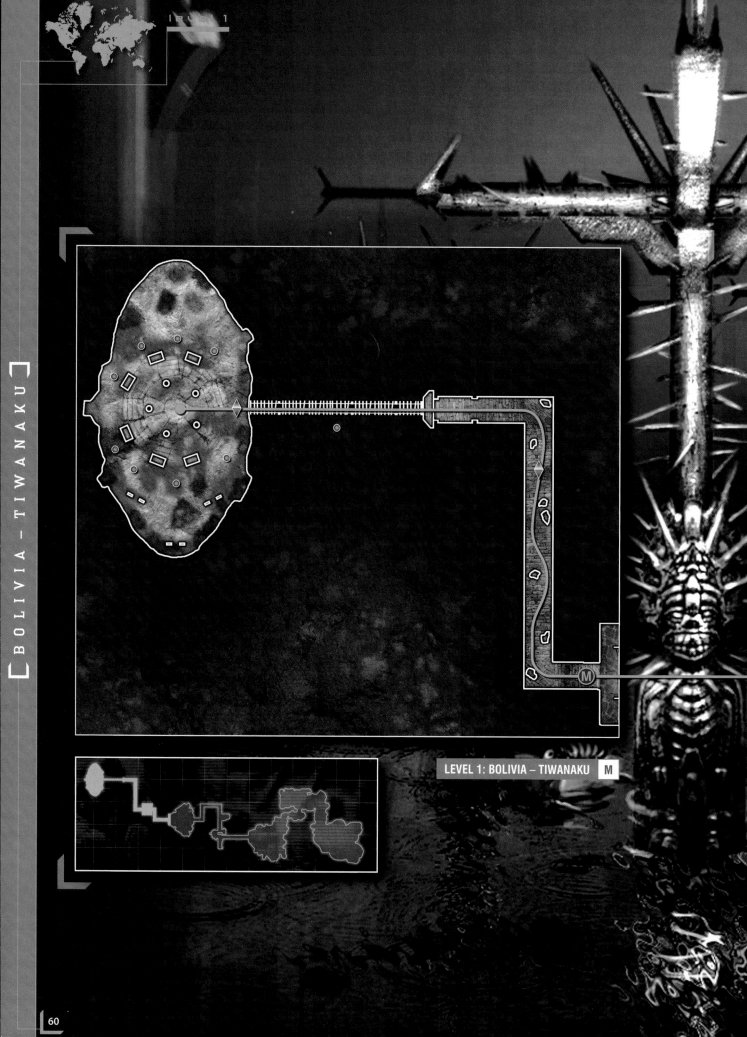

LEVEL 1: BOLIVIA — TIWANAKU **M**

TOMB RAIDER LEGEND

HOW TO PLAY

WALKTHROUGH

EXTRAS

INTRODUCTION

LEVEL 1

LEVEL 2

LEVEL 3

LEVEL 4

LEVEL 5

LEVEL 6

LEVEL 7

LEVEL 8

AREA MAP

A – B

C – D

E

F – G

H

I – J

K

L – M

L As soon as you walk through the exit, a Super Action will begin. In order to survive, you must press the button that corresponds with the symbol displayed on the screen (in this instance, ◎, then ⊗). Follow the corridor and, after passing the checkpoint, slowly approach the abrupt drop that leads to the room below. There is a jaguar at the bottom; if you can get a clear shot, it's prudent to kill it from here in Manual Aim mode. Walk forward slowly so that Lara takes hold of the ledge, then climb along to the right. Drop down, continue right, and then release your grip twice to safely reach the floor below. If you didn't kill the jaguar before, do so now: there's plenty of room to maneuver here as you shoot it (1-O).

Move onto the raised area (Fig. 12) in the corner of the pit. From there, jump towards one of the horizontal poles on the nearest of the four cruel-looking devices situated around the room – it doesn't matter if you choose the left or right pole. When Lara lands, the device will rotate by 90° and then stop. Swing around it and jump again to the next one. Repeat this process until you reach a wall ledge. Move along to the right until you encounter a gap, then jump over to reach the ledge on the opposite side (1-P). Move as far to the right as you can, jump up to the ledge above, move right, and then jump vertically again. Now move left, jump at the end to grab the ledge on the opposite side, and move around the corner until you can go no further. Leap to the left to land on a platform safely above the pit. Walk over to the wall, jump vertically to grab its ledge and pull yourself up.

[12]

LEVEL 1: BOLIVIA – TIWANAKU L

M Follow the corridor until you reach a checkpoint and, beyond it, a bridge. After the cutscene, Lara finds herself in a decidedly precarious situation. As soon as control of her is returned to you, run forward and jump the gaps as they appear to avoid being killed by the helicopter. Jump over the final gap (Fig. 13), and pull yourself up onto the platform. You now have to defeat no less than eight mercenaries. Move and dodge constantly to avoid their attacks, use cover when required, and remember that the combination of a sliding tackle followed by a burst of bullets as an opponent lies prone can be a highly effective combat technique.

[13]

PERU – RETURN TO PARAÍSO

LOCATION	PARAÍSO (PERU)
WEATHER	PARTLY CLOUDY
TERRAIN	SOUTH AMERICAN VILLAGE, EXCAVATION SITE
TIME	AFTERNOON
LARA'S OUTFIT	LEGEND

EXTRAS

INTRODUCTION

LEVEL 1

LEVEL 2

LEVEL 3

LEVEL 4

LEVEL 5

LEVEL 6

LEVEL 7

LEVEL 8

AREA MAP

A – B

C – D

E – G

H – J

K

L – M

PERU – RETURN TO PARAÍSO

LEVEL 2: PERU – RETURN TO PARAÍSO `A-B`

MISSION DETAILS

A You take control of Lara in the village's main street (**2-A**). Follow the road until you reach the large door that leads to the market square. You will cross a checkpoint on the way. After the cinematic interlude, you must defeat two successive groups of soldiers. To avoid having to fight all members of the first wave simultaneously, you can take cover in the areas either side of the steps leading to the church entrance. Keep moving, pick off your adversaries methodically, and try to shoot the truck's fuel tank (and, of course, the explosive barrels littered around the area) if you have the opportunity to take soldiers out with the resultant explosion. After the first group of enemies has been defeated, a brief cutscene will show the arrival of a second wave of soldiers.

Once you have eliminated the majority of your foes, emerge from cover and dispatch any remaining soldiers. Now run around and collect as much rifle ammunition as Lara can carry – you'll need it for the forthcoming battles. As you saw in the brief cutscene, a man equipped with a shotgun is waiting for Lara on one of the balconies. Climb on the vertical pole with a flag at the top (Fig. 1), jump to the adjacent balcony, and then kill him from there (**2-B**, **2-C**, **2-D**). Approach the second gap in the railings and grapple swing across to the balcony where the man with the shotgun previously stood. Go through the smashed door. You will reach a checkpoint inside the house, and will find a set of grenades. Collect them, then kick the door to exit.

INTRODUCTION

LEVEL 1

LEVEL 2

LEVEL 3

LEVEL 4

LEVEL 5

LEVEL 6

LEVEL 7

LEVEL 8

[0 1]

CAN I KICK IT? (YES YOU CAN!)

At the village entrance, you will find a soccer ball on the ground to the right of Lara. Feel free to kick it around. Lara doesn't have the skills of a professional player, but she can still bounce the ball against walls or even volley it. You can also practice Lara's combat skills (including kicks) on the training dummy just ahead of the entrance. Further into the village, Lara can also put her feet to good use by kicking doors and closets open. You never know what might be hidden inside...

AREA MAP

A – B

C – D

E – G

H – J

K

L – M

B In this next section of the village, your goal is to follow the street to its end. There are many solders to fight – indeed, you will see one the very moment you step out of the door. From your position on the rooftop, immediately kill the enemy standing on the small balcony. Now drop to the lower level and use the nearby alley for cover while picking off your assailants one by one; there are explosive barrels that you can shoot to kill or injure nearby enemies. Be very careful to avoid any grenades thrown in your direction. It's also worth remembering that you can use the Magnetic Grapple to pull soldiers down from rooftops and balconies if you wish. Now move cautiously forward to the corner of the street – there may well be another solder on the balcony beside the blue-grey building – collecting ammunition, grenades and Health Packs as you progress.

Three more enemies will ambush Lara as she walks around the corner. Immediately throw a grenade at the man hiding behind the barrels and market stall, then shoot his partner as he emerges from the alleyway (**2-E**). Have a weapon at the ready as you run towards the next junction. A truck will screech to a halt in front of you. The easiest way to kill the man behind the turret is to immediately shoot the power transformer above him (Fig. 2). Now quickly take cover behind the sheet of corrugated iron and dispatch the pair of soldiers that run in from the left and right. The final group of soldiers can be found around the corner to your left. As they are taking cover behind destructible crates, the most efficient way to dispatch them is by using grenades. Stock up on items dropped by the soldiers, then run over to the motorbike to continue.

[0 2]

GRENADES

This section of Tomb Raider Legend is the first to feature combat involving hand grenades. Grenades are a powerful tool: they can be used to dispatch entire groups of soldiers, flush assailants from cover, and destroy destructible items that enemies are hiding behind. Soldiers will generally attempt to dive for cover when they see Lara throw a grenade in their direction. You can often prevent this by firing a short, controlled burst of fire to stun them long enough for the device to explode. When facing soldiers that use grenades, always listen out for the telltale sound that the devices make when thrown, as they can be very hard to spot in the heat of battle.

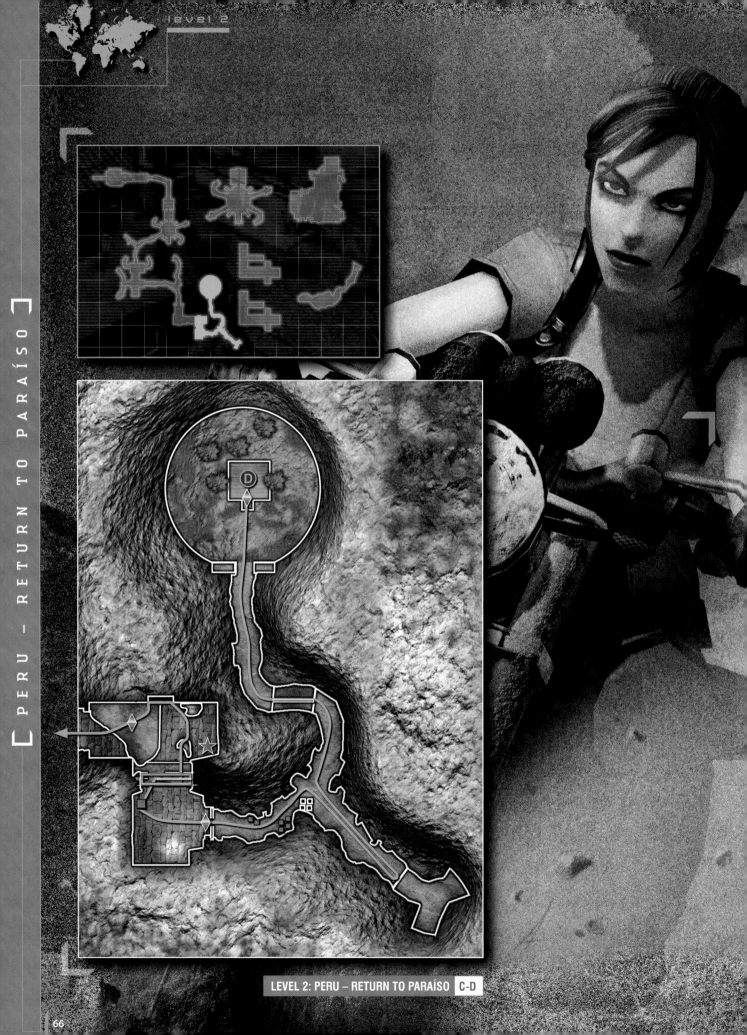

[PERU – RETURN TO PARAÍSO]

D

…

 C The motorbike ride en route to the excavation site is divided into three sections by two checkpoints, and contains a number of specific hazards and set pieces. Before we discuss these, there are a few things that you should bear in mind. First and foremost, Lara will lose energy if she crashes, so keep your eye on the road ahead at all times. That doesn't mean that you should drive slowly, though: although it may not be immediately apparent, you are working against a time limit. Secondly, look out for red and white Health Packs: you can collect these by running over them (Fig. 3). Finally, remember that you can heal Lara at any time by pressing ✛.

When the motorbike sequence begins, you are given a short amount of time to become accustomed to the controls. Measured use of 🄻 is the key to successfully navigating obstacles – such as rocks and generic crates – and safely making your way around bends. After a short time, you will encounter a ramp in front of a wooden fence: use the former to jump the latter. This is followed immediately by another wooden fence. Immediately shoot the explosive barrel when the button icon appears to pass through safely. You now have to fight a number of enemies riding motorbikes. Tackle them one at a time, driving close enough to increase the accuracy of Lara's pistols, but not so close that she's an easy target when they return fire. Get used to regulating your speed, releasing the accelerator to allow enemies to pull ahead if they are too close, or braking to allow them to overtake you. Be quick to dodge when they fall from their bikes – Lara will slow down and sustain damage if she hits them – and avoid situations where you face two or three riders simultaneously. Occasionally, you will see explosive barrels on either side of the track. You can use these to knock nearby riders from their bikes, but be careful not to shoot them if Lara could be caught in the blast. On the Tomb Raider difficulty or while racing a Time Trial, it can help to weave erratically while riding

close to enemy riders to confuse them. This can prevent Lara from sustaining too many hits, but is very much an expert tip for players with prior experience of this section.

You will reach the first checkpoint of the motorbike sequence when you reach a burning bridge. Jump from the ramp on the left-hand side, then use the ramp on the right-hand side to cross it safely. The following section features pitched battles against numerous riders: don't be surprised to face more than three at any one time. Try to maintain a safe distance, always aiming to kill the enemy at the rear of the pack first. You should also be especially careful when fighting the riders armed with shotguns: at close range, their weapons can inflict large amounts of damage. After the second checkpoint, you will encounter a group of three trucks. Move over to the left to dodge the crates dropped by the rearmost vehicle. Now drive alongside it, and then move over to the right to avoid crates dropped by the truck furthest forward. Kill the two soldiers on the back of the truck, then drive up the ramp to initiate a cutscene.

[03]

 D From the wooden platform, run straight ahead. Crouch or roll through the low gap to enter the tunnel, and get into the habit of regularly throwing flares to illuminate the dimly lit passages. Follow the corridor and jump vertically to hang onto the horizontal bar when you reach the gap. Move along the bar, then let go once you have crossed the pit. When a cave-in blocks the left-hand route, backtrack and pick a path through the stalactites and stalagmites. Crouch or roll under the iron spikes – you will pass a checkpoint as you do so – and then grab hold of the nearby crate and push it onto the floor switch. This activates a trap that fires spears from the walls. Don't worry: Lara cannot be injured by this. Climb onto the crate and jump from there to the only spear that remains in a horizontal position (Fig. 4). Swing on it and jump to the nearby platform (2-F). Run and jump over to the ledge just above the face carved into the

brickwork. Move along to the left and jump laterally to reach the exit to the room and a checkpoint.

[04]

HOW TO PLAY

WALKTHROUGH

EXTRAS

INTRODUCTION

LEVEL 1

LEVEL 2

LEVEL 3

LEVEL 4

LEVEL 5

LEVEL 6

LEVEL 7

LEVEL 8

AREA MAP

A – B

C – D

E – G

H – J

K

L – M

LEVEL 2: PERU – RETURN TO PARAÍSO **E-G**

[05]

E In the next room, light the way forward with a flare and drop down just in front of the activated trap. You can then walk under the spears on the right-hand side (Fig. 5). Pull the round boulder backwards and leave it in the corner. Be cautious now: by removing the boulder from the floor switch, you have reactivated the trap! Cross the floor switch by retracing your steps to avoid being gored by the spikes as they emerge. Now jump onto the platform in the corner and leap over to the rope hanging from the small crane. Climb higher on the rope, then swing and jump onto the platform on the upper level. Go through the open door to reach a checkpoint.

F As soon as you drop down to the ground, a cutscene begins. Once it ends, you are pursued by the Unknown Entity. Run forward and jump above the two piles of debris, then drop down into the room below. You will reach a new checkpoint. Move over to the left of the room, climb the two small steps, then jump vertically and pull yourself onto the platform above. Push the round boulder down to the lower level, then maneuver it onto the floor switch: this activates the dilapidated trap. Climb back onto the platform in the corner. Jump onto the central platform, and from there to the spear. Adjust your position so that Lara is in alignment with the rope (Fig. 6), and then jump over. Move to a slightly higher position on the rope, swing, and then jump to the far platform to reach a checkpoint (**2-G**).

[06]

THE "UNKNOWN ENTITY"

Once you have reached the upper platform above the spear trap after positioning the boulder on the switch below, Amanda appears behind the bars to the left of Lara. Take the time to pause and view an atmospheric aside before you jump over to the horizontal pole. After Amanda flees in terror, wait for a moment, and you can watch the fearsome Unknown Entity run through the corridor in fast pursuit of Lara's friends.

G Run through the corridor, hopping over the debris, until you reach a metal pipe. Jump up and grab it, then cross the pit (Fig. 7). Release your grip and run forward to initiate a cutscene. After it ends, the action returns to the present day...

[07]

HOW TO PLAY

WALKTHROUGH

EXTRAS

INTRODUCTION

LEVEL 1

LEVEL 2

LEVEL 3

LEVEL 4

LEVEL 5

LEVEL 6

LEVEL 7

LEVEL 8

AREA MAP

A – B

C – D

E – G

H – J

K

L – M

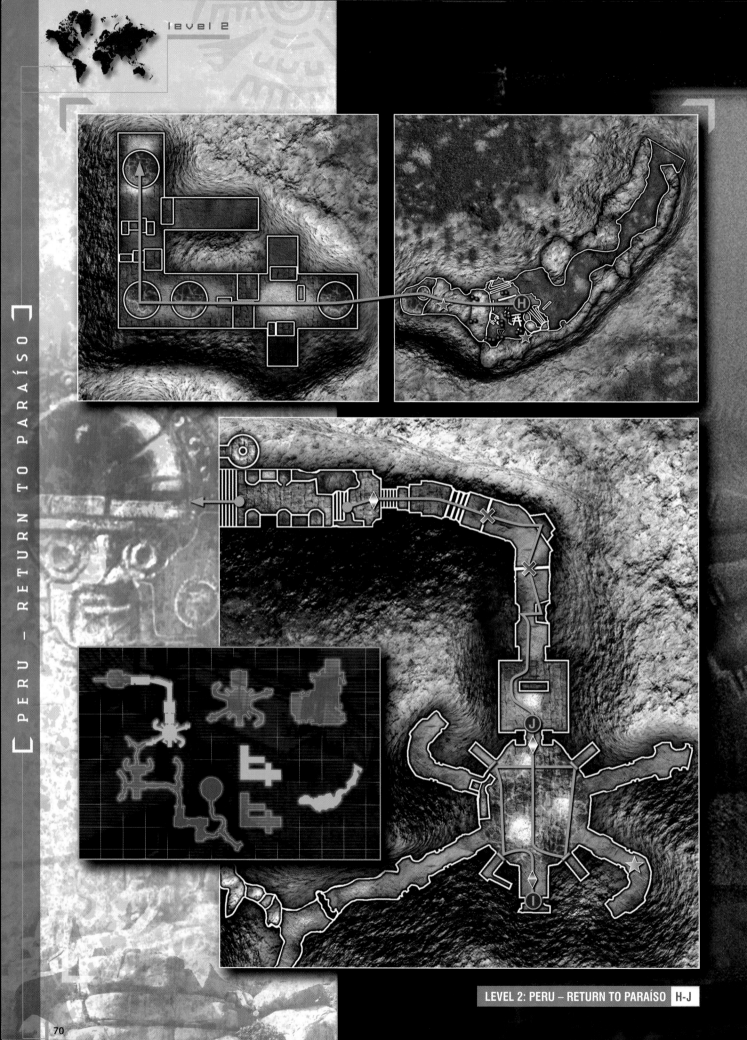

PERU – RETURN TO PARAÍSO

HOW TO PLAY

WALKTHROUGH

EXTRAS

INTRODUCTION

LEVEL 1

LEVEL 2

LEVEL 3

LEVEL 4

LEVEL 5

LEVEL 6

LEVEL 7

LEVEL 8

AREA MAP

A – B

C – D

E – G

H – J

K

L – M

H You resume the adventure at the excavation site (**2-H, 2-I.**) Head towards the pool and dive in, then swim straight to the bottom. Now swim horizontally into the only available passage. At the end of it, quickly swim up to the air pocket. Take the time to allow Lara's oxygen gauge to fill, then dive to the bottom again. Swim through the broken iron bars, and then immediately swim up to the surface again. Breath, dive to the bottom and go through the passage opposite the broken bars. Return to the surface for more air, then plunge back to the depths and swim through the small arch (Fig. 8). After the checkpoint, you'll find yourself inside a large, water-filled room.

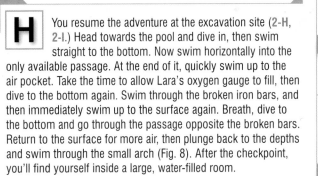

[0 8]

SWIM FASTER

When you are going through the submerged maze (paragraph **H**) and solving the puzzle in the large room (paragraph **I**), you will find your task much easier if you swim faster by repeatedly pressing ▲. This will help you to reach the required destination at greater speed, and is essential if you are to solve the approaching underwater puzzle...

I Look under the water, and you will see four blue stones beneath the surface. Your goal here is to activate all four of these switches. However, they only remain in their glowing "active" state for a short period of time. To solve the puzzle, you need to interact with all four with only one intake of breath to sustain Lara as she swims between them. Dive and swim from one gem to the next, using ▲ to both increase your swimming speed and pull each glowing switch (Fig. 9). Don't worry if Lara's oxygen gauge is almost empty as you approach the last one, as a cutscene will resolve the situation on your behalf (**2-J**). Jump through the hole in the wall to reach a checkpoint.

[0 9]

J Continue forward after the cutscene until you reach a slope that is too steep for Lara to climb. Grab the wall ledge on the left, jump up again, then leap backwards to grab the ledge opposite. Pull yourself up onto the platform. Run, jump and grapple swing from the shimmering beam above to reach the flat area. Another slope prevents further progress. This time, grab the wall ledge on the right-hand side, jump up and climb onto the platform. Swing over the slope with your grapple to reach the safety of the steps (Fig. 10). Climb them to pass a checkpoint. The next room features an interactive cutscene. You will first need to make Lara run (**L** ↑), jump (❌), then finally grab the ledge safely (▲).

[1 0]

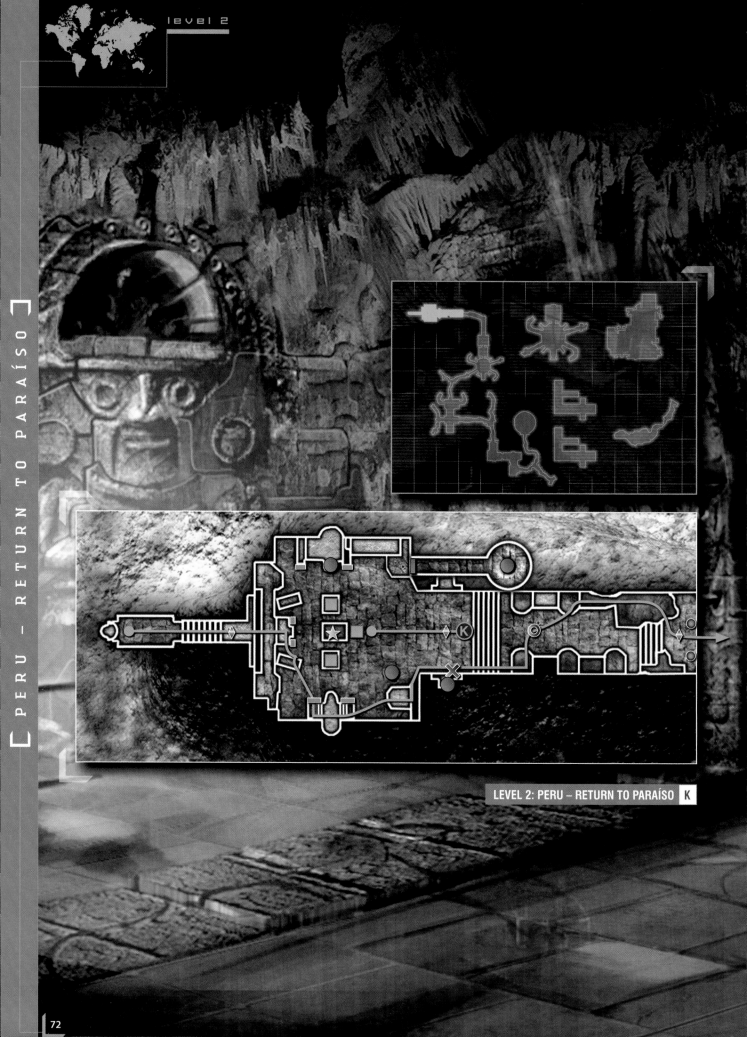

PERU – RETURN TO PARAÍSO

LEVEL 2: PERU – RETURN TO PARAÍSO K

HOW TO PLAY

WALKTHROUGH

EXTRAS

INTRODUCTION

LEVEL 1

LEVEL 2

LEVEL 3

LEVEL 4

LEVEL 5

LEVEL 6

LEVEL 7

LEVEL 8

AREA MAP

A – B

C – D

E – G

H – J

K

L – M

K In order to solve the puzzle in this area, you will need three round boulders – only one of which is initially at your disposal. The second is very easy to obtain when you know how. Move to the top of the steps, and cast Lara's gaze at the pillar to the left. Fire the Magnetic Grapple at the shimmering plate near its top (Fig. 11), then pull it: the pillar will fall forward and release the boulder that lay on top of it. Grab the boulder, then roll it onto the floor switch to the right of the small statue.

[1 1]

Climb one of the new ladders on the right-hand side of the area – these are the "arms" of the statue that were opened during the cutscene. Jump horizontally to grab the middle ledge, move to its central point, and jump vertically twice to hang from the statue's "head". Jump laterally (either direction is fine) to reach one of the upper ladders, climb up, and you'll find the third boulder at the top. Push it over the edge. You can either retrace your steps to return to the ground below or, alternatively, jump onto the upper platform that extends from the far wall, slide down the slope beside it, then climb down one of the two ladders to achieve the same (but more immediate) result.

Move the two boulders onto the remaining floor switches. As the last one is moved into position, the puzzle is solved. Climb one of the ladders in front of the statue to reach the passage that opened moments before.

After the cutscene, a checkpoint is activated. Jump to grab the ledge on your right (when facing in the direction of the altar beneath). Jump again and pull yourself up onto the platform. From there, jump over to the ladder and climb to the top of the statue. Cross it and jump to the pillar. Grab the wall ledge just above it, and move along it towards the left. Jump laterally across the two gaps and keep going until Lara hangs above another pillar, then drop down to reach it (**2-K**). Jump to the hanging rope, swing in the direction of the pillar in front of you and jump over to it. Leap over to the next pillar and you'll see two guards. Slide down the slope and fight them at close quarters; this is quicker and potentially less damaging than trading shots in Manual Aim mode from above. A checkpoint is triggered as you reach the platform below.

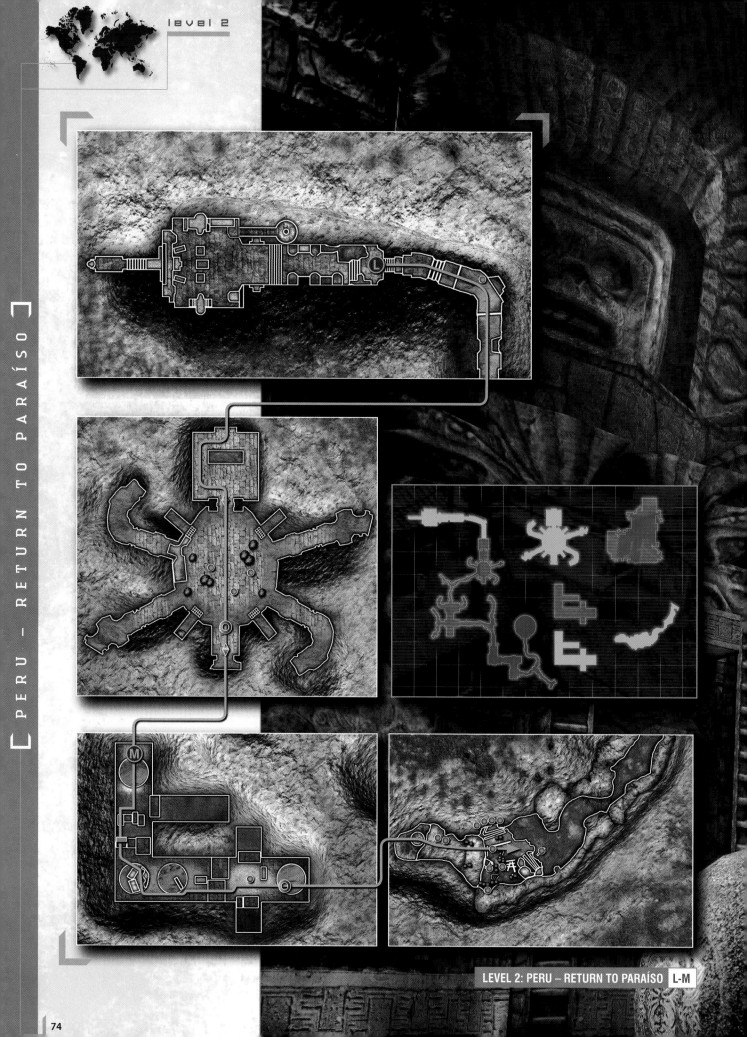

PERU – RETURN TO PARAÍSO

HOW TO PLAY

WALKTHROUGH

EXTRAS

INTRODUCTION

LEVEL 1

LEVEL 2

LEVEL 3

LEVEL 4

LEVEL 5

LEVEL 6

LEVEL 7

LEVEL 8

AREA MAP

A – B

C – D

E – G

H – J

K

L – M

L Run forward, slide down the slope and simultaneously eliminate the soldier at the foot of the steps. Retrace your steps until you reach a checkpoint. There are three mercenaries waiting for you in the big round room. Approach the cracked wall, switch to Manual Aim mode, and throw a grenade through to make them dive for cover (Fig. 12). Now jump through the hole and open fire. When the chamber is cleared of enemies, grab the rope hanging opposite the cracked wall panel, then climb it and swing to reach the arch you swam through earlier. Walk through it to reach a checkpoint.

[12]

M Run up the passage until you reach a ladder. Climb it and go through the broken iron bars. Grab the ledge to the left, jump vertically, and then pull yourself up onto the platform. Draw a weapon immediately and dodge as you shoot at the soldier in front of you (Fig. 13). Jump on the rope that hangs from above, and climb it. When you reach the top, jump over to solid ground (there's a checkpoint here) and launch an assault on the enemies located in this area. There's plenty of cover to hide behind, so use it wisely: the old shack is a good spot to begin your attack. When the first group of soldiers has been eliminated, reinforcements will arrive and drop down from the ledge. You can either fire at them with Manual Aim mode from a distance, or run over and engage them at close range. After a brief cutscene, a final enemy will appear and begin firing at Anaya's jeep. Kill him to end the level.

[13]

TEMPORARY COVER

At the excavation site there are small crates to hide behind, but you should remember that they are eminently destructible and will not survive many bullet impacts. Don't linger too long behind them: they offer temporary refuge from incoming fire, and little more.

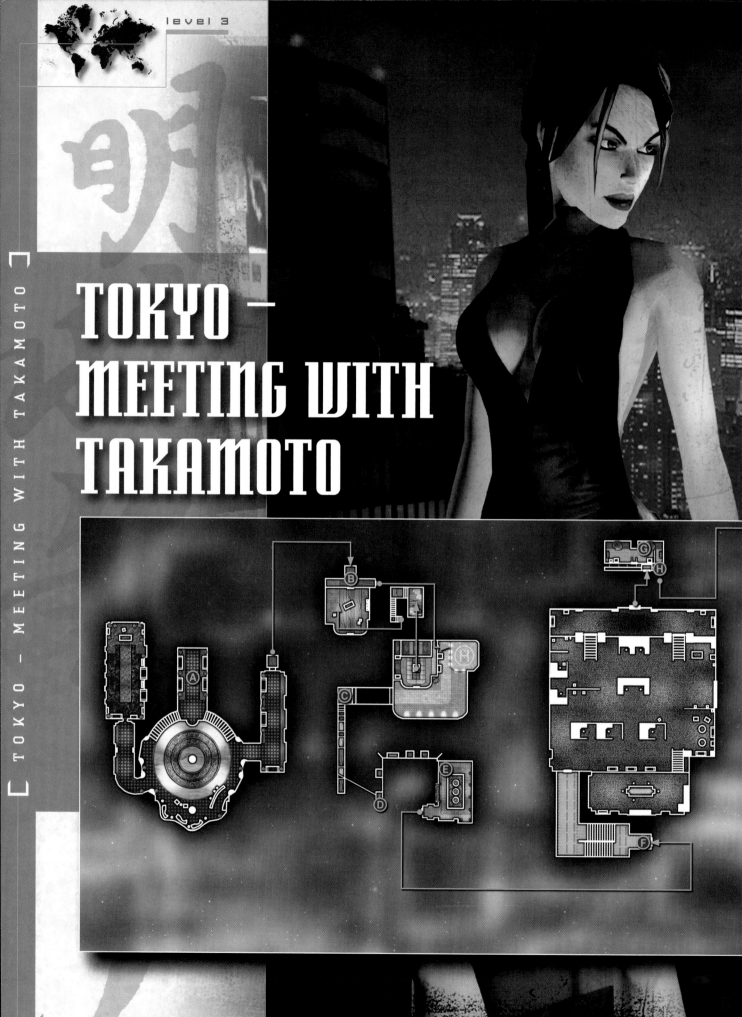

TOKYO – MEETING WITH TAKAMOTO

HOW TO PLAY

WALKTHROUGH

EXTRAS

INTRODUCTION

LEVEL 1

LEVEL 2

LEVEL 3

LEVEL 4

LEVEL 5

LEVEL 6

LEVEL 7

LEVEL 8

AREA MAP

A – B

C – E

F – H

I – J

K – L

AREA MAP

LOCATION	TOKYO (JAPAN)
WEATHER	CLEAR
TERRAIN	BUILDINGS AND ROOFTOPS
TIME	LATE EVENING
LARA'S OUTFIT	EVENING GOWN

MISSION DETAILS

HOW TO PLAY

WALKTHROUGH

EXTRAS

INTRODUCTION

LEVEL 1

LEVEL 2

LEVEL 3

LEVEL 4

LEVEL 5

LEVEL 6

LEVEL 7

LEVEL 8

AREA MAP

A – B

C – E

F – H

I – J

K – L

A Walk downstairs and talk to the bartender. Facing the bar, walk to your right. Enter the corridor and open the door at the end. After the cutscene, return to the party to meet a new group of guests. As soon as the fight against Takamoto's henchmen begins, run back to the corridor leading to Nishimura's office to avoid being shot at from all sides. Make well-timed sorties from cover, firing at any adversaries that have the foolish temerity to stand within shooting range (Fig. 1), then carefully make your way out into the bar area to kill any remaining Yakuza. Remember to dive behind cover every time you need to reload, and grab weapons dropped by slain foes whenever you can. After the cutscene that follows the battle, enter the elevator – it's at the end of the corridor to the left as you face the bar.

[01]

B Having left the elevator, run through the glass door at the end of the corridor to reach a checkpoint. Look to your right, and you'll see a fuel barrel beneath the metal structure. From a safe distance, draw your pistols and shoot it. Climb the vertical pole revealed by the explosion and jump over to the platform on your right. Pull yourself up, and then climb onto the rooftop (**3-A**). You should notice that the raised portion of the skylight is shimmering. This indicates that you can move it with the Magnetic Grapple. Stand to the left-hand side of it, attach the grapple, then pull to create an opening (Fig. 2). Drop into the room below and go down the stairway (**3-B**, **3-C**). Now jump on the motorcycle. It's a powerful machine: occasional taps of the accelerator button will be more than sufficient as you maneuver it into position. Ride it out of the hangar, turn right and turn to face the incomplete bridge between the two buildings. Hold the accelerator for full throttle, and be ready to participate in an interactive cutscene (the buttons are ⬜, ⨯ and ◎). After this dramatic interlude, you will reach a new checkpoint.

[02]

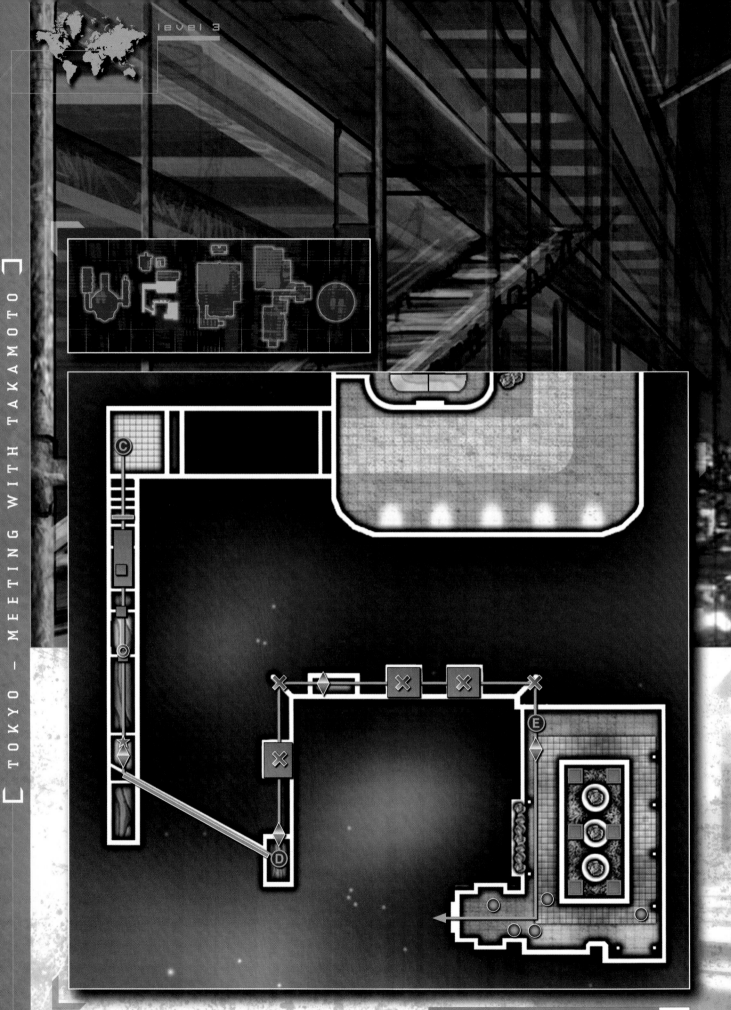

TOKYO – MEETING WITH TAKAMOTO

LEVEL 3: TOKYO – MEETING WITH TAKAMOTO   C-E

[03]

C

Jump to the yellow and black vertical bar (**3-D**), swing around it and jump over to the wooden scaffolding. The first scaffold is not firmly secured, so its far edge will tip when Lara walks on it; for that reason, you should run forward and quickly jump to the second scaffold. Once there, switch to Manual Aim mode and shoot at the base of the rope to release the glass panel (Fig. 3). Now jump onto the rope. Swing over to the next platform. Kick the barrel aside, then make a vertical jump to grab hold of the zip line. Lara will slide down it and trigger a checkpoint as she lands.

[04]

D

Turn to the left from your position facing the wall of the building. Throw your Magnetic Grapple at the window-cleaning platform, pull it all the way towards you, then release the grapple (see "Swinging Platforms" for further advice). The platform will swing back and forth. As soon as it moves back in your direction, jump over to it (Fig. 4). As the platform swings towards the corner of the building, run, jump and attach the Magnetic Grapple to the light. Now turn to your right, swing, and jump to the nearby platform to reach a checkpoint. Two more window-cleaning platforms lie ahead. Use the same technique as previously to reach the second of these. Now jump and attach your Magnetic Grapple to the light as before, turn to face the broken safety barrier, retract your grapple cord a little, then swing safely onto the roof terrace. You will pass a checkpoint as you land.

SWINGING PLATFORMS

If you have a hard time making the jump to the window-cleaning platforms, there is an easy way to make them swing with greater vigor. Throw the grapple and pull the platform towards your position. As soon as it begins to swing away, stop pulling. Once it heads back towards you, resume the button presses. Repeat this two or three times to build sufficient momentum, then make the required leap.

E

Eliminate the enemies that rush to greet you on the roof terrace; they have two attack dogs that should be your first priority. You can shoot the six gas lanterns that surround the raised central area (Fig. 5). Destroy one whenever a henchman or dog is close to inflict damage, but be careful to ensure that Lara isn't caught in the explosion. After the battle, head to the far right-hand corner and open the door.

[05]

HOW TO PLAY

WALKTHROUGH

EXTRAS

INTRODUCTION

LEVEL 1

LEVEL 2

LEVEL 3

LEVEL 4

LEVEL 5

LEVEL 6

LEVEL 7

LEVEL 8

AREA MAP

A – B

C – E

F – H

I – J

K – L

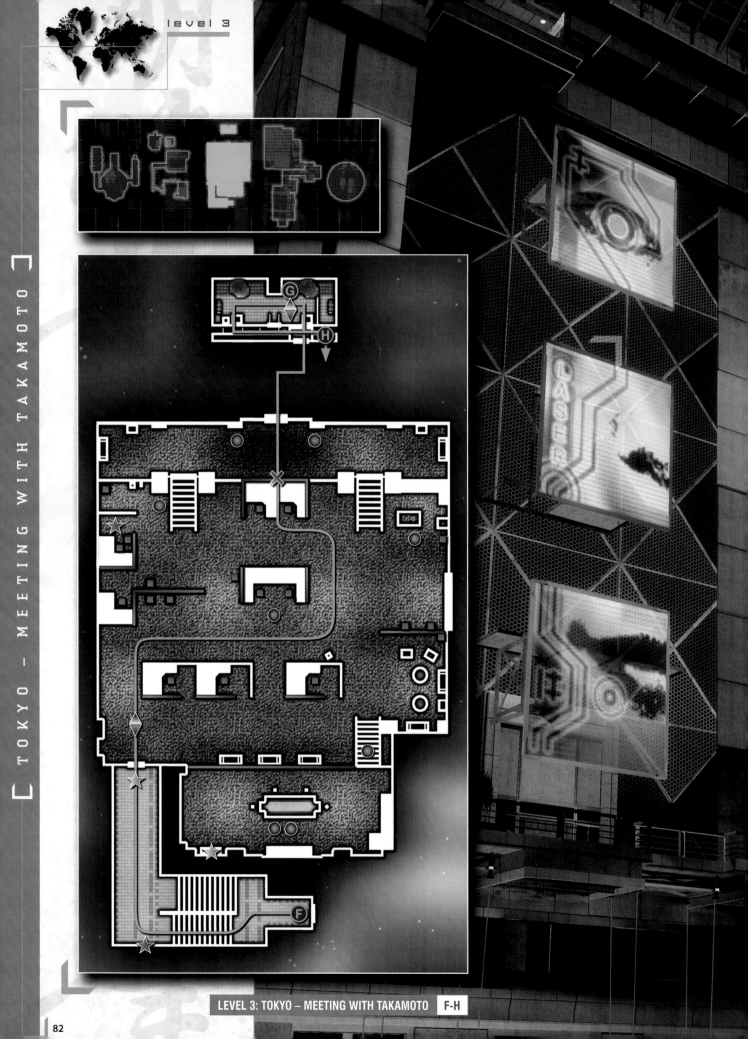

TOKYO – MEETING WITH TAKAMOTO

LEVEL 3: TOKYO – MEETING WITH TAKAMOTO F-H

HOW TO PLAY

WALKTHROUGH

EXTRAS

INTRODUCTION

LEVEL 1

LEVEL 2

LEVEL 3

LEVEL 4

LEVEL 5

LEVEL 6

LEVEL 7

LEVEL 8

AREA MAP

A – B

C – E

F – H

I – J

K – L

[06]

F Climb the stairs (3-E) and you'll see a corridor to your right (3-F). Walk along it and open the door to reach a checkpoint. There are several henchmen to fight in this room, but there is also plenty of cover. If you sneak in quietly, you can pick a good defensible position before you begin your attack. The partition wall just in front of the entrance is a good spot. Once the battle begins, don't allow the Yakuza with shotguns to approach you: they can be extremely dangerous at close range. Once the battle is over, face the huge monitor screen. Shoot at the clasps that secure it to the ropes on both upper corners (Fig. 6), then throw your grapple at the central "T" symbol and pull (3-G, 3-H). Two highly aggressive henchmen will appear after the screen falls. The most direct way to deal with them is to jump onto the makeshift platform, throw a grenade at one, then open fire on his partner. Go through the door to reach a checkpoint.

THE ELEMENT OF SURPRISE

When Lara enters certain areas that feature enemies, they will not attack until they actively notice her arrival. This applies to the battle described in paragraph **F**. Use the element of surprise to your advantage. After entering the room, hide behind the partition wall just in front of you. Turn to your right: you will see that two Yakuza are congregated on the upper area of the office, while the others pace around the office cubicles. If you wish, you can switch to Manual Aim mode and hurl a couple of well-placed grenades to initiate your attack, potentially catching your enemies off-guard.

[07]

G Jump onto the drainpipe (it's to your left as you walk outside). Climb as far as you can, jump towards the nearby ledge, and move around the corner. Jump up, then pull yourself up onto the platform above. Throw the Magnetic Grapple at the shimmering metal plates, then pull to rotate the neon sign and move a new platform into position (Fig. 7). Jump over to it and, from there, to the subsequent platform. You'll reach a checkpoint at the top of the ladder.

[08]

H Turn around, throw your grapple at the shimmering target as before, then pull to rotate the sign. Jump to the horizontal pole, swing around it and jump over to the platform ahead. Climb to the top of the vertical pole, then jump over to the platform behind (Fig. 8) and pull yourself up. Jump onto the vertical pole, climb it, then jump over to the horizontal bar. Once the third neon sign has moved into position, jump back to the vertical pole and, from there, to the new platform above. Now run and jump to the next platform, but don't linger at the far edge; the mechanism is not secured, and Lara's weight will tip the platform downward if she pauses there. You reach a checkpoint as you reach the (relative) safety of the next small platform. Jump onto the vertical pole in front of you, and climb it rapidly: it isn't entirely secure, and can only bear Lara's weight for a very limited period of time. As soon as you are level with a horizontal pole, jump over to it. Quickly swing from each of the four poles before they snap, to reach a balcony. Pass through the door to activate a checkpoint.

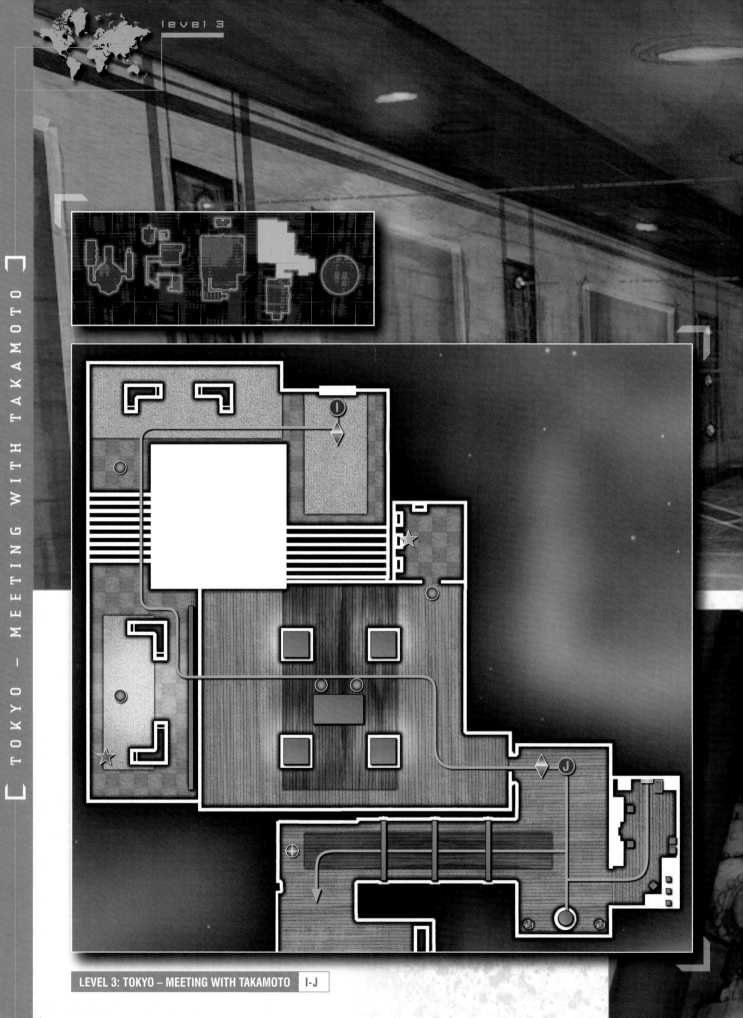

LEVEL 3: TOKYO – MEETING WITH TAKAMOTO I-J

HOW TO PLAY

WALKTHROUGH

EXTRAS

INTRODUCTION

LEVEL 1

LEVEL 2

LEVEL 3

LEVEL 4

LEVEL 5

LEVEL 6

LEVEL 7

LEVEL 8

AREA MAP

A — B

C — E

F — H

I — J

K — L

[09]

I From the entrance, you can see a few men engaged in conversation at the end of the corridor; several others are out of sight. Toss a grenade at the trio in front of you, then run to the area over to the right. Run around the corner to reach the mezzanine and kill the two Yakuza there. From this raised vantage point, you can attack the enemies on the lower level from where you are, or leap down and wreak havoc at close range. Note that you can also shoot the chandelier (Fig. 9) to make it fall and crush any opponents below (**3-I**, **3-J**). Once you have dealt with the henchmen, go through the open glass door to trigger a checkpoint.

[10]

J Run into the small room to your left. Activate the switch next to the fire extinguisher: this reveals a series of laser tripwires in the nearby corridor. If any of the beams are interrupted, a turret on the far wall is activated and will open fire on Lara. The solution is to grab hold of the round ***objet d'art*** to the left of the corridor. Roll it in front of Lara, and it will shield her from the bullets fired by the turret (Fig. 10). Once you reach the other side, wait until the turret stops firing before you release your grip and resume your chase after Takamoto. Note that you can actually perform well-timed rolls to pass the beams if you prefer.

SECURITY CAMERAS

In the control room before the corridor with the laser security system (paragraph **J**), you will find a screen that enables you to view three security cameras in turn. On one of these, pay attention to the shimmering object on the underbelly of the dragon statue; this is a clue that will help you to find the exit in that room when you reach it. On another, you will see a crate; this object is the key to obtaining a well-hidden surprise.

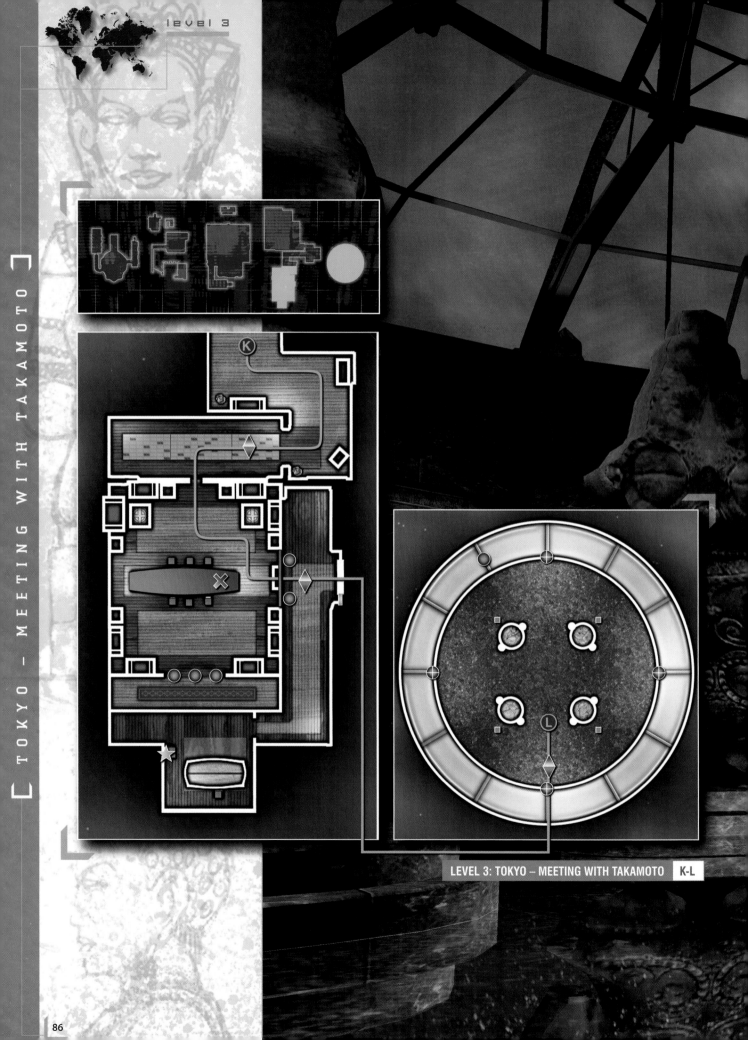

TOKYO – MEETING WITH TAKAMOTO

LEVEL 3: TOKYO – MEETING WITH TAKAMOTO K-L

86

HOW TO PLAY

WALKTHROUGH

EXTRAS

INTRODUCTION

LEVEL 1

LEVEL 2

LEVEL 3

LEVEL 4

LEVEL 5

LEVEL 6

LEVEL 7

LEVEL 8

AREA MAP

A – B

C – E

F – H

I – J

K – L

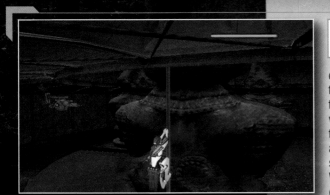

[11]

K Follow the corridors until you reach a door to your left, then go through it. After the cutscene, Takamoto's henchmen will attack. As the room is small and your opponents fierce, throw a grenade immediately to distract them at the very least, then use your best available weapon to dispatch the trio swiftly. Try to maintain as much distance between Lara and them as you can: their shotguns are less effective at range. Now place Lara near the table's end, beneath the dragon's tail. Throw your Magnetic Grapple at the shimmering grapple point and pull the dragon towards you. As soon as it can't go any further (Fig. 11), release the grapple and the dragon will swing forward and smash the window opposite. Two new henchmen will immediately appear either side of the empty pane. Once they are dead, jump from the table or the chest to grab the ledge of the window you smashed. Pull yourself up to reach a checkpoint (3-K). There are three assault rifles on the desk inside Takamoto's office, which is just along the corridor. If you are already carrying one and need more ammunition, or are low on shotgun ammo, we advise that you collect them. The shotgun is by far the most effective weapon you can have for the forthcoming battle, though. When you are ready for the final showdown with the Yakuza boss, press the elevator button to open the door, then walk inside.

L When the cutscene ends, Lara is on the lower level of the room, with Takamoto on the upper walkway. The orange bar in the top right-hand corner of the screen represents his current health. There are turrets on the lower level, and you need to reach the upper walkway to escape them immediately. To do so, you should climb one of the vertical poles behind the four statues (Fig. 12), then jump backwards to reach the circular platform above. Takamoto has three distinct attacks. From a distance, he will send out low and high energy shockwaves that can be dodged by, respectively, jumping or rolling. When you move close to him, he will fire a more focused beam of energy; this is easy to avoid as long as you stay mobile.

[12]

To defeat Takamoto, you need to avoid his shockwaves while shooting at him whenever you can. Run towards him, firing as soon as you have a clear shot; you can also roll when it is safe to do so, as this makes Lara move fractionally faster. When you draw near, he will begin to use his "vertical" shockwave. Keep shooting, and don't stand still for a second: his close-quarters attack *hurts*. After a short period of time, he will retreat at a surprising pace to another position on the walkway. Give chase, dodging the shockwaves as he sends them in your direction. If you're suitably patient, this isn't a massively difficult battle. When Takamoto finally collapses, a cutscene marks the end of the level.

GHANA – PURSUING JAMES RUTLAND

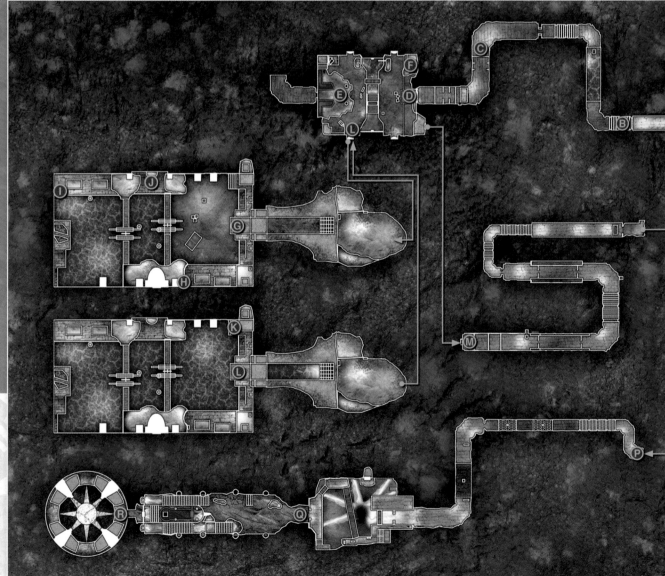

TOMB RAIDER
LEGEND

HOW TO PLAY

WALKTHROUGH

EXTRAS

INTRODUCTION

LEVEL 1

LEVEL 2

LEVEL 3

LEVEL 4

LEVEL 5

LEVEL 6

LEVEL 7

LEVEL 8

AREA MAP

A – C

D – F

G – J

K – L

M – O

P – R

AREA MAP

LOCATION	AMAHLIN (GHANA)
WEATHER	SUNNY
TERRAIN	RAINFOREST AND TEMPLE INTERIORS
TIME	MORNING
LARA'S OUTFIT	LEGEND

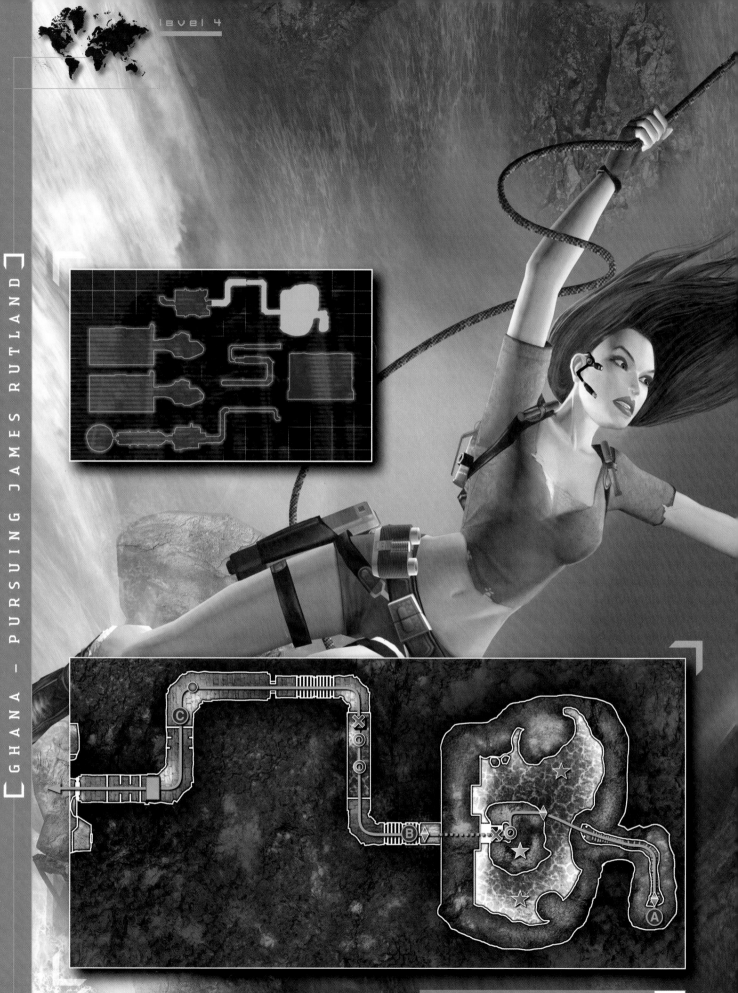

GHANA – PURSUING JAMES RUTLAND

LEVEL 4: GHANA – PURSUING JAMES RUTLAND   A-C

MISSION DETAILS

HOW TO PLAY

WALKTHROUGH

EXTRAS

INTRODUCTION

LEVEL 1

LEVEL 2

LEVEL 3

LEVEL 4

LEVEL 5

LEVEL 6

LEVEL 7

LEVEL 8

AREA MAP

A – C

D – F

G – J

K – L

M – O

P – R

[01]

A Follow the path until you face the huge waterfall. Dive from the cliff in any way you see fit, but remember that this is a great opportunity to perform a spectacular swan dive. To do so, run forward, jump, and then immediately press ◎ (4-A). Swim back to the surface and climb onto the central islet to reach a checkpoint. Run to your right, jump on the rock ledge, pull yourself up, and then jump to the upper platform (Fig. 1). Now jump to the hanging rope to remove the locking mechanism that holds the bridge in place. You can then lower the bridge in one of three ways: slide down the rope and swing towards the bridge until Lara kicks it, jump down and immediately either use your Magnetic Grapple to pull it back, or shoot at it. You'll need to be quick if you choose one of the last two methods – the lock will soon drop down into position (4-B, 4-C). Either way, step onto the bridge and enter the temple to reach a checkpoint.

B Run along the corridor until you reach a pool. The current here is too strong for Lara to swim against, so throw your grapple at the raft and pull it over (Fig. 2). Walk onto it, jump over to the first hanging rope, swing, and jump to the second rope. Now swing and jump again to reach the opposite platform. You should see a henchman through the doorway at the top of the stairs. He has a shotgun, so attack from (and maintain) a safe distance.

[02]

C Jump above the extended blades of the (harmless) trap. When you stand on the pressure plate around the corner, the gate at the end of the hallway will rise and then steadily fall back into place. To get through it on time, you'll need to make a precise dash through the small obstacle course ahead. Place Lara just in front of the pressure plate. Run over the switch to activate the gate, jump over the spiked bar, squeeze between the next bars, roll beneath the final obstruction (Fig. 3), and then quickly roll through the gap beneath the gate.

[03]

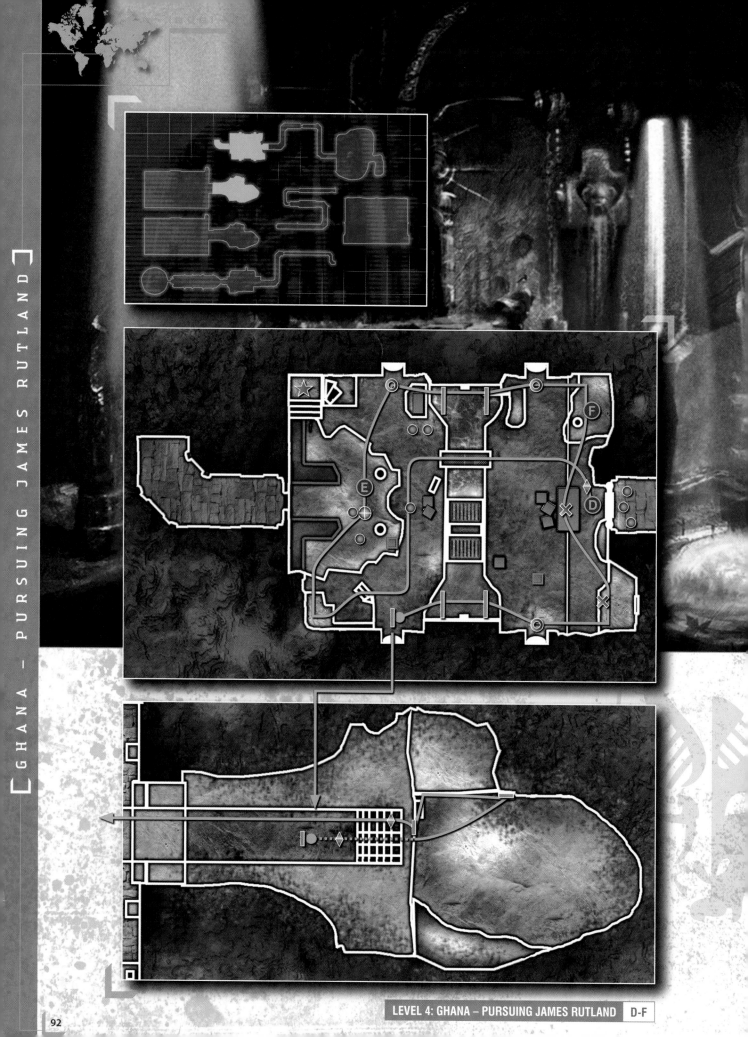

LEVEL 4: GHANA – PURSUING JAMES RUTLAND D-F

HOW TO PLAY

WALKTHROUGH

EXTRAS

INTRODUCTION

LEVEL 1

LEVEL 2

LEVEL 3

LEVEL 4

LEVEL 5

LEVEL 6

LEVEL 7

LEVEL 8

AREA MAP

A – C

D – F

G – J

K – L

M – O

P – R

[04]

D There is a checkpoint as you enter this room. Hide behind the stack of crates in front of you. Note the locations of the soldiers patrolling the area. You can either begin your assault by throwing a grenade at the two solders on the right-hand side, or by shooting the explosive barrel to the left of the pillar on the other side of the room to cause part of the platform above to collapse (Fig. 4). For a *really* spectacular entrance, try to achieve both. Now dash over to the far side of the room, firing as you move, to avoid the attentions of the soldier manning the turret on the raised area. Kill all adversaries on the lower level, climb to the upper platform – use the broken staircase in the far right-hand corner of the room to jump to a ledge to reach it – and then dispatch any remaining soldiers up there. Once this first wave of enemies has been defeated, three more soldiers arrive on the far side of the room. From your position on the upper platform, you can now use the turret to eliminate them with ease. A checkpoint is activated as the last mercenary falls.

[05]

E Standing on the upper platform, run and jump over to the rope, then swing and push against the pillar on the left-hand side of the room to free the waterwheel (4-D). Still hanging on the rope, swing again, jump, and grab one of the horizontal poles on the moving waterwheel (Fig. 5); you can also reach these from the lower level if you prefer. Wait until you reach the other side, then jump over to the rope. Finally, swing forward – you may need to move Lara up the rope slightly before you begin – and then jump to the platform ahead.

F Jump over to the hanging platform. Throw your Magnetic Grapple at the shimmering metal band on the broken pillar and then pull to move the hanging platform. Hop onto the platform to your left, then turn and face the hanging rope. Jump over to it, swing and jump to the horizontal bar on the waterwheel; from there, swing and leap to the second bar, and then over to the ladder. Climb all the way to the top (there is a checkpoint here) and then move over to the second ladder. Climb it and then jump over to the ledge to your left (Fig. 6). Move a little to the left, then jump vertically to grab the ledge above. Move to the left, and then jump up to grab the ladder. Climb to the top to reach another checkpoint.

[06]

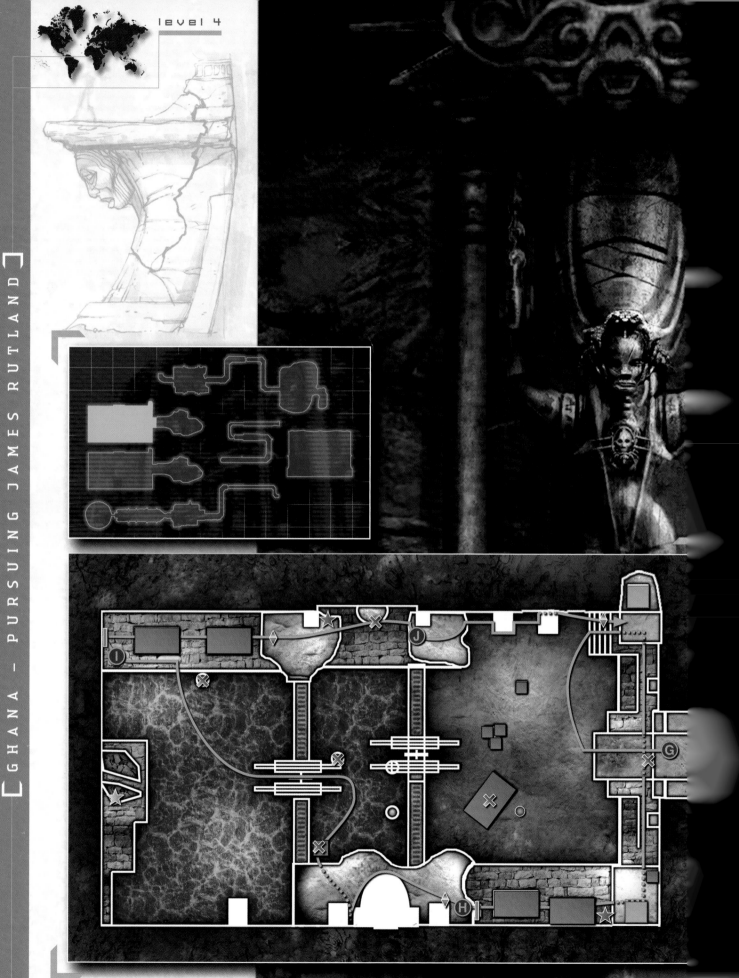

[07]

G Kill the lurking jaguar before you drop down into the next room, then run to the right and pull yourself up onto the broken steps. Climb the steps, then take the next set down to the other side of the room (**4-E**). Climb up onto the raised rock platform. Now jump onto the block of stone supported by a pulley. Lara's weight causes a second block of stone to rise; as soon as it is higher than your current platform, jump over to it (Fig. 7). Quickly jump onto the ladder and climb to the top of it to activate a checkpoint.

[08]

H Run forward after the cutscene and jump to the wall ledge at the end of the platform. Move around the corner, and then drop down once. Jump to the ledge to your left; now drop down twice to reach the ground. Jump over to the raft. Throw your grapple at the metallic section of the broken column, pull yourself forward, and allow the current to take the raft through the gap to your left (**4-F**). Throw the Magnetic Grapple at the shimmering section of the broken column to your right (Fig. 8), and then pull yourself over. Now jump onto the platform to continue.

[09]

I Climb the ladder to the top, then jump backwards to land on the block of stone attached to the pulley (Fig. 9). Wait until both blocks are level, hop over to the second one, and then quickly jump to the platform ahead to pass a checkpoint (**4-G**). Now use the Magnetic Grapple to swing across the gap to reach the next platform.

[10]

J Prepare yourself for an extended climbing session. Jump to the ledge ahead, then move around the corner and drop to the ledge below. Move right, around the corner, and then jump vertically to grab the small ledge above. Now jump backwards to reach the next ledge (Fig. 10). From your position holding onto the crack in the wall, drop down to the ledge below. Now move over and jump to the ledge on the right. Jump to the crack above, then move to the right of the ledge and jump over to the platform to activate a checkpoint.

INTRODUCTION

LEVEL 1

LEVEL 2

LEVEL 3

LEVEL 4

LEVEL 5

LEVEL 6

LEVEL 7

LEVEL 8

AREA MAP

A – C

D – F

G – J

K – L

M – O

P – R

GHANA – PURSUING JAMES RUTLAND

LEVEL 4: GHANA – PURSUING JAMES RUTLAND K-L

HOW TO PLAY

WALKTHROUGH

EXTRAS

INTRODUCTION

LEVEL 1

LEVEL 2

LEVEL 3

LEVEL 4

LEVEL 5

LEVEL 6

LEVEL 7

LEVEL 8

AREA MAP

A – C

D – F

G – J

K – L

M – O

P – R

K Step on the floor switch to your left to dislodge the stone block on the small platform. Now use it to jump over to the central platform once it stops rotating. Your goal in this puzzle is to free the "arms" of the statue from the restraining clasps, which will enable you to pull the switch at the centre with the Magnetic Grapple. Use a second small platform to reach the far platform. Grab the block and position it on top of the floor switch to open the first clasp. Make your way back to the first floor switch and stand on it. The second clasp will open (this takes a couple of seconds), but will begin to close the moment you leave the pressure plate. To complete the puzzle, you need to get across to the central platform and pull the switch before the clasp closes completely. However, this means that you need to reach it while the small platform is rotating. To do this, jump over just before it briefly returns to a horizontal position (Fig. 11), then immediately leap again before you fall. Now fire your grapple at the switch, and pull quickly.

SAFETY NET

From paragraph **K** onwards, if you accidentally fall, you can use the stone block dislodged by the first pressure pad to gain easy access to the upper area. Just jump on the block, grab the nearest wall ledge, and jump vertically to grab the ledge above. Move to your left, jump vertically once again, and then pull yourself up onto the platform.

[11]

L Dive into the pool below. Turn around and swim towards the tunnel, then pull yourself up onto the ledge on the right. Follow the water to the ladder, then climb down. Drop to the ledge below. Move to the right (and around the corner), then drop to the ledge beneath. Go right again and jump over to the ladder, then climb down – you'll reach a checkpoint in the area below. Now run over and climb down the ladder next to the waterfall. After the brief cutscene, jump over to one of the poles on the waterwheel (Fig. 12). Wait until you reach the other side, then swing and jump over to the rope; now jump to the platform ahead and run through the door to activate a checkpoint.

[12]

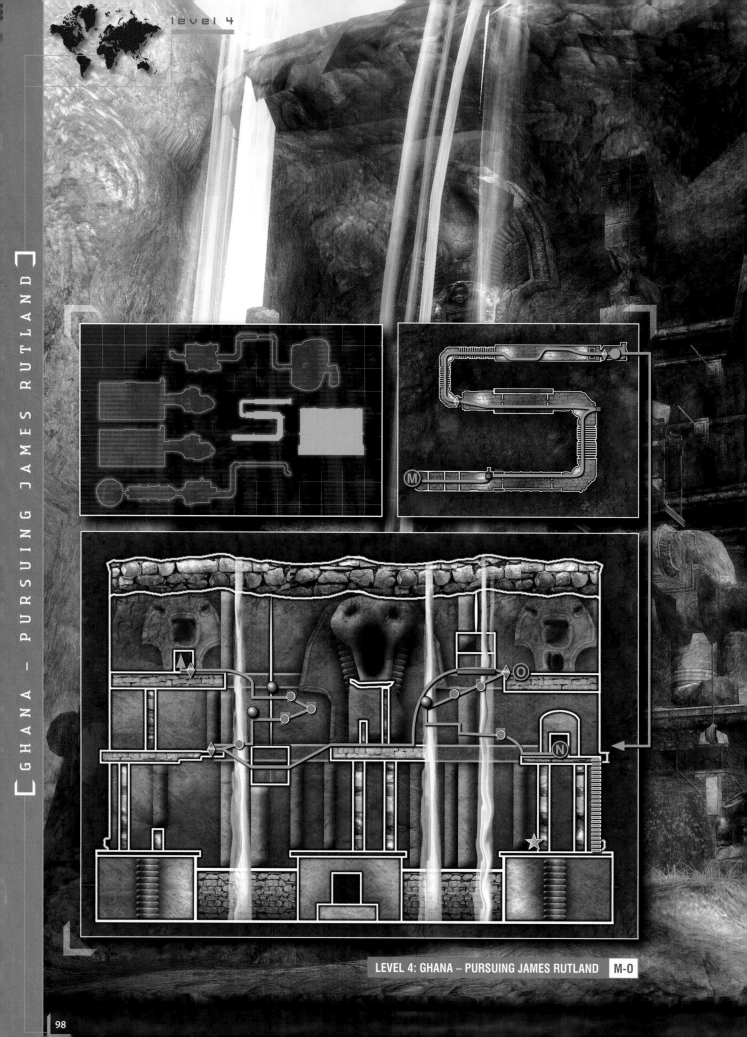

LEVEL 4: GHANA — PURSUING JAMES RUTLAND M-O

GHANA — PURSUING JAMES RUTLAND

TOMB RAIDER
LEGEND

HOW TO PLAY
WALKTHROUGH
EXTRAS

INTRODUCTION
LEVEL 1
LEVEL 2
LEVEL 3
LEVEL 4
LEVEL 5
LEVEL 6
LEVEL 7
LEVEL 8

AREA MAP
A – C
D – F
G – J
K – L
M – O
P – R

M To get past the three spear traps, run (or roll) through as they are retracted into the walls. When you reach the rotating blades, grab the block of stone (Fig. 13) and push it ahead of you along one side of the corridor. When the blades hit the stone, their progress will be halted. You can now climb on top of the block and jump off it to proceed. Go up the steps, then pull the small block from the wall to your right. Again, push the block along the corridor to halt the blades, then climb up and jump over to continue. You can also jump over the low spinning blades and roll under the high spinning blades to get past these traps, if you prefer. You will pass a checkpoint as you run through the next doorway. Continue forward until you reach a cutscene. With the boulder rolling behind you, quickly run towards the doorway. Jump above the spears to the right and roll beneath the next set of spears to the left; finally, leap over the gap to safely reach the next checkpoint (**4-H**).

[1 3]

[1 4]

N Facing the temple, jump to the horizontal bar on your left. Swing around it and jump to the wall ledge in front of you. Move to your left, around the corner, then jump vertically to grab the ledge above. Head left again, around the corner, and then jump backwards to grab the ledge behind you. Jump vertically to the ledge above, but be ready to react swiftly: a rock is dislodged from its precarious position above. To avoid it, jump backwards to reach a horizontal pole (Fig. 14). Swing from this pole to the next one, and then jump over to the platform; doing so will activate a checkpoint.

[1 5]

O Jump to the hanging platform: it will move to a lower position, which enables you to jump to the platform ahead. Run and leap to a second hanging platform, then jump over to the platform beyond it. Jump to the horizontal pole, swing around it, and jump again to reach the opposite ledge. Move to your left, around the corner. Jump vertically to grab the ledge above, but watch out: another rock is poised to fall from above, so you need to quickly jump over to the horizontal pole to your right. From the first pole, swing and jump to the next pole; turn around (Fig. 15), swing and jump towards the third pole, then over to the wall ledge. As soon as you land on it, move around the corner to your left to avoid the rock that falls from above. Jump vertically, go around the corner to your left, and then jump backwards to land on the platform behind you. A checkpoint is activated as you pass through the doorway.

LEVEL 4: GHANA – PURSUING JAMES RUTLAND **P-R**

HOW TO PLAY

WALKTHROUGH

EXTRAS

INTRODUCTION

LEVEL 1

LEVEL 2

LEVEL 3

LEVEL 4

LEVEL 5

LEVEL 6

LEVEL 7

LEVEL 8

AREA MAP

A – C

D – F

G – J

K – L

M – O

P – R

[16]

P Move along the corridor and activate your Personal Light Source as you run down the steps. Swing across the two spike pits with the Magnetic Grapple. There are two soldiers on a bridge through the doorway, with a third on the opposite side. While you can engage them in a gunfight (there's a metal box you can use as cover), it's easier to simply destroy the bridge by either throwing a grenade, or by shooting the section of rock above it; the rock will fall, sending the first two soldiers to their deaths below. You can then use Manual Aim mode to kill the remaining enemy on the far side of the pit. Swing over with the Magnetic Grapple. Run through the doorway to reach a checkpoint, then use the two horizontal bars on your right to reach the wall ledge (4-I). Jump vertically to grab the ledge above. Move to your left, around the corner, and then jump vertically twice. Move to your right, around the corner. Jump to the ledge above, then jump backwards to the horizontal bar. Use it, and the next bar, to reach the platform. Now stay low and quiet, and be careful not to fall into the water.

There are a number of soldiers in this area, and you'll need to decide how best to launch your attack. You can kick (or use the Magnetic Grapple to pull) one of the nearby barrels into the water (Fig. 16) to destroy the bridge below and thus kill a number of men instantly. This makes the battle ahead a little easier, but you will need to finish off the remaining soldiers on the far side of the chamber in Manual Aim mode, or at close quarters after swinging across on the ropes. Alternatively, you can simply run forward and take on each solider in turn, making your way over the bridge to attack the enemies on the other side. Don't linger on the bridge – a single grenade will cause it to collapse. Pay special attention to the man wearing a white T-shirt: he wields a grenade launcher. Stock up on as much Assault Rifle ammunition as you can find before you continue: it will come in handy soon. Go through the doorway to reach a checkpoint.

Q Kill the jaguar, and then climb onto the broken stairs. A boulder will roll down from above, so quickly jump towards the hanging rope to avoid it. Climb higher on the rope, then swing and jump towards the opposite set of steps. Move forward a little, then retreat quickly as soon as another boulder rolls towards you and hide in the recess opposite the rope (Fig. 17). Once the boulder has passed, climb the stairs and step on the floor switch until the door is completely open (4-J). Run forward and roll under it before it closes.

[17]

R You should stick to Lara's pistols for the first part of this battle. Rutland uses two kinds of attack. From a distance, he tosses grenades at you, but the delay before explosion makes them easy to dodge. At close quarters he will slash at Lara with the sword fragment he holds. This move is harder to avoid, but if you maintain your Combat Lock, jump away and continue to fire regularly, you can prevent him from getting too close.

Rutland can be hurt but, as you will soon notice, he periodically jumps onto one of the four platforms to heal. When he does so, take the opportunity to shoot the four stones at the front of each one (you can use ◬ to do this) to reveal grapple points. Wait until he next leaves the battle, then attach your Magnetic Grapple to each platform in turn and pull to destroy them (Fig. 18). Denied the space to retreat and heal, Rutland can now be defeated. Switch to your secondary weapon and show him no mercy.

[18]

KAZAKHSTAN – PROJECT CARBONEK

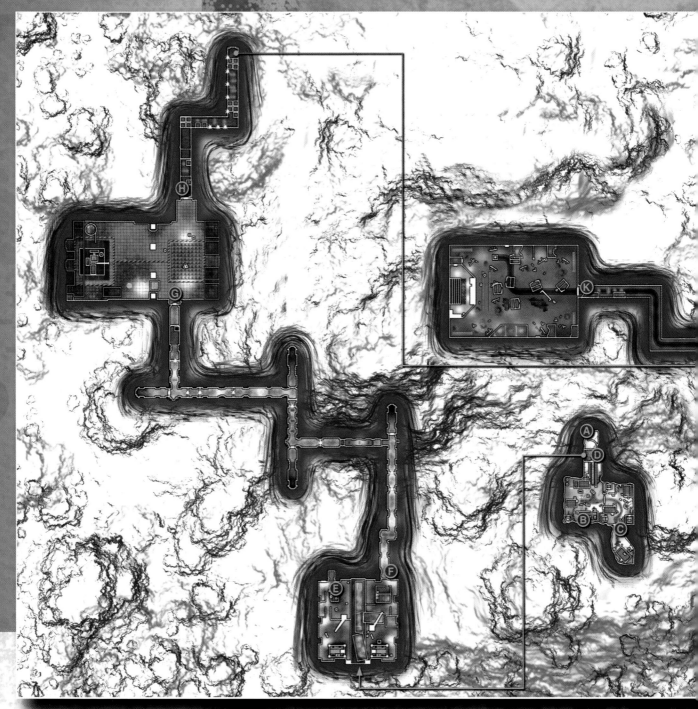

HOW TO PLAY

WALKTHROUGH

EXTRAS

INTRODUCTION

LEVEL 1

LEVEL 2

LEVEL 3

LEVEL 4

LEVEL 5

LEVEL 6

LEVEL 7

LEVEL 8

AREA MAP

B

E

H

J

L

N

AREA MAP

LOCATION	EASTERN SIBERIA (KAZAKHSTAN)
WEATHER	SNOWY
TERRAIN	MILITARY OUTPOST, ABANDONED LAB
TIME	AFTERNOON
LARA'S OUTFIT	WINTER

KAZAKHSTAN – PROJECT CARBONEK

LEVEL 5: KAZAKHSTAN – PROJECT CARBONEK **A-B**

MISSION DETAILS

INTRODUCTION

LEVEL 1

LEVEL 2

LEVEL 3

LEVEL 4

LEVEL 5

LEVEL 6

LEVEL 7

LEVEL 8

AREA MAP

A – B

C – E

F – H

I – J

K – L

M – N

 Jump from the top of the cliff and be ready for a test of your reflexes. As soon as Alister says "Now Lara!" and a ⃝ icon appears, press that button to open your parachute. You'll reach a checkpoint when you land safely on the roof. Immediately run forward and take control of the turret. You now need to eliminate all enemies in the area. With Lara a static target behind the gun emplacement, you'll need to do this quickly and efficiently. Try to target the explosive barrels when soldiers move close to them for instant kills, and watch out for enemies sniping from inside the building (**5-A**).

When this first wave of enemies has been dispatched, drop down to the ground to initiate a second battle. Once the dust settles, collect any Health Packs, grenades and ammunition that you need, then enter the building ahead (**5-B**). Now climb the ladder to reach a checkpoint on the roof (Fig. 1).

[01]

 When you arrive on the roof, you can see a man on the watchtower behind the two ventilation stacks. A great way to kill him is to wait until he turns his back to you, then quietly approach and toss a grenade at his feet (Fig. 2). Once he's dead, jump over to the tower. This will trigger the arrival of a group of soldiers below. Either slide down the plank to reach the nearby roof, or ride the cable to ground level, and deal with them in any way you see fit. You should, however, prioritize the mercenary manning the turret and the soldier using a grenade launcher (**5-C**). After the fight, enter the medical building (there's a spotlight above the door) to trigger a cutscene, then leave through the only exit. There is another group of soldiers outside. You can either engage them with guns blazing as normal, or quickly run over and use the turret. When the mercenaries are dead, use the keypad to open the gate. You'll cross a checkpoint on the other side.

[02]

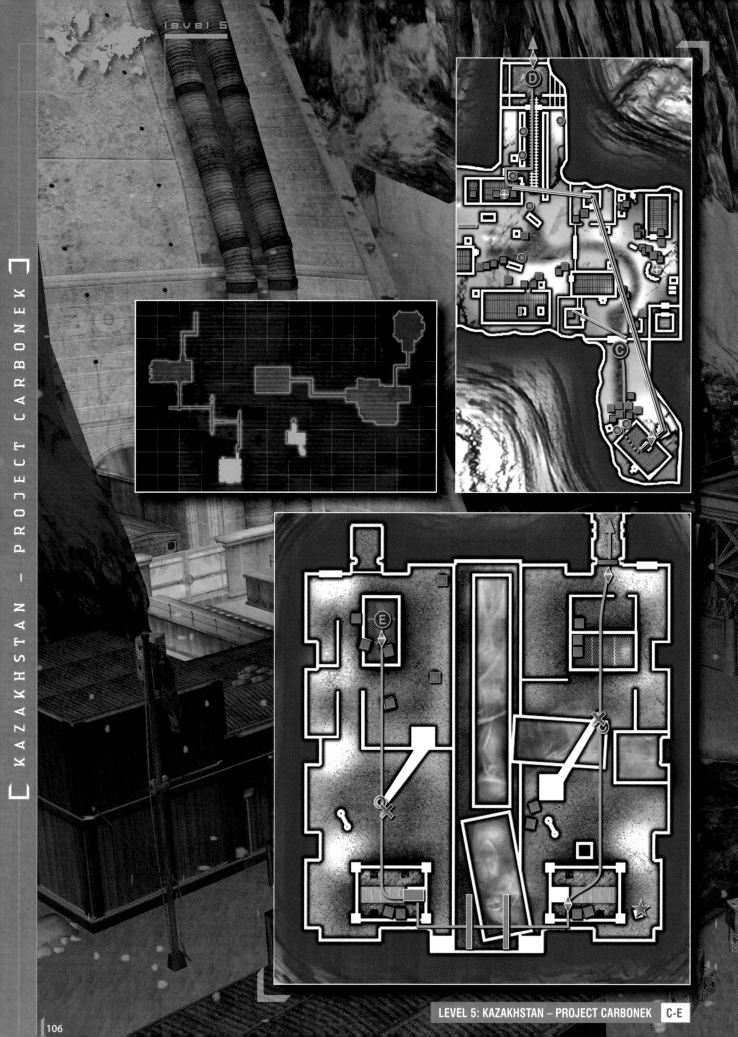

KAZAKHSTAN – PROJECT CARBONEK

LEVEL 5: KAZAKHSTAN – PROJECT CARBONEK **C-E**

[0 3]

C After you pass through the gate, soldiers at the top of the slope will immediately begin to roll fuel barrels towards you. Draw your weapons and use ④ repeatedly to destroy them immediately; if you're quick enough, the mercenaries will be killed in the explosions (Fig. 3). Now enter the building, approach the main screen to initiate a cutscene, and then climb the ladder to pass a checkpoint. Leap over to the next ladder and climb to the top. Now hop up and grab the cable: Lara will slide to a watchtower. Use the next cable to return to the roof you landed on at the beginning of the mission. Now drop to the ground and open fire on the soldiers below. As soon as a brief cutscene shows the train leaving, there is a tight time limit to beat: you need to reach the motorbike at the tunnel entrance and set off in pursuit as quickly as possible. It's not actually necessary to kill all the guards. Just run to the bike, press ④ to jump on, then ⊗ to accelerate along the tunnel.

HOW TO PLAY

WALKTHROUGH

EXTRAS

INTRODUCTION

LEVEL 1

LEVEL 2

LEVEL 3

LEVEL 4

LEVEL 5

LEVEL 6

LEVEL 7

LEVEL 8

AREA MAP

A – B

C – E

F – H

I – J

K – L

M – N

[0 4]

D This motorbike sequence is similar to the one played during the Peru mission, but there are some key differences. Most importantly, you need to be very careful not to hit the trees: this can spell instant death for Lara. Fight the waves of mercenaries on motorbikes until the train enters a tunnel. On the mountainside track, keep to the left path at all times (you can simply smash through the barriers) for the safest journey. The path on the right is much more dangerous, and is for thrill-seekers only, but has more health packs to pick up if you are running low.

After the train emerges from the tunnel, you again need to fight men on motorbikes, but you also have to face soldiers firing from SUVs (Fig. 4). When you kill the latter, you may need to turn quickly to avoid crashing into the vehicle as it swerves to a halt. This section can be quite difficult due to the sheer number of enemies you face, so scan the environment closely for Health Packs. After the train enters a second tunnel, you need to follow the track to the right again and then jump the train twice before driving onto it when Lara draws level with the carriages. Be quick: you only have a short window of opportunity to achieve this. Accelerate forward to initiate a cutscene. This is followed by a Super Action where Lara needs to duck beneath the tunnel roof girders (◎), shoot the rope holding the hanging pipe (④), and then throw her grapple at the crane (▣).

[0 5]

E From your position on the platform, throw your grapple at the crane just above the hanging rope. Pull back, then release the grapple and quickly jump to the rope before it swings away from you. Wait until the crane returns to its previous position, then jump over to the platform ahead. Climb the ladder, and then jump to your right to grab the sign. Move to your left and jump over to the horizontal pole. Swing and jump forward twice and Lara will automatically grab the sign; don't adjust your position while swinging on the poles, or she might miss it (Fig. 5). Drop down to the platform below to reach a checkpoint (5-D). Again, pull the crane towards you with the grapple, release it and quickly jump to the hanging rope. Swing and jump forward to reach the hanging platform. Jump to the ledge ahead of you (if you miss, you can use the movable crate below to get back up), jump vertically, and then pull yourself into the opening to trigger a checkpoint. Draw your guns and destroy the propeller blades just inside the ventilation shaft, then run forward.

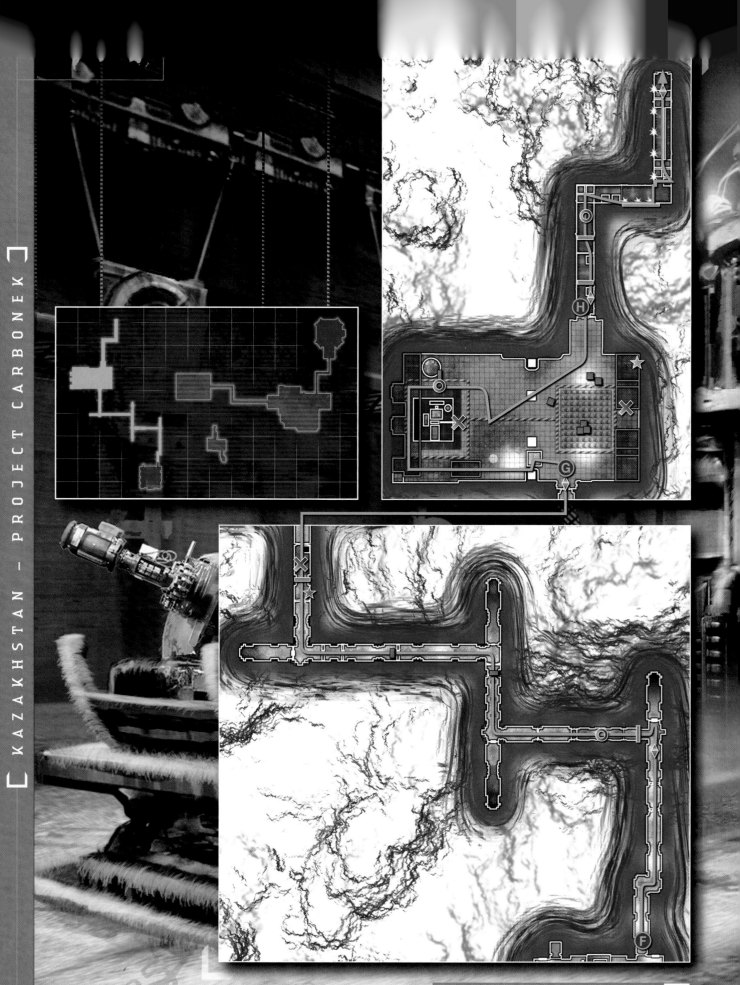

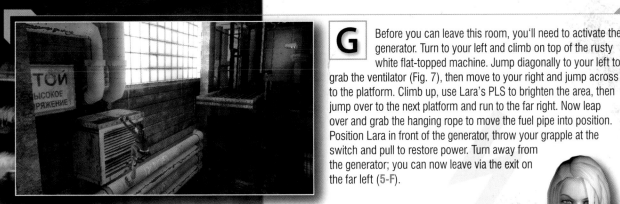

[06]

F Follow the path and slide down the icy ramp. Jump above the electric cable, roll beneath the next one, then collect the glowing piece of paper to learn about the death of the man behind the gate. Turn to your left, jump to the horizontal bar, and from there to the hanging rope; now swing and jump to the opposite ledge. Slide down the slope, being quick to jump above the cables during your descent. Roll under the next set of electric cables, then shoot the fan. Slide down the next slope, jump above the cables, and then immediately press Ⓐ to shoot the fan. Jump above, then roll beneath, the cables in the corridor. On the next slope, hop over the cables, then jump at the last second to grab the horizontal pole (**5-E**). Jump forward and throw your grapple (Fig. 6), then swing and jump over to the platform ahead. Destroy the fan with Ⓐ as you slide down the slope. A checkpoint awaits as you drop into the room.

[07]

G Before you can leave this room, you'll need to activate the generator. Turn to your left and climb on top of the rusty white flat-topped machine. Jump diagonally to your left to grab the ventilator (Fig. 7), then move to your right and jump across to the platform. Climb up, use Lara's PLS to brighten the area, then jump over to the next platform and run to the far right. Now leap over and grab the hanging rope to move the fuel pipe into position. Position Lara in front of the generator, throw your grapple at the switch and pull to restore power. Turn away from the generator; you can now leave via the exit on the far left (**5-F**).

[08]

H After reaching the checkpoint in the corridor, pull yourself up onto the platform to your right. Jump over to the horizontal pole, and from there to the platform ahead. Now leap over to the next horizontal pole, from there to the rope, and swing over to the platform. If you fall to the ground below, just jump to grab the raised area at the end of the corridor. Turn to your right, hop over to the small platform ahead, and from there to the platform above. As soon as the electrical discharge moves beyond the beginning of the bar on the right, jump over and grab it. Move quickly along to the left (but not so quickly, of course, that you catch up with the electricity), then jump backwards once you reach the end to grab the ledge behind Lara (Fig. 8). Move to your right, around the corner, drop down once, jump backwards, then release your grip to land on the platform below. If you fall down at any point, hurry and pull yourself up onto the platform here before Lara succumbs to the deadly effects of the gas. Grab the metal bar as soon as the electrical discharge moves forward from the start of it, then swing forward quickly and drop to the platform on the other side. Go through the door to reach a checkpoint and trigger a cutscene.

HOW TO PLAY

WALKTHROUGH

EXTRAS

INTRODUCTION

LEVEL 1

LEVEL 2

LEVEL 3

LEVEL 4

LEVEL 5

LEVEL 6

LEVEL 7

LEVEL 8

AREA MAP

A – B

C – E

F – H

I – J

K – L

M – N

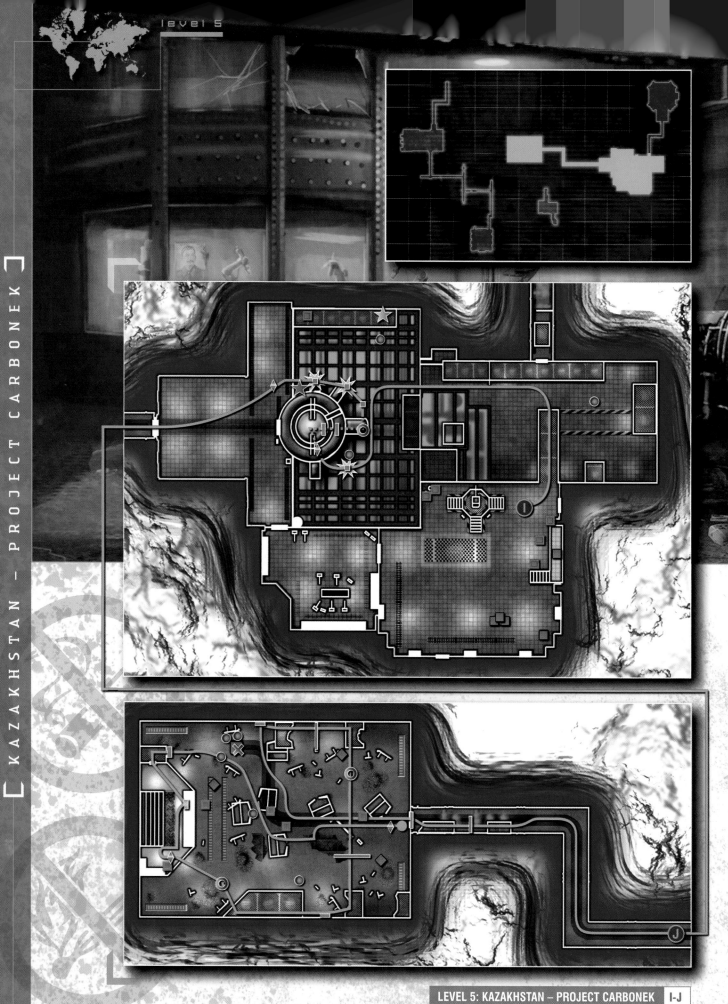

LEVEL 5: KAZAKHSTAN – PROJECT CARBONEK **I-J**

KAZAKHSTAN – PROJECT CARBONEK

HOW TO PLAY

WALKTHROUGH

EXTRAS

INTRODUCTION

LEVEL 1

LEVEL 2

LEVEL 3

LEVEL 4

LEVEL 5

LEVEL 6

LEVEL 7

LEVEL 8

AREA MAP

A – B

C – E

F – H

I – J

K – L

M – N

[0 9]

I Kill any soldiers you can see from the upper level, then run down the broken bridge and dispatch any remaining enemies; there are three in total (**5-G**). As soon as the electrical discharge on the vertical pole moves up by a safe distance, jump onto the pole and climb to the top. Leap from the pole to the nearby platform (a checkpoint is activated as Lara lands), then to the upper level above it. Turn around and jump to the horizontal bar. Jump from the first bar to the second one, and then to the rope. Turn to your left, swing and jump from the rope to the vertical pole (Fig. 9). Now jump from pole to pole, timing your jumps carefully to avoid the electrical discharge. You will find this easier if you position the camera so that your current pole and the next one are in line. As long as you're patient, this really isn't as difficult as it may seem. You will pass a checkpoint when you reach the upper platform; pick up the shining note to learn more about the events that took place in the facility (**5-H**). Go through the unlocked door at the centre of the area to continue.

NOTE ON RIOT SHIELDS

Whenever Lara faces a soldier equipped with a riot shield, try to use a sliding tackle or a jump-kick to knock them off their feet before you open fire. You can also use the second type of slow-motion attack (jump towards their upper bodies with weapons drawn, then jump again to launch Lara over the top of their heads) to shoot them from behind. See page 18 of the How to Play chapter for more information on Lara's assorted attacking moves.

J Follow the corridor until you reach the toxic gas, then pull yourself onto the platform above. Jump over to the horizontal bar and then jump to the platform ahead. Now use the subsequent horizontal bar to enter the next room. Kill the soldiers here; there are a few fuel barrels that can assist you in this task. Grab and push the cage containing the Plasma Focal Point along the track until its path is obstructed by debris. Jump onto the top of the device, then leap over to the ladder. Climb to the top, then hop over to the platform to your right. Jump over to the horizontal pole, then swing and jump to the next platform.

Jump over to the hanging rope and then leap to reach the ledge above the blue ball (Fig. 10). Move to the ledge on the opposite side, then leap backwards, swing around the bar, and jump to the platform ahead. Jump over to the ladder – it will be fully extended as you land on it, creating a shortcut – climb to the top, then hop over to your right. Run to the end of the platform and press ⊕ to destroy the fuel barrel behind the window. Use the rope to swing over and jump through the opening to reach a checkpoint.

Read the notes beside the scientist's body, then pull the lever to activate the plasma ball at the centre of the room. Now climb down the broken ladder, throw your grapple at the plasma cage – don't get too close to it! – and pull it along the rails. It will blast aside any debris it encounters. When the cage reaches the door, it will begin to move automatically; you will reach a checkpoint as it passes through the exit.

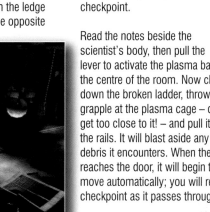

[1 0]

111

KAZAKHSTAN – PROJECT CARBONEK

LEVEL 5: KAZAKHSTAN – PROJECT CARBONEK K-L

INTRODUCTION

LEVEL 1

LEVEL 2

LEVEL 3

LEVEL 4

LEVEL 5

LEVEL 6

LEVEL 7

LEVEL 8

AREA MAP

A – B

C – E

F – H

I – J

K – L

M – N

K Your goal is to follow the plasma cage along the corridor, but there's no hurry: take as much time as you need. Pull yourself up onto the platform. Jump to the next platform via the horizontal pole. Drop to the floor and approach the electric field. Pull the electrified orb towards you with your grapple – it will cease to crackle with energy – and then quickly release it and roll underneath before it returns to its original position. Repeat this trick to pass the second orb. In the next section of the corridor, the situation is similar, but the orbs are positioned in pairs. You must make them swing both at the same time and, if possible, in corresponding directions. To do so, pull one of them with your grapple and make it swing as vigorously as it can. Now let go of it and do the same with the second one, but try to make it reach the peak of its swing as the first one does (Fig. 11). The electric field will thus disappear intermittently, enabling you to roll through without sustaining any damage. Repeat this process with the second pair of orbs. You will reach a checkpoint as you return to the large chamber containing the Tesla tower.

[11]

PLASMA ORBS

When you face the twin plasma orbs described in paragraph **K**, you will need to switch swiftly from one orb to the other with your grapple. As using Manual Aim mode is impractical (it takes too long), use ⑱ to select the orb you want to target. Practice changing your current target before you begin: it makes this hazard much easier to pass.

[12]

L Open the sliding door by pulling it with your grapple from the left side: the Plasma Focal Point will automatically move into place. Carefully run (or roll) through the malfunctioning door – don't touch it, or Lara will be electrocuted – to initiate a cutscene where Lara discovers an ancient shield. After it ends, pick up the notes beside the dead scientist. Roll through the next malfunctioning door and use the magnetic gun. As soon you are inside it, use it to pick up (hold Ⓛ1) and fire (press Ⓡ1) objects at the soldiers on the far platform (5-I). Now use the device to move the hanging platform as far to the right as it will go (Fig 12). You can now use it to reach the door on the other side of the room.

KAZAKHSTAN – PROJECT CARBONEK

LEVEL 5: KAZAKHSTAN – PROJECT CARBONEK M-N

HOW TO PLAY

WALKTHROUGH

EXTRAS

INTRODUCTION

LEVEL 1

LEVEL 2

LEVEL 3

LEVEL 4

LEVEL 5

LEVEL 6

LEVEL 7

LEVEL 8

AREA MAP

A – B

C – E

F – H

I – J

K – L

M – N

M Jump up onto the platform. Switch to Manual Aim mode and shoot the two metal bars that are in the way. The path being clear, you can now use the Magnetic Grapple to move the platform along the corridor. Leap to the second platform and target the metal device at the end of the corridor – you'll need to stand at the very edge to reach it. Throw the grapple at it and pull quickly to build up momentum, then release and crouch to avoid the electrified pole (Fig. 13). Jump to the next platform and destroy the metal bar. Throw your grapple at the metal object, pull hard, but this time jump over the electrified pole. You'll pass a checkpoint as you hit the floor. Now go through the door at the end of the hallway.

[13]

N The Unknown Entity is immune to standard weapons, and can inflict large amounts of damage on Lara if given the opportunity to do so. As soon as the cutscene ends, run over and get inside the magnetic gun at the centre of the room. Press and hold **L1** with the creature in your sights to take hold of it. Now aim at one of the bursts of electrical energy crackling between two small orbs (there are four of these around the chamber) and fire. If your aim was true, the Unknown Entity will disappear for a short period of time. This is your opportunity to jump out and pull one of the four levers situated on the walls of the room (Fig. 14). Now turn tail and run as quickly as you can to get back inside the magnetic gun before the creature can attack. You must to repeat this process until all four levers have been activated; bear in mind that levers that have already been activated are marked with a green light.

[14]

Note that it *is* possible, if you're sufficiently quick and agile, to activate all four levers without using the magnetic gun during this opening section of the battle. The strategy outlined above is merely a safer way, so feel free to opt for this "speedy" solution if you prefer. Stay in motion to avoid attacks; moving from side to side works well to confuse the Entity. If you see a glowing fiery point on the floor, immediately jump or roll away from it before the Entity attacks that spot.

[15]

During a cutscene, the sword fragment is revealed (it's still surrounded by an energy protection shield), followed by four additional large orbs that are lowered from the ceiling. You now have to remount the magnetic gun and shoot each of these four large orbs with **R1** until they swing into the electrical discharge crackling between the eight smaller orbs (Fig. 15). You need to move all four into position quickly, as they will soon swing back to their previous positions.

Once all four large orbs are in position, the electrical discharge grows stronger and the energy protection shield that protects the sword fragment disappears. Immediately dismount the magnetic gun, throw your Magnetic Grapple at the sword fragment, and pull to trigger the final cutscene of this level. Again, don't waste any time: after a few seconds, the four large orbs will swing away from the electrical discharge, and the energy protection shield will reactivate.

ENGLAND – KING ARTHUR'S TOMB?

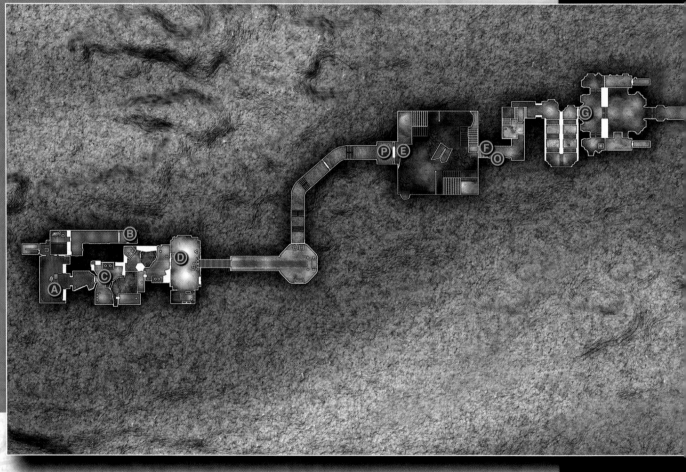

AREA MAP

LOCATION	CORNWALL (ENGLAND)
WEATHER	STORMY
TERRAIN	CATACOMBS, NATURAL CAVERNS
TIME	NIGHT
LARA'S OUTFIT	BIKER

HOW TO PLAY

WALKTHROUGH

EXTRAS

INTRODUCTION

LEVEL 1

LEVEL 2

LEVEL 3

LEVEL 4

LEVEL 5

LEVEL 6

LEVEL 7

LEVEL 8

AREA MAP

A – B

C – E

F – H

I – J

K – L

M – P

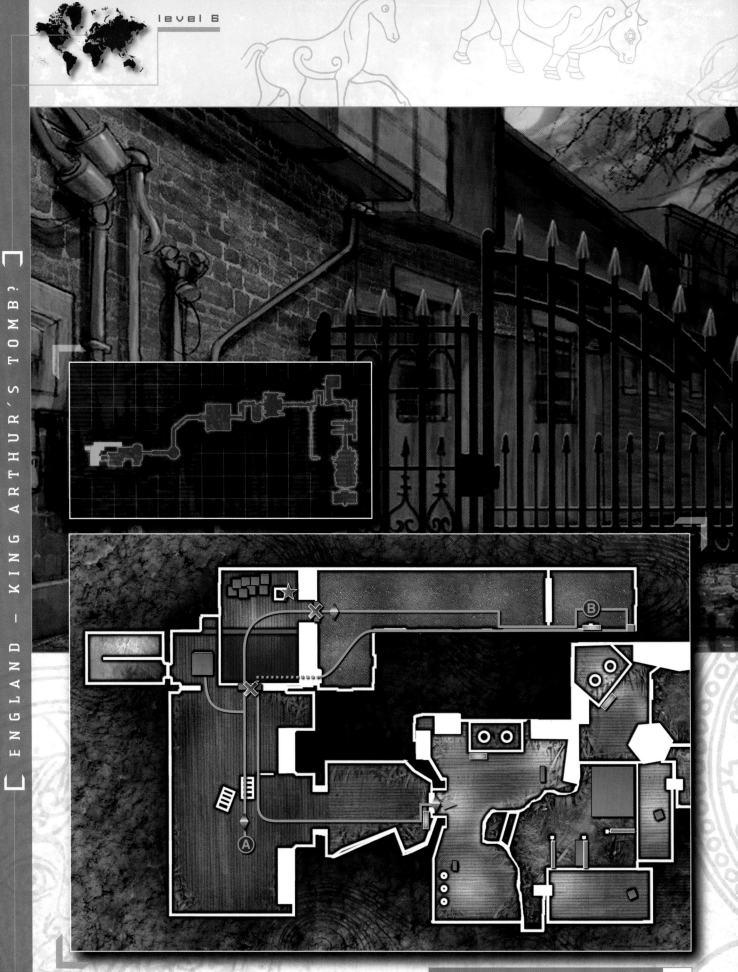

LEVEL 6: ENGLAND – KING ARTHUR'S TOMB?   A-B

MISSION DETAILS

HOW TO PLAY

WALKTHROUGH

EXTRAS

INTRODUCTION

LEVEL 1

LEVEL 2

LEVEL 3

LEVEL 4

LEVEL 5

LEVEL 6

LEVEL 7

LEVEL 8

AREA MAP

A – B

C – E

F – H

I – J

K – L

M – P

A Throw the Magnetic Grapple at the shimmering vent cover just above the Gift Shop entrance and pull to remove it. Position the nearby crate below the opening, and then climb up into the room (**6-A**). Either shoot the vent cover between the shelves or pull it aside with the Magnetic Grapple to reveal a route to the alley below. Roll through it to reach a checkpoint. Run along the back alley and jump up to grab the lintel above the window closest to the gate (Fig. 1). Jump vertically, then move along the ledge, above and past the metal gate. Drop down when you reach the other side. You can now pull the lever to restore power to the building.

[01]

LIGHTS ON

This level is very dark in places, so you will often need to activate your Personal Light Source. Take the time to allow its power gauge to refill completely when you suspect that there is a critical moment approaching: it can be enormously frustrating to have it cut out during combat, or while making a series of death-defying leaps. Remember that you do not need to wait for the PLS to completely recharge before you reactivate it. If you only (and urgently) need a few seconds of light, a split second will suffice.

B Climb the drainpipe to the left of the power box, then jump to the ledge on your right. Move over the metal gate, and continue to the end of the ledge. Drop down to grab the lintel below. Be careful to not fall or drop into the pool of water in the alley below: Lara will be electrocuted if she touches it. Jump laterally twice to reach the far lintel, then jump to the right to land on the ground beyond the electrified puddle (Fig. 2). Open the unlocked door and head over to the "sword in the stone" switch just beyond the ticket booths. Activate it to open the door, and walk through to reach a checkpoint.

[02]

119

LEVEL 6: ENGLAND – KING ARTHUR'S TOMB?   C-E

HOW TO PLAY

WALKTHROUGH

EXTRAS

INTRODUCTION

LEVEL 1

LEVEL 2

LEVEL 3

LEVEL 4

LEVEL 5

LEVEL 6

LEVEL 7

LEVEL 8

AREA MAP

A – B

C – E

F – H

I – J

K – L

M – P

C Run to the wooden plank that serves as a small bridge above the gap (6-B). Jump to the horizontal bar in front of you, swing on it and jump to the next pole. As soon as you grab it, Lara's momentum makes it swing by ninety degrees. Now quickly spring backwards (the wooden board enables Lara to jump from this position) to reach the horizontal bar behind her. If you hesitate, the first bar will swing back to its original position, which means that you'll need to jump back to the previous bar and try again. If you fall, Lara will be injured as she lands in the area below, but you can climb back up via the wooden ledges.

Swing on the horizontal bar and jump over to the drawbridge. As soon as you grab the edge of the drawbridge, immediately jump backwards to return to the pole. Wait until the drawbridge falls into position, then turn around and jump onto it. If you wait too long, it will return to an upright position, and you'll have to start all over again.

In the next room you will find a wooden casket secured in an upright position. Switch to Manual Aim mode, then shoot the base of the rope to release it (Fig. 3). Now jump to the makeshift platform and, from there, to the other side of the room (6-C). When you attempt to activate the sword switch, the mechanism will break. To open the exit, attach the Magnetic Grapple to the counterweight and pull to raise the barrier. Once it's sufficiently high, quickly detach the grapple and roll beneath the barrier before it closes to reach a checkpoint.

[0 3]

HISTORY LESSONS

As you make your way through the derelict museum, activate the switches beside each exhibit to view short performances of moments from the Arthurian legend. These will inspire conversations between Lara's assistants.

[0 4]

D Jump behind the controls of the forklift. Its controls will be instantly familiar; however, this time you also have the fork at your disposal, which you can use to move crates around. Raise and lower the fork with L1/R1 and L2/R2 respectively (6-D). Use it to move the crates aside to create a gap, then drive down the stairway to reach the room below (6-E). Now either move or barge aside the crates in front of the weak wall section (to your left as you enter the room), then smash through to reach a checkpoint (Fig. 4). You can also destroy crates in this area with grenades, which is especially useful during Time Trials. Stay in the vehicle and cruise through the passage. You can simply drive through the spear traps – you will be protected as long as you are inside the forklift. Lower the fork before you reach the metal gate, and then use it to raise the barrier. Drive through the final spike trap, then head for the wall ahead. As soon as the forklift smashes through it, an interactive cutscene begins: Lara has to jump (⊗) from the vehicle. If you succeed, you will reach a new checkpoint.

E The staircase that once offered easy access to the distant floor below has, as you can plainly see, fallen into a state of disrepair; be ready for a perilous climb down (6-F). Run to your left and go down the stairs (6-G). Jump to the wall ledge to your left. Move to the right, jump over to the next ledge, and then quickly move to your right again before it crumbles. As soon as you land on the platform below, run – be quick, as it will fall after a set (and short) period of time – and jump to the next section of the ruined staircase. Now leap over to the horizontal bar that extends from the wall. Swing around the pole and jump to the recess in the far wall. Carefully drop down and hang from the ledge. Jump right to reach the next ledge, then quickly move along to the end before it falls (6-H). Drop down to the floor below, then jump over to the hanging rope. Now swing over to the next section of the staircase. As soon as you land, run and leap to the next platform before it collapses. Now jump and grab the wall ledge to your left (Fig. 5). Move to the right, around the corner; drop down to the platform below and, from there, to the ground.

[0 5]

SHAKY SCREEN?

Every time you notice the screen shaking, you can be sure that the ledge or platform you have just reached is about to break or fall. Don't pause for a second: immediately leap, run or use fast traverse (by tapping △ repeatedly) to move to a more secure position.

LEVEL 6: ENGLAND – KING ARTHUR'S TOMB?   F–H

HOW TO PLAY

WALKTHROUGH

EXTRAS

INTRODUCTION

LEVEL 1

LEVEL 2

LEVEL 3

LEVEL 4

LEVEL 5

LEVEL 6

LEVEL 7

LEVEL 8

AREA MAP

A – B

C – E

F – H

I – J

K – L

M – P

F A checkpoint is activated as you climb the stairs and enter the corridor. Run forward and jump across the burning river of oil. Follow the passage until you reach a flaming floor trap. The dark areas burn constantly; the two metal areas only intermittently. You can carefully time a sequence of jumps to cross it if you wish, but there is an easier way: use the Magnetic Grapple to pull the metal crate towards you until it stands on the first section of the hazard. Now climb on it (Fig. 6) and, when the second metal section of floor bursts into flames, jump over to it. The fire will go out before Lara lands. Quickly leap over the last strip of boiling oil to reach the safety of the stone floor beyond it.

Turn around and pull the crate back over. Push it onto the first flaming floor panel in the next corridor section, then jump on top of it. Again, time your leap so that you run and take off as the intermittent jets of flame on the metal floor tiles begin, then jump once again when you land. Finally, use the Magnetic Grapple to

[0 6]

pull the crate over once again, and position it at the foot of the stone barrier. Use it to climb over into the room beyond and, as you land on the other side, reach a checkpoint.

[0 7]

G Pull the nearby lever to move the barrier up, then grab the crate and pull it into the room (6-I). Now push it underneath the spinning propeller blades to your left to halt their rotation, but position it to one side so that there is room to pull a second crate through. Now run into the small room and pull the second crate through the gap, and place it underneath the blade trap blocking the entrance to the central chamber – again, positioning it to leave room for Lara to push another crate through. Return to the first crate and pull it from beneath the blades. Now push it into the central chamber and, beyond that, underneath a final set of spinning blades. Grab the second crate and push it onto the flaming floor section just past the last set of blades, creating a makeshift platform over the fire hazard (Fig. 7). Pull the lever to your right, and then run (or roll) beneath the door before it closes.

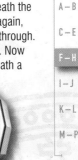

H Follow the passage all the way to the checkpoint and the large floor switch. The portcullis ahead only remains open while this pressure pad is activated, so you need to find an object to place on top of it in order to proceed.

Go left and swim across the pool of water (6-J). Take note of the shimmering casket inside an alcove behind metal bars on the wall above the pool. Position Lara so that she, the chandelier above the water and the casket are in alignment. Pull the chandelier with the Magnetic Grapple until it dislodges the barrier in front of the casket. Now pull the casket with the grapple to make it fall into the pool (Fig. 8). Jump onto the casket, and use the Magnetic Grapple to pull your makeshift raft over to the far side of the pool using, in turn, the lantern to the left, then the lantern on the right-hand wall, and finally the lantern just beyond the pressure pad. As soon as the casket touches the ramp at the edge of the pool, jump over to solid ground, turn around, and then pull it up before the current takes it away. Stand to the rear of the floor switch, and then drag the casket into position. Now continue forward, via the exit, until you reach another checkpoint.

[0 8]

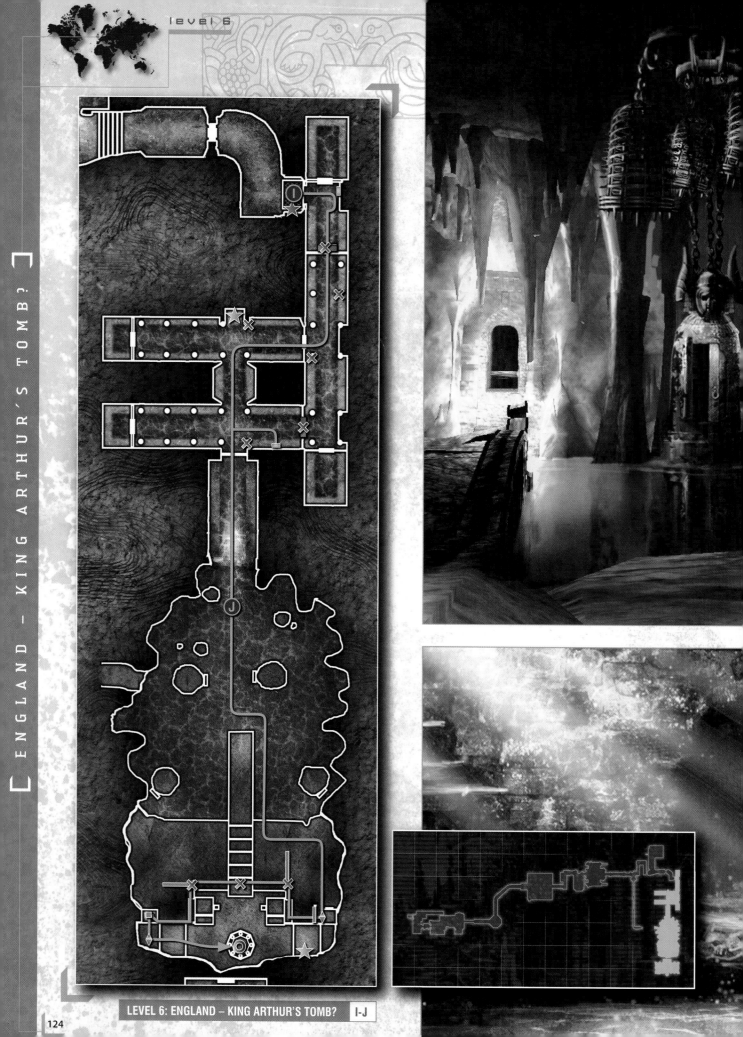

LEVEL 6: ENGLAND – KING ARTHUR'S TOMB? I-J

I Jump down into the water (**6-K**). Swim against the current and activate the lever next to the metal gate. The portcullis will open, and a casket will drift along the passageway. Quickly climb on top of it, and then jump over to the opening on your right (above the metal gate) when you reach it (Fig. 9). If you can't achieve this before the casket floats past, you can stand on top of it and pull it back against the current by attaching your Magnetic Grapple to the lanterns. Drop down into the water on the other side, swim forward to the junction, then take the left passage. At the next junction, head left again, then activate the lever. Climb on top of the casket as it floats towards you (**6-L**).

From your position on top of the casket, jump over to the opening on your left. If you fall into the water, you can again pull the casket back into position by firing the Magnetic Grapple at the lantern on the wall. Once on the other side, swim forward to reach an underwater lake.

[09]

INTRODUCTION

LEVEL 1

LEVEL 2

LEVEL 3

LEVEL 4

LEVEL 5

LEVEL 6

LEVEL 7

LEVEL 8

J Swim across the lake and climb onto the shore when you reach it. Use the Magnetic Grapple to rotate the two lantern poles at either side of the building's entrance by 90° in a clockwise direction. Now run over to the left side of the building. Use the ledges to jump vertically until you reach the platform above (and, on top, a checkpoint). Jump over to the horizontal pole, swing around it, and jump forward to reach the slope on the other side. Slide down and time your jump carefully in order to grab the lantern pole you moved into position earlier (Fig. 10). After it rotates back to its original position, swing around it, jump forward and immediately throw the Magnetic Grapple at the lantern above. Build sufficient momentum while swinging, then jump over to the second lantern pole: it will also rotate to its original position. Swing around it and jump to land on the slim platform ahead. Hop over to the next small platform, then jump vertically to reach the wall ledge. Move to your right, jump vertically to grab the ledge beneath the window, then move and jump to your right to reach the chain. Climb to the top of it, and jump from there to reach the roof and another checkpoint (**6-M**). Jump to the rope hanging from the small dome, slide down, and finally drop to the floor below.

[10]

AREA MAP

A – B

C – E

F – H

I – J

K – L

M – P

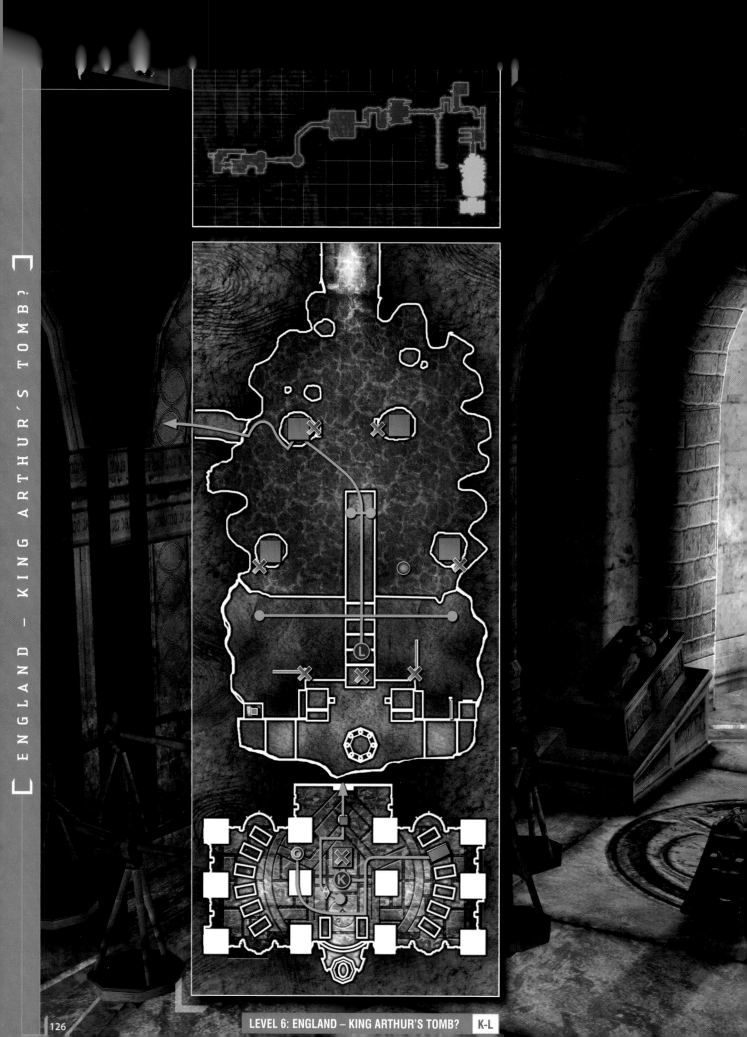

LEVEL 6: ENGLAND — KING ARTHUR'S TOMB? K-L

HOW TO PLAY

WALKTHROUGH

EXTRAS

INTRODUCTION

LEVEL 1

LEVEL 2

LEVEL 3

LEVEL 4

LEVEL 5

LEVEL 6

LEVEL 7

LEVEL 8

AREA MAP

A – B

C – E

F – H

I – J

K – L

M – P

[11]

K Facing the luminous "egg", turn to your left and head towards the second sarcophagus from the left. After the short cutscene, grab the front section of it and pull it across the room. Now position it in front of the broken stone pillar with its lower end pointing outward and its higher edge touching the stone (Fig. 11). Position Lara in front of the luminous "egg", then turn around to face the chandelier. You should have Lara, the chandelier, and the bell on the floor on the same axis. Attach the Magnetic Grapple to the chandelier and pull to make it swing vigorously. Now detach the grapple and quickly run to the broken pillar. Use the broken sarcophagus section to climb up, then jump over to the pulley rope with the stone counterweight at its base. Lara's weight will make the pulley go down and the bell go up. If the chandelier still has sufficient momentum, it will strike the bell; as it tolls, a cutscene will begin. You'll reach a checkpoint as it ends; now run outside to continue.

[12]

L This creature is far too hardy to be damaged by Lara's weapons, so don't waste a single bullet on its tough hide. The only way that you can harm it is by luring it to a position beneath one of the suspended metal cages, then use the Magnetic Grapple to pull a nearby lever and drop the cage from above.

While moving up and down the path that extends into the lake to avoid the creature's attacks, target the tower nearest to it (Fig. 12) and begin firing with Lara's pistols. The creature will become briefly mesmerized by the dull ringing of the bullets as they hit home. When this happens, immediately put the pistols away and fire the Magnetic Grapple at the lever beside the tower, then pull to bring the cage above crashing down on top of the monster's head. You need to do this immediately. If the creature turns away before the cage hits home, move to another location and try this elsewhere to allow time for the cage to return to its previous position.

You need to hit the creature with all four cages in order to continue. As long as you are quick enough to shoot the towers to distract the monster and you avoid falling into the water (Lara will sustain a lot of damage if this happens), this should only be a moderately challenging battle. Once your massive adversary falls, use its body as a bridge to reach a ledge, then jump up to reach the exit.

LEVEL 6: ENGLAND – KING ARTHUR'S TOMB? M-P

[13]

M Follow the corridor to reach a checkpoint, and then swing over the pit with the Magnetic Grapple. Now jump to the horizontal pole, swing around it and jump forward. Slide down the slope, jumping above the gap when you reach it. Now get ready for an interactive cutscene. Lara will need to jump (⊗), swing from the gate with her grapple (▣), and then fire at the chain clasp holding the gate in place (▲). When play resumes, switch to Manual Aim mode and shoot the base of the rope to release it from the top of the portcullis. Jump up and grab either of the shields (Fig. 13). Jump vertically, then move across and jump vertically once again to reach the rope (**6-N**). Now swing forward and jump to the platform ahead to reach a checkpoint. Pull the lever to open the portcullis, then run through the exit.

[14]

N Slide down the slope to return to an area visited earlier. Your goal is to retrace your steps to reach the room where you found the forklift. For now, drop down to the corridor. There are two soldiers that will open fire if they spot Lara. You can fight them conventionally, but there is an easier way. As you hit the ground, wait until they walk over the metal grille in the corridor, then activate the fire trap with the lever. Pull it again to disable the flames. Once you run through the disabled blade trap, two more soldiers will attack from the raised platform to your left (**6-O**). After you clear the area, move the crate in the centre of the room to halt the propeller trap in order to reach the stone gate and a checkpoint. Fire through the bars to kill the soldier that attacks (Fig. 14), then throw a grenade to kill the soldier waiting on the other side of the flaming floor panels. The intermittent fire jets that were active before have now been disabled; make your way through the corridor by carefully jumping over the remaining flames. Once you reach the flaming oil pit, kill the enemy on the other side (you can surprise him with a grenade if you like), then jump over.

[15]

O When you enter the deep chamber with the elevator, immediately kill the soldier that awaits your arrival: he carries a grenade launcher that you may wish to collect to use in the forthcoming battles. Jump over to the elevator and press the button to ride it to the top of the chamber, then kill the soldier that attacks you from the ledge above. Now throw your grapple at the shimmering casket behind the bars. Pull it to make the platform swing forward, stop as it swings backwards, and continue until it gains plenty of momentum. Now release the grapple and make a carefully timed jump to the staircase (Fig. 15).

[16]

P Numerous soldiers (and two dogs) will attack you on this final section of the level. Dodge their attacks, get behind cover whenever possible, target any destructible objects you find, toss grenades when you encounter more than one assailant (Fig. 16), and pick up weapons left by your victims. You should also remember to replenish your life gauge by using Health Packs whenever necessary. Once you enter the area where you first discovered the forklift, kill the two remaining soldiers to end the mission.

HOW TO PLAY

WALKTHROUGH

EXTRAS

INTRODUCTION

LEVEL 1

LEVEL 2

LEVEL 3

LEVEL 4

LEVEL 5

LEVEL 6

LEVEL 7

LEVEL 8

AREA MAP

A – B

C – E

F – H

I – J

K – L

M – P

NEPAL – THE GHALALI KEY

AREA MAP

LOCATION	HIMALAYAS (NEPAL)
WEATHER	SUNNY
TERRAIN	SNOWY MOUNTAINS
TIME	EVENING
LARA'S OUTFIT	WINTER

HOW TO PLAY

WALKTHROUGH

EXTRAS

INTRODUCTION

LEVEL 1

LEVEL 2

LEVEL 3

LEVEL 4

LEVEL 5

LEVEL 6

LEVEL 7

LEVEL 8

AREA MAP

A – C

D – F

G – I

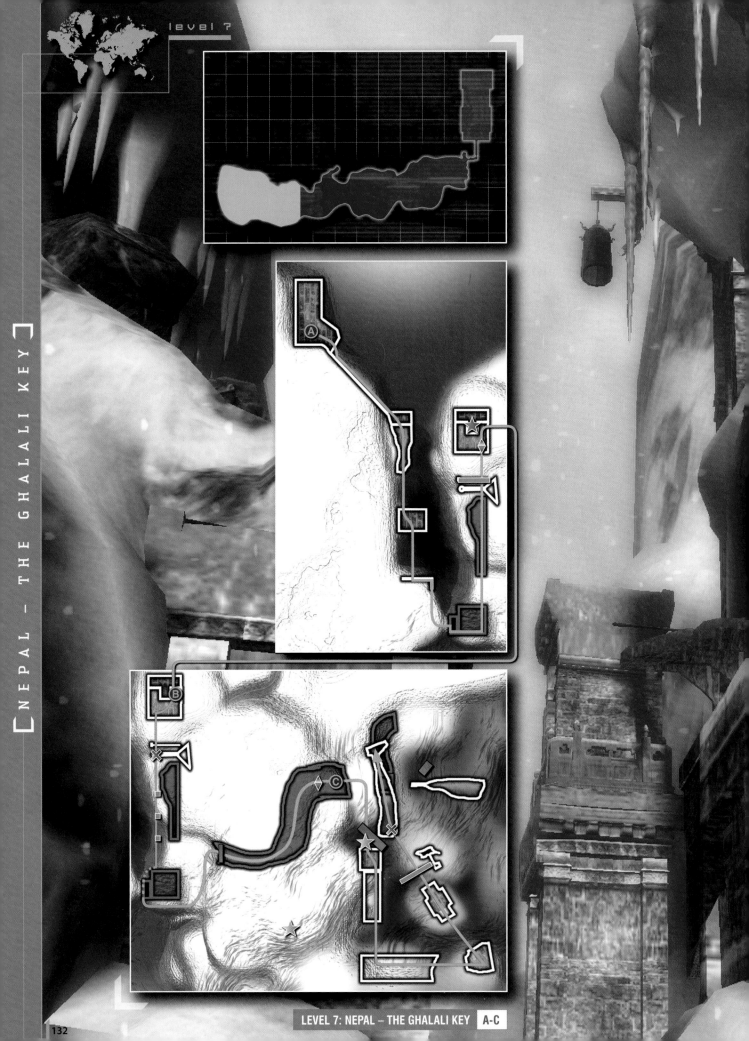

NEPAL – THE GHALALI KEY

A

B

C

HOW TO PLAY

WALKTHROUGH

EXTRAS

INTRODUCTION

LEVEL 1

LEVEL 2

LEVEL 3

LEVEL 4

LEVEL 5

LEVEL 6

LEVEL 7

LEVEL 8

AREA MAP

A – C

D – F

G – I

J – K

L

[01]

A Jump to the ledge in front of you. Head left until you reach its end, moving at maximum speed as you reach the crumbling section. Pull yourself up twice to reach the top platform. Slide down the slope and leap at the last second to grab the ledge ahead. Pull yourself up, then jump forward. From the ledge, drop down to the ledge below and move to your left, around the corner. Once you can't go any further, spring backwards (Fig. 1), then immediately move to your right before the wall section crumbles. Pull yourself up twice to reach the large platform above. Jump to the sloping platform, swiftly run across it – it will soon crumble and fall – and jump to the horizontal pole. Swing around and quickly leap to the opposite ledge before the pole breaks, then jump vertically to reach a checkpoint on top of the pillar (**7-A**).

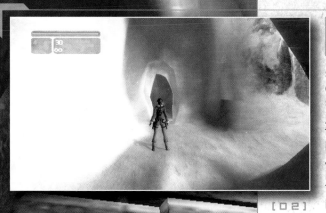

[02]

B Turn around and swing towards the icicles by throwing the Magnetic Grapple at the bell above. Jump over to the first icicle and, from there, quickly hop over to the second, then the third, and finally leap to the safety of the ledge, as all three icicles will drop after a short period of time. Don't try to reposition Lara: just jump straight ahead. On the ledge, move to the far right. Jump vertically to hang from the ledge above and move across to the end of it. Jump up again to grab the ledge above (**7-B**). Pull yourself up to reach a snowy platform. Turn to your right: you will see a block of ice in the snow wall. Shoot it in Manual Aim mode to reveal a passage (Fig. 2). Run through it and continue until you reach a checkpoint.

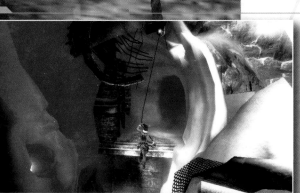

[03]

C Facing the wrecked plane below, turn to your right. Leap over to the pillar in front of you. Slide down the short slope and jump as you reach the bottom; repeat this on the next slope to reach a small platform. Jump to the next platform, then run and quickly leap over to the horizontal bar before it falls. Swing around the bar, jump forward and immediately throw the Magnetic Grapple at the section of fuselage above (Fig. 3). Now jump to the tunnel in front of you (**7-C**).

NEPAL – THE GHALALI KEY

LEVEL 7: NEPAL – THE GHALALI KEY D-F

HOW TO PLAY

WALKTHROUGH

EXTRAS

INTRODUCTION

LEVEL 1

LEVEL 2

LEVEL 3

LEVEL 4

LEVEL 5

LEVEL 6

LEVEL 7

LEVEL 8

[0 4]

D Run through the tunnel. On the other side, turn to your right and jump over to the wing of the ruined plane. Drop down once to the ledge below, then jump backwards to the wall ledge behind you. Move to your right and drop down twice to reach the lower level (7-D). Follow the path to the left, then drop down one level (but not to the very bottom). From here, try to locate the snow leopard below and kill it in Manual Aim mode to deny it the opportunity to retaliate (Fig. 4). Now jump down and head over to the fuselage (7-E). The wreck is far too dangerous for Lara to enter in its current state, so you need to find "ballast" to secure it in place. Attach the Magnetic Grapple to the engine, then pull it into position just in front of the plane. Now climb inside – don't move too far along! – and then pull the engine onto the back end of the plane. This will stabilize the fuselage and enable you to enter it safely. Once inside, walk forward to begin an interactive cutscene. Lara has to pick up the artifact (△), run (🕹 ↑), roll beneath the chair (◎), and finally jump out of the wreckage (✗).

E When you take control of Lara after the cutscene, leap over to the slope and slide down, then jump at the last second to reach a horizontal pole. Swing and immediately jump to reach the slope ahead before it breaks. Slide down and jump over to the subsequent slopes; when you reach the third, you'll need to press △ to shoot the ice wall (Fig. 5). Now jump across the next gap and then jump over to the horizontal pole. As previously, the pole is about to break, so quickly swing around it and leap to the safety of the platform ahead (7-F).

AREA MAP

A – C

D – F

G – I

J – K

L

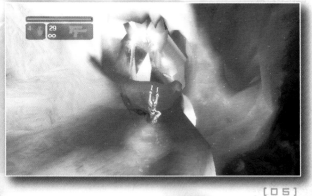

[0 5]

[0 6]

F Run through to the small tunnel; you'll pass a checkpoint on the way. Jump to the platform ahead, then to the horizontal bar on your right, and then to the wall ledge in front of you. Move to your left and jump across to the next ledge, then continue swiftly to your left – it will soon crumble. At the end, drop down to the ledge below. Jump backwards to the horizontal pole. Swing around it and jump to the long icicle ahead. Climb to the top, and then jump over to the next one. Turn to your right and jump to the nearby platform. It is precariously balanced, and will lean over to the side that you land on (Fig. 6) (7-G). Immediately move to the opposite end and jump over to the wall ledge. Move to your right and pull yourself up onto the platform at the end (7-H).

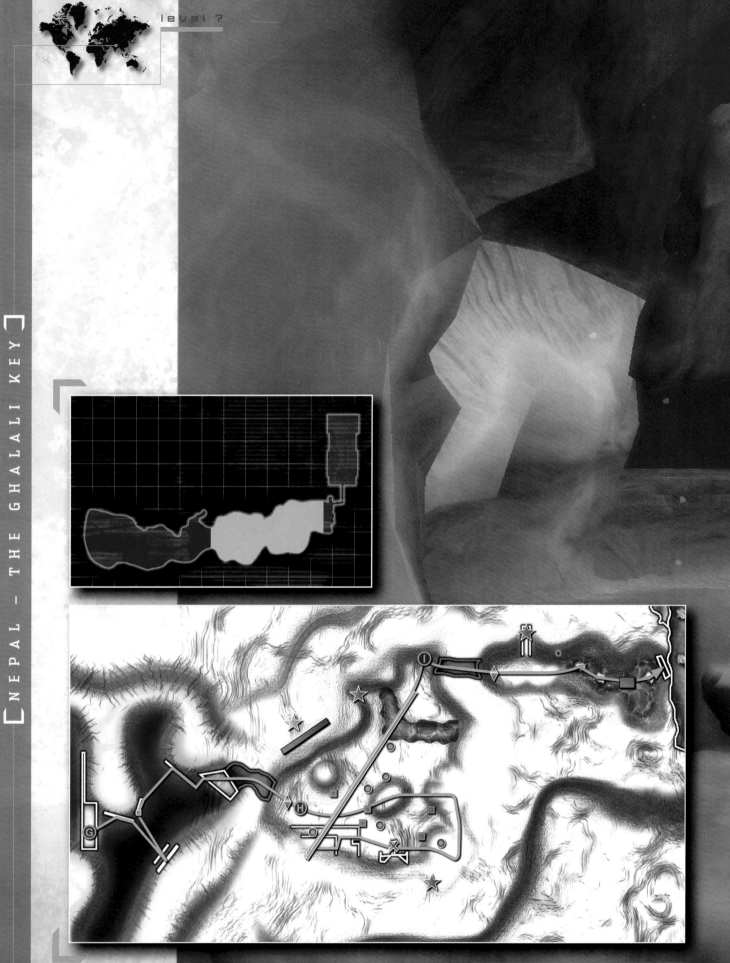

LEVEL 7: NEPAL – THE GHALALI KEY   **G-I**

[07]

G Jump to the wall ledge to your left. Move to your right and jump across to the ledge on the nearby wall. Drop down once to the ledge below, move to its left end then jump backwards to grab a vertical pole. Climb to its top, spring to your right and move to the end of the ledge. Once you can't go any further, leap laterally to the next ledge (Fig. 7). This will soon crumble, so immediately move to your right after landing and jump vertically to the ledge above. Pull yourself up onto the platform and run through the passage. A checkpoint awaits you outside.

[08]

H You now have to confront Rutland's henchmen. Destroy the canisters: they will explode violently, killing anyone within the vicinity of the blast (Fig. 8). You can therefore win this fight rapidly if you dispatch the soldiers on the lower level first, then turn your attention to enemies on the raised platforms (7-I, 7-J). Pull yourself up onto the small central platform. From there, jump to the platform at the foot of the blue ice wall. Turn to your right and jump to the slightly higher platform (7-K). Turn to your right again, throw your grapple at the hanging bell and swing over to the brick platform. Climb onto the small raised area, jump up to grab the cable just above you, and then slide down it to reach the far platform.

RESISTANCE TO COLD

Whether it is due to her outfit or her natural hardiness, Lara has a remarkable resistance to cold. However, if you let her fall into freezing water, its effects can be deadly: her life gauge will constantly decrease until you return her to dry land.

I Slide down the slope to reach both a cave and a checkpoint (7-L). Follow the passage to discover a pool of water. Don't fall in! The water is lethally cold in this area. Switch to Manual Aim mode and shoot at the block of ice hanging from the ceiling. You must now jump from one floating platform to the next until you reach the cavern exit (Fig. 9).

[09]

HOW TO PLAY

WALKTHROUGH

EXTRAS

INTRODUCTION

LEVEL 1

LEVEL 2

LEVEL 3

LEVEL 4

LEVEL 5

LEVEL 6

LEVEL 7

LEVEL 8

AREA MAP

A – C

D – F

G – I

J – K

L

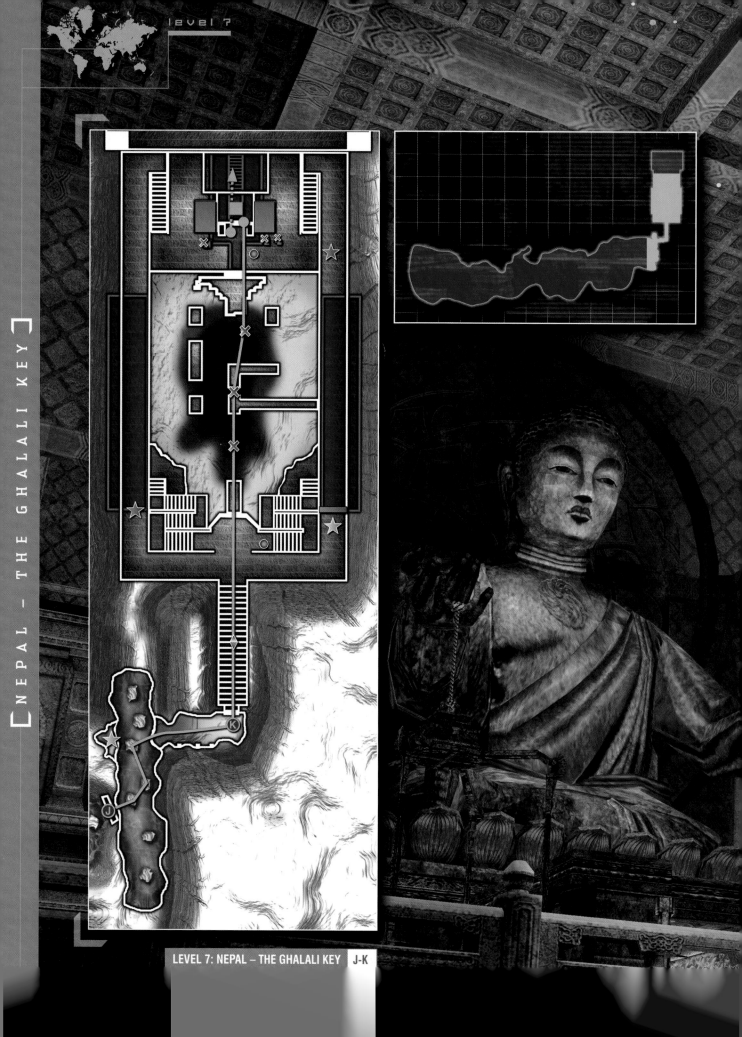

NEPAL – THE GHALALI KEY

HOW TO PLAY

WALKTHROUGH

EXTRAS

INTRODUCTION

LEVEL 1

LEVEL 2

LEVEL 3

LEVEL 4

LEVEL 5

LEVEL 6

LEVEL 7

LEVEL 8

AREA MAP

A – C

D – F

G – I

J – K

L

J From the ledge, drop down to the small bank below. Your goal is to reach the exit on the other side of the stream, which you can see in the distance to your left. To do so, you need to move upstream by jumping from one floating ice platform to the next until the exit is within range. The current is fairly slow, so there's really no need to rush.

Wait on the starting platform until you see a number of the floating platforms drift towards you. Patiently make your way from one ice platform to the next, only jumping if you are sure you can make a safe landing (Fig. 10). If there are no further platforms within reach, you may need to return to the starting position and try again. When you reach the opposite bank (**7-M**), you should continue along the tunnel until you come to a staircase on your left.

[1 0]

K Climb the steps and kill the snow leopard waiting for you at the temple entrance (**7-N**). Walk to the broken balustrade, then jump over the edge and throw the Magnetic Grapple at the bell hanging from the ceiling. Now swing across from bell to bell until you reach the other side. As soon as you land on the platform at the foot of the Buddha statue, be ready to fight another snow leopard. Dodge its attacks, and dispatch it as quickly as you can. You can actually jump to the raised platform from the last grapple point, if you prefer, which makes this fight much easier (**7-O**, **7-P**).

Facing the statue of Buddha, you will notice a door beneath it. To open it, you will need to place the golden box on top of the floor switch on the platform above the door. This can be achieved by using the scales hanging from the statue's hands, and the three available crates (one small, one medium, and the large golden box). The solution is as follows:

- Jump onto the scale hanging from Buddha's left hand (on your right): it will move down to the floor. Pull the small crate onto the scale with your grapple.

- Jump onto the other scale hanging from Buddha's right hand (on your left): it will move down to the floor. Pull the golden crate onto the scale with your grapple.

- Jump back to the first scale (in Buddha's left hand): it moves down to the floor. Pull the medium crate onto the scale with your grapple.

- With the two smaller crates as counterweights, the golden crate will remain in a raised position even after you leave the scale (Fig. 11). Jump up to the central platform and place the golden crate on top of the floor switch.

The door below will open. Go through it and run down the stairs.

[1 1]

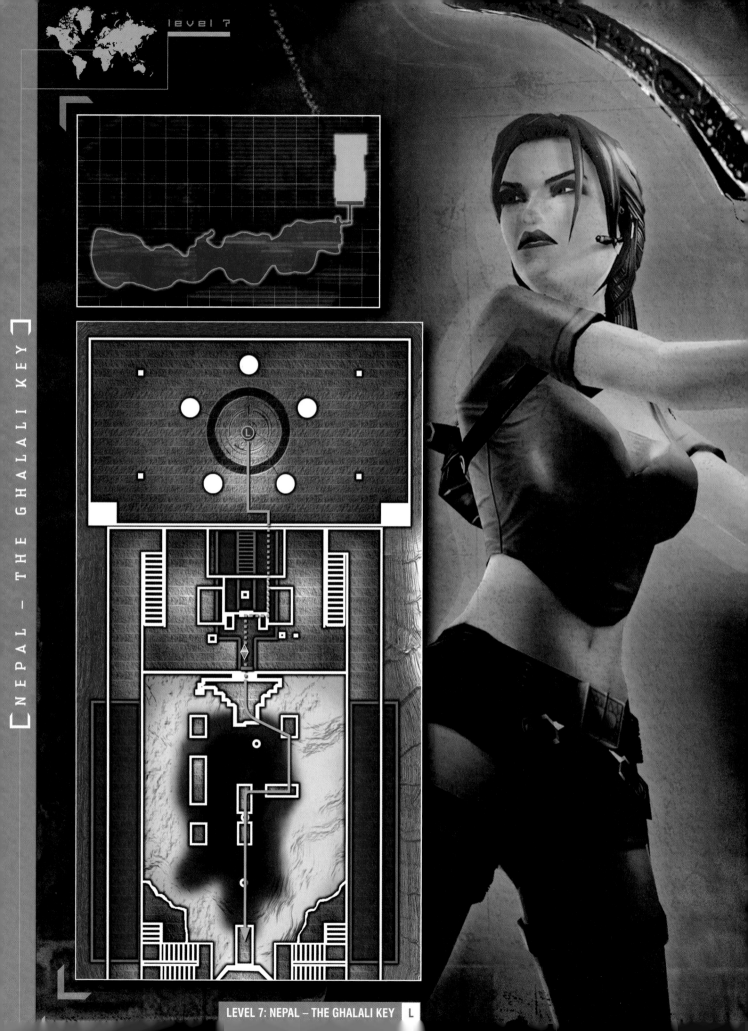

HOW TO PLAY

WALKTHROUGH

EXTRAS

INTRODUCTION

LEVEL 1

LEVEL 2

LEVEL 3

LEVEL 4

LEVEL 5

LEVEL 6

LEVEL 7

LEVEL 8

AREA MAP

A – C

D – F

G – I

J – K

L

L As the door that you entered through is now closed, you'll need to leave via an exit on the lower level. Use Excalibur to smash down the door. As soon as you run through the gap, the temple's lower level begins to fall apart. You need to time the next sequence of jumps precisely, and there really isn't a second to spare. Proceed in the following order: jump to the platform on the left (Fig. 12), then jump to the platform on your right. Now jump to the platform to the right, turn to the left and jump straight ahead to the next platform and, after pausing for a moment to let it tip forward, jump to the final ledge to end the level.

[12]

BOLIVIA – THE LOOKING GLASS

MISSION DETAILS

A Your goal in this first stage of the final level is very simple: to survive an enormous battle against numerous opponents. The following tips and tricks will help you to defeat the largest group of mercenaries you have faced so far.

- Excalibur is inordinately powerful: a single hit from one of its shockwaves is enough to kill any soldier. This is the only weapon you'll need to use during this final stage: even grenades are a comparatively weak and feeble attacking option by comparison.

- Despite their weight of numbers, your assailants are at a distinct disadvantage. Shockwaves from Excalibur are fast and wide, and can smash through (or simply penetrate) certain items of scenery: your rather unfortunate opponents have almost nowhere to hide (Fig. 1).

- With so much firepower at your disposal, there's little point in seeking cover. Sheer aggression is your best form of defense. The sooner you reduce the number of enemies you face, the easier the battle will become.

- Your priority should be to eliminate the enemies that pose the greatest danger – specifically, the soldiers manning the two turrets, and those wielding grenade launchers. It's difficult to spot grenades while swinging Excalibur, so don't stay in any one spot for more than a second or two. Given the number of opponents you face simultaneously, this is just good common sense. Run, dodge, jump, and generally try to make yourself a hard target to follow at all times.

- Additional mercenaries will join the fray by sliding into battle on the zip cords situated around the platform. Don't assume that an area cleared of mercenaries will remain free of enemy activity for long. Keep moving, and always be ready to turn and dispatch any sneaky soldiers that are preparing to attack Lara from behind.

- Don't stand too close to the edge: falling from the platform will lead to instant death for Lara.

- Although this opening section of the final battle is fairly easy, the fight that follows is rather more challenging. For that reason, you should take the time to collect Health Packs (Fig. 2) and ensure that Lara is at full fitness before you kill the last mercenary.

As soon as you kill the final soldier, a cutscene (and a checkpoint) follows before you fight Tomb Raider Legend's ultimate battle...

[01]

[02]

HOW TO PLAY

WALKTHROUGH

EXTRAS

INTRODUCTION

LEVEL 1

LEVEL 2

LEVEL 3

LEVEL 4

LEVEL 5

LEVEL 6

LEVEL 7

LEVEL 8

AREA MAP

A – B

B Once again, Amanda summons the ancient and malevolent Unknown Entity with murderous intent. Unlike your previous encounter, however, you can now attack it directly with the mighty Excalibur.

The Unknown Entity will circle the platform and launch projectiles at Lara (Fig. 3). Many of these explode when they hit the ground or scenery. If Lara is caught within the blast radius of these energy waves, she will be knocked off her feet and lose health; direct hits can be ***extremely*** damaging, and should be avoided at all costs. The outer ring of pillars (or the ruins that remain if they are destroyed) can offer a degree of cover, but this isn't something you should rely too heavily on. If the Unknown Entity pulls both arms back, it is preparing to make a slow yet devastating attack that is, nonetheless, easy to dodge if you read the signs in time. When it pulls one arm back, it will perform a much weaker but faster assault. Stay mobile at all times and maintain a reasonably safe distance between Lara and her adversary, and be ready to jump to avoid its attacks at a moment's notice. Again, you should also avoid the edge of the platform: if Lara falls, you'll be sent back to the start of the battle.

You should hold **L1** throughout this fight to maintain a lock-on and track the Unknown Entity's progress. It is highly agile, and can dodge many of Excalibur's shockwaves, but rest assured: those attacks that do hit home cause damage, as the health bar in the top right-hand corner of the screen will attest. The trick is to stay sufficiently far away to have time to dodge the creature's attacks, but not so far that blasts from Excalibur become ineffective.

When its energy gauge is very low, the Unknown Entity will collapse to the ground. Make your way over to it and launch a close-quarters melee attack with **△** (Fig. 4). Speed is of the essence: if you are too slow, the Unknown Entity will rise again and you will lose the opportunity to strike. Rolling towards it is marginally faster than running; it's also useful if you quickly identify that your nemesis is about to fall, and begin your dash before it hits the ground.

The Unknown Entity's health bar will be replenished when it resumes its attack. If you managed to strike it with a melee attack, the health bar will be lower than before. Move quickly to a safe distance, then resume your assault. You now need to repeat the above process at least three

more times: knock the Unknown Entity to the ground, stab it, then retreat and begin again. Each time it collapses, the Unknown Entity will become weaker. When its energy gauge is virtually empty, Lara can finally inflict a killing blow. Now sit back and enjoy the concluding cutscene...

[0 3]

[0 4]

LAST SAVE

Remember to use the "Save & Quit" option to record your progress once the adventure ends! If you don't, you'll miss out on unlockable bonuses that can be found in the Extras menu. Turn to page 164 for further details.

3ʳᵈ CHAPTER

EXTRAS

If you think you're au fait with everything there is to know about Tomb Raider Legend, think again. In this chapter we reveal the locations of the Bronze, Silver and Gold Rewards, explore the manifold secrets they unlock, take an exhaustive tour of Croft Manor, and explain how to beat each level's Time Trial. As an added bonus, we also speak to the Crystal Dynamics team in a revealing (and exclusive) "Behind the Scenes" article, and take a look back at Lara's previous adventures. Naturally, this section of the guide contains countless **spoilers**. If you're a purist seeking to finish Tomb Raider Legend without help on your first playthrough, you may prefer to wait until you complete the game before reading any further!

SECRETS

Completing Tomb Raider Legend is an admirable accomplishment, but there's still plenty of fun to be had once you beat its eight exhilarating levels. If you want to experience everything the game has to offer, you'll need to collect every last Reward, finish every stage in the demanding Time Trial mode, and explore every inch of Croft Manor. Over the following pages we explain how you can achieve a 100% completion rating, and also take a look at the many hidden features this will enable you to enjoy...

CROFT MANOR

Packed with 27 Rewards to locate, and a host of puzzles to complete in order to find the most artfully concealed Gold Reward in the entire game, the Croft Manor level is an engaging treasure hunt that takes place in Lara's home. This section details the location of every single Reward in a step by step walkthrough accompanied by annotated maps and illustrative screenshots.

GETTING STARTED

You can access Croft Manor from the title screen once you complete the opening Bolivia level for the first time and, more specifically, save your progress. To play the level, select Croft Manor from the Main Menu. You will be asked to choose a save file. Pick your most "current" save – again, it's a requisite that this file specifies that you have beaten the Bolivia stage – and Croft Manor will load.

Lara will begin in the Foyer area of her not-so-humble abode. You can now explore as you please, collecting Rewards and other items as you find them. To store your progress, select Save Rewards from the Pause menu, then choose the save file that you wish to add the collected rewards to. This should obviously be your most

"current" saved position. You will be asked for confirmation before the overwrite takes place. Don't worry: your progress in the main adventure will not be affected by adding this record of your achievements at Croft Manor.

To leave Lara's home and return to the title screen, select Exit Croft Manor, then confirm your decision. You will be offered another opportunity to save any collected Rewards. Select Quit to exit the level.

TREASURE HUNTING TIPS

Should you opt to explore Croft Manor without consulting the walkthrough, you should bear in mind the following useful tips.

- You can find four items of Lara's equipment either lying around or hidden within the manor's rooms. The Magnetic Grapple and Pistols are vital: you will not be able to collect many Rewards without them. The Personal Light Source is extremely handy (though *technically* not essential) for collecting two rewards, while the Binoculars are merely useful to have.

- Pay attention to visual cues and clues. If Lara turns her head, she may well be looking at a point of interactivity. Look closely for the distinctive shimmer that indicates that an item can be used with the Magnetic Grapple, and watch the gun reticle closely while looking around in Manual Aim mode. If it turns red or blue, you've discovered a place where you can put the Pistols or Magnetic Grapple to good use.

- You cannot use the Magnetic Grapple to collect Rewards during the Croft Manor level. You may be able to see and reach a Reward with the device, but the grapple head will stubbornly refuse to acquire a purchase when you fire it.

- There are no specific hazards or enemies in the Croft Manor level, but Lara can still be harmed by falling from great heights – and, of course, by drowning. There are no drops that are instantly fatal, but you may find that Lara sustains minor cuts and bruises as you attempt to negotiate the walls of the Obstacle Course area. If that should be the case, you have one Health Pack that you can use when required. You can also completely refill Lara's health gauge by changing her outfit in the Bedroom area. If Lara is killed – and it takes a special brand of either negligence or malice to achieve that here – then play will resume from the last activated checkpoint.

- Don't forget to save your Rewards before you turn off your console!

- The walkthrough offers the fastest and most efficient route through Croft Manor. It's designed to be followed on a step by step basis, but it's also arranged in a manner that makes it a useful reference tool. There's really no shame in quickly referring to it if you're having difficulty finding a particularly elusive Reward...

HOW TO PLAY

WALKTHROUGH

EXTRAS

SECRETS

PREVIOUS
ADVENTURES

BEHIND THE
SCENES

CROFT MANOR

REWARDS

UNLOCKABLES

CAST

FOYER

FIRST THINGS FIRST: As the map shows, there are five distinct areas in Croft Manor. The Foyer – Lara's starting position on every visit to this level – acts as a central hub and provides access to another four areas: Bedroom, Study, Swimming Pool and Obstacle Course. Your first visit to the Foyer is necessarily brief, but rest assured that you'll return here shortly to collect hidden Rewards.

COLLECTING THE MAGNETIC GRAPPLE: Turn around and enter the Tech Center through the door in the glass wall and use the computer on the floor to the right of Zip (Fig. 1). This opens a safe in the far wall. Walk over and collect the Magnetic Grapple. Now take the staircase and head left. Go through the door at the far end of the balcony, then follow the corridor to reach the Bedroom.

BEDROOM

COLLECTING THE PISTOLS: Turn to your left as you enter the room: you will see a round plaque featuring the head of Medusa with two switches either side of it (Fig. 2). Pull both of them to reveal the Pistols. Remember to actually pick them up before you continue!

BRONZE REWARD #1: Look behind Lara's bed to find a Bronze Reward (Fig. 3).

DRESSED TO KILL: You can change Lara's current outfit in the room to the right of the entrance. Simply run to the wardrobe at the far end, and then follow the onscreen prompt when it appears (Fig. 4). Note that the range of attire available to Lara is dictated by your performance and progress in the main game – see page 168 for details.

MOVING SWIFTLY ON: Leave via the exit and follow the corridor to return to the Foyer. Run along the upper balcony and take the first door on your left. Now continue along the next corridor to reach the Study.

[02] [03] [04]

STUDY

COLLECTING THE PLS: Collect the Personal Light Source from the edge of the desk where Alister is working (Fig. 5).

BRONZE REWARD #2: Run upstairs and follow the balcony to reach a smaller room. There is a Bronze Reward in plain view in the corner – it's to your right as you enter (Fig. 6).

BRONZE REWARD #3: In the upstairs room, pull the switch in the far left-hand corner to reveal a Bronze Reward hidden behind a set of shelves (Fig. 7).

SILVER REWARD #1: Return to the lower level of the study and shoot the wooden boards adjacent to the entrance to find a Silver Reward behind a small shelving unit (Fig. 8).

[05] [06]

GOLD REWARD PUZZLE #1: Grab the shelving unit uncovered by shooting the wooden planks while acquiring **Silver Reward #1** and push it on top of one of the two gray switches either side of the desk. Facing Alister, turn 90 degrees to the right: you should see the second small shelving unit sitting on a metal-rimmed ledge. Fire the Magnetic Grapple at this shimmering platform and pull to remove the unit from the wall (Fig. 9). Now push it on top of the second of the two gray switches. This will open a wall panel to the right of Alister's desk. Activate the PLS and enter the secret tunnel. Pull the tongue of the wall plaque beside the pile of crates (Fig. 10) to reveal an inscription that you can read with ◎: "Above the Waters, Twin Sisters turn their backs one upon the other to leave the Ambages unguarded." This is the first clue in your quest for the Gold Reward.

[07]   [08]   [09]

[10]   [11]   [12]

HOW TO PLAY

WALKTHROUGH

EXTRAS

SECRETS

PREVIOUS
ADVENTURES

BEHIND THE
SCENES

CROFT MANOR

REWARDS

UNLOCKABLES

CAST

SILVER REWARD #2: There is a Silver Reward in plain view inside the secret corridor (Fig. 11). You should have seen (and, hopefully, collected) it en route to the wall plaque described in **Gold Reward Puzzle #1**.

BRONZE REWARD #4: Shoot the wooden boxes in the corner of the secret corridor as it turns to the left to find a Bronze Reward (Fig. 12).

LAST BUT NOT LEAST: Pull the tongue of the wall plaque at the far end of the corridor. This opens the door that leads to the Bedroom. You've achieved all you can on this side of the house for now, so make your way back to the Foyer.

FOYER REVISITED

BRONZE REWARD #5: Go down to the lower area. Face the stairs, then run to the corner to your left to find a Bronze Reward situated in front of a door (Fig. 13).

BRONZE REWARD #6: Run up the stairs and then head left. From the balcony, turn and face the shimmering switch on the wall adjacent to the stairs (Fig. 14). Fire the Magnetic Grapple at it and pull to reveal a Bronze Reward in a hidden alcove.

SILVER REWARD #3: Now head over to the opposite balcony. Turn to face the switch protruding from the square hole in the wall adjacent to the stairs (Fig. 15). Use Manual Aim to shoot it until the panel below opens to reveal a Silver Reward.

TIME FOR A SWIM: Run down the stairs and take the second door on your left (it's just beside the glass wall) and follow the corridor to reach the Swimming Pool area.

[13]

[14]

[15]

SWIMMING POOL

BRONZE REWARD #7: Jump into the pool and swim down to find a Bronze Reward (Fig. 16).

BRONZE REWARD #8: From the entrance, run over to the deckchairs in the far left-hand corner of the room to find a Bronze Reward (Fig. 17).

BRONZE REWARD #9: Run over to the fish statue on the left-hand side of the room and pull it from its position to reveal a Bronze Reward (Fig. 18). Now push the statue as close to the pool as you can: this is prep work for a later puzzle (Fig. 19).

PREPARING A PATH: Remaining on the left-hand side of the room, use the Magnetic Grapple to pull the spears forward on the two statues at either end of the room (Fig. 20) to create horizontal poles for Lara to swing from at a later date.

REACHING THE FIRST RAISED AREA: From the entrance to the room, run to the right-hand side of the pool and pull the two fish statues out as far as they will go. Jump from the top of the fish statue in the far right-hand corner of the room (Fig. 21) to reach the nearby spear, then jump from there to the ledge beneath the balcony. Move around to the opposite side, then spring backwards to land on top of the second fish statue. Hop over to the spear, and then swing to the platform ahead.

BRONZE REWARD #10: After reaching the upper area, you can collect a Bronze Reward from the diving board (Fig. 22).

OPENING THE SECRET TUNNEL, PART 1: On the upper area, rotate the two statues until they face each other: this will reveal a plaque with a tongue switch identical to that found in the secret tunnel leading from the Study to the Bedroom. Pull it, and a cutscene will show a barrier moving aside beneath the waters of the pool.

[16]

[17]

[18]

150

[19]

[20]

[21]

SECRETS

PREVIOUS
ADVENTURES

BEHIND THE
SCENES

CROFT MANOR

REWARDS

UNLOCKABLES

CAST

[22]

[23]

IMPORTANT NOTE: You *must* do this before you perform the actions described in **Gold Reward Puzzle #2**. Once the puzzle clue appears, you cannot trigger the appearance of the tongue switch!

GOLD REWARD PUZZLE #2: Remember the clue found in the secret passageway earlier? You are now "Above the Waters", and the statues before you are the "Twin Sisters". Rotate both statues so that they face away from each other ("...turn their backs one upon the other") to reveal a new cryptic clue ("...the Ambages unguarded"). This reads: "Within the Hall of Knowledge, Tomes of Cerulean, Topaz, Viridian and Crimson in turn reveal their Arcanum."

COLLECTING THE BINOCULARS: Move over to the other side of the platform and jump over to the spear. Now jump forward and immediately fire the Magnetic Grapple to swing from the metal object hanging from the ceiling (Fig. 23). Swing over to the next spear, and from there to the second upper area. Run over to the horse statue to collect the Binoculars.

SILVER REWARD #4: Look behind the far fish statue to find a Silver Reward (Fig. 24).

SILVER REWARD #5: Use the Magnetic Grapple to pull the blue ball from its position on top of the fish statue (Fig. 25), then roll it on top of the round floor switch to lower a hanging platform above the pool. Return to the lower level. Now climb on top of the fish statue you moved to find **Bronze Reward #9** earlier, then jump over to the hanging platform. Use the Magnetic Grapple to make it swing towards the balcony, then jump over. Collect the Silver Reward (Fig. 26).

OPENING THE SECRET TUNNEL, PART 2: Jump into the pool below. Swim over to the lever and pull it to open the second barrier blocking the opening to your left (or, actually, to your right as you turn around after using the lever). This is a secret tunnel that leads to the Obstacle Course area.

SILVER REWARD #6: Take a deep breath, then swim through the secret tunnel to find a Silver Reward (Fig. 27). After you collect it, continue forward to reach the Obstacle Course area.

[24]

[25]

[26]

[27]

OBSTACLE COURSE

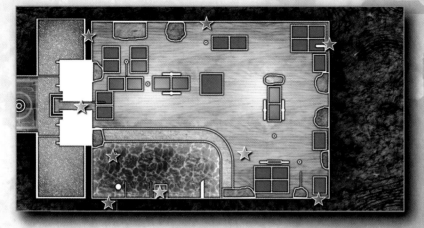

A FEW WORDS ON INTERACTIVE SCENERY: The Obstacle Course room features interactive scenery that can be moved between two positions with the Magnetic Grapple. This enables you to create new routes to reach previously inaccessible Rewards, but can also remove a vital step on the path to reach other Rewards. To avoid potential confusion and frustration, we advise that you refrain from moving anything unless instructed to do so.

BRONZE REWARD #11: Collect the Bronze Reward at the bottom of the pool as you enter the Obstacle Course area (Fig. 28). Note: if you're not making your way through from the Swimming Pool area, the pool is just to your right as you enter this room.

[28]

[29]

[30]

[31]

BRONZE REWARD #12: Jump onto the ledge on the stone towards the far end of the room (Fig. 29), then spring backwards to reach the horizontal bar. Jump from there to the vertical pole, then to the horizontal beam, then over to the pole attached to the wall. Jump to your right to reach the ledge in the rock, and then move around the corner. Jump up to reach the ledge above, then move around to the right. Drop to the slope, then immediately jump to grab the rock beam jutting out from the wall. Move around to the ledge in the wall, then jump up to grab the hand-holds. Climb to the top of these, then leap over to the ledge to your right. Move right and jump to the first horizontal pole (again, to your right); from there, swing over to a second pole. Position yourself close to the wall, then jump over to the ledge. Move to the left, then drop into the alcove to collect the Bronze Reward (Fig. 30).

SILVER REWARD #7: From your position in the alcove after collecting **Bronze Reward #12**, hop up to grab the wall ledge. Move out of the alcove, then spring backwards to reach the horizontal pole; from there, swing to the next horizontal pole. Turn to face the wall and move as close as you can, then release your grip to grab the ledge below. Move to the left, then drop to the next ledge down; finally, release your grip above the small rock platform and collect the Silver Reward after you land (Fig. 31). You can also, of course, simply jump across to the small island from the ground floor, but it's *much* more fun if you do it our way...

[32]

BRONZE REWARD #13: Use the Magnetic Grapple to move the horizontal pole near the entrance by 90 degrees in an anticlockwise direction (Fig. 32). Now use the blue ramp at the centre of the room to jump to the horizontal bar; from there, jump to the vertical pole; now jump to the horizontal bar you repositioned a moment ago. Swing over to the slanted stone set against the wall, then jump to grab the ledge before Lara falls to the floor. Hop up to the ledge above, then spring backwards to grab the vertical pole. Jump to the next

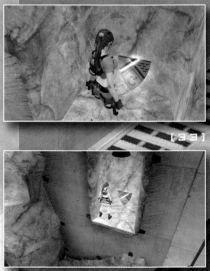

[33]

[34]

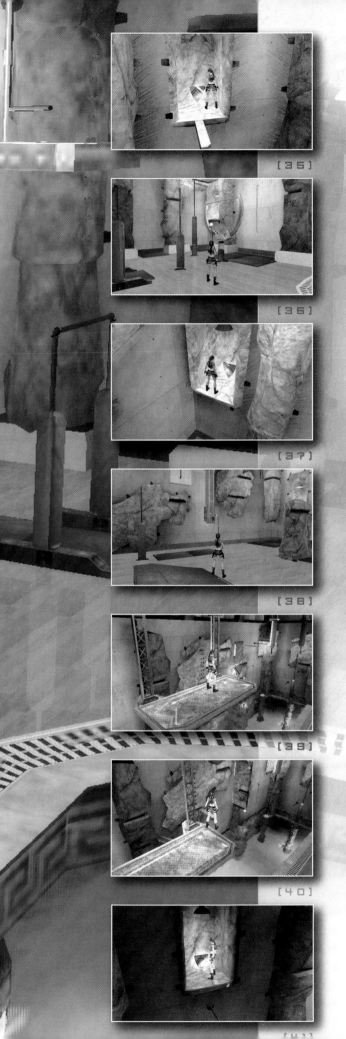

[35]

[36]

[37]

[38]

[39]

[40]

HOW TO PLAY

WALKTHROUGH

EXTRAS

SECRETS

PREVIOUS
ADVENTURES

BEHIND THE
SCENES

CROFT MANOR

REWARDS

UNLOCKABLES

CAST

vertical pole, then release your grip to drop to the slope below. Jump immediately to grab the ledge ahead, then climb up to collect the Bronze Reward (Fig. 33).

BRONZE REWARD #14: The vertical pole by the door must be in the position described at **Bronze Reward #13**. Use the blue ramp at the centre of the room to jump to the horizontal bar. Swing to the vertical pole, then hop over to the horizontal bar. Jump over to the slanted stone set against the wall, then jump to grab the ledge before Lara falls to the floor. Move to your right, around the corner, and then jump to your right to reach the vertical pole. From here, jump to the pole attached to the wall. Climb to the top, then leap to the ledge to your right, then jump over to the ladder. Climb up and then spring to the vertical bar on the wall to your left; now jump over to the alcove and climb up to collect the Bronze Reward (Fig. 34).

BRONZE REWARD #15: After collecting **Bronze Reward #14**, drop and hang onto the alcove ledge, then use the vertical pole to return to the ladder. Climb down until Lara is aligned with the lower of two ledges on her right, then jump over to it. Jump to the ledge above, then jump over to the ledge on your right. Move around the corner, then spring backwards to reach the horizontal pole. Turn Lara so that she is facing the small ledge protruding from the wall below, then drop down to grab it. Move right and climb up into the alcove to pick up the Bronze Reward (Fig. 35).

BRONZE REWARD #16: Attach the Magnetic Grapple to the grapple point on the device supporting the horizontal bar in the far right-hand corner of the room (Fig. 36), and then pull to convert it to a vertical bar. Now jump onto the ledge on the nearby stone, then spring backwards to reach the horizontal bar. Jump from there to the vertical pole, then over to the vertical pole you moved into position a moment ago. Hop over to the next vertical pole, and then over to the wall ledge. Now jump to your right to reach an alcove containing the final Bronze Reward (Fig. 37).

SILVER REWARD #8: Use the Magnetic Grapple to move the ladder positioned against (facing into the room from the entrance) the left-hand wall (Fig. 38). The horizontal pole close to the door should be in the position described at **Bronze Reward #13**. Use the blue ramp at the centre of the room to jump to the horizontal bar; from there, jump to the vertical pole; now jump to the horizontal bar. Swing over to the slanted stone set against the wall, and then jump to grab the ledge before Lara slides to the floor. Move around the corner, then jump over to the vertical pole. Now jump to the pole attached to the wall. Climb to the top, leap to the ledge to your right, then jump over to the repositioned ladder. Climb to the top, then jump to your right to reach a hanging platform. Wait for it to finish moving, then jump to the next platform to collect the Silver Reward (Fig. 39).

SILVER REWARD #9: From your position on the raised platform, turn to face the small pool below. Fire your Magnetic Grapple at the interactive wall above it, then pull to change its position (Fig. 40). Now leap from the platform to the ledge on the wall. It's a dangerous stunt, but well within Lara's capabilities. Move around the corner and then drop to the slope; jump before Lara falls and grab the ledge. Jump up to the hand-holds, climb them, then leap over to the ledge on your right. Move along it, then spring backwards to grab the horizontal pole. Now use the next two horizontal poles to reach the hanging platform. Fire the Magnetic Grapple at the shimmering metal plate beneath the alcove, then pull to move the platform. Hop over the short gap to collect the Silver Reward (Fig. 41). Your work here is done! Your next task is to return to the Study.

STUDY REVISITED

GOLD REWARD PUZZLE #3: The clue in the Swimming Pool area specified a "Hall of Knowledge"; this is the Study. The "Tomes of Cerulean, Topaz, Viridian and Crimson" are, respectively, blue, yellow, green and red books that can be pushed in turn to open a hidden compartment containing another inscription. Push the blue book on the ground floor, just beside the entrance; go upstairs and push the yellow book in the small room; push the green book on the balcony; finally, push the red book in the downstairs area. When the shelves move aside, you can read the following clue: "Above the Hearth, revealed visage and countenance touched in haste raise up the Steward."

SILVER REWARD #10: You can collect the tenth and final Silver Reward from in front of the inscription (Fig. 42) after completing **Gold Reward Puzzle #3**.

[42]

FOYER FINALE

GOLD REWARD PUZZLE #4: As you return to the Foyer area, you will notice that plaques with "switch" tongues have now replaced the pictures that were once hanging at the end of both balconies. From your position on the balcony, use the Magnetic Grapple to pull the vertical poles above the glass wall to a lower position, creating a row of three horizontal bars (Fig. 43). Now go over to the opposite balcony ("Above the Hearth..."), then approach and activate the plaque switch ("...revealed visage..."). You now face a tight time limit: immediately jump to the horizontal pole and swing to the opposite balcony via the horizontal beams to pull the second switch ("...and countenance touched in haste..."). A statue of Athena will rise from the floor in the room below, and you will receive a final clue: "The risen Athena turns to face the Sun, whose burden then reveals the Golden Laurel."

GOLD REWARD PUZZLE #5: Run downstairs and rotate the statue of Athena to face the floor switch ("...turns to face the Sun...") in front of the staircase. Now run and stand on the floor switch ("...whose burden then reveals the Golden Laurel"). The Gold Reward will rise up on a pedestal, but it is out of Lara's jumping range. Run upstairs to either balcony and make your way over to the central horizontal pole. Move along to the end nearest the pedestal and, facing it, drop down. Now collect the Gold Reward to conclude the treasure hunt (Fig. 44).

[43]   [44]

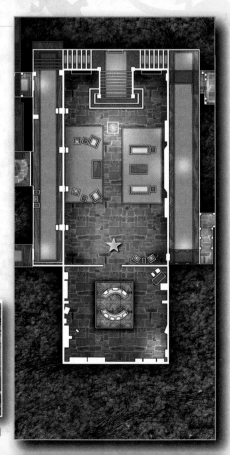

TOMB RAIDER LEGEND

HOW TO PLAY

WALKTHROUGH

EXTRAS

SECRETS

PREVIOUS ADVENTURES

BEHIND THE SCENES

CROFT MANOR

REWARDS

UNLOCKABLES

CAST

REWARDS

INTRODUCTION

Designed to be used in conjunction with the main walkthrough, the following section reveals the location of every Bronze, Silver and Gold Reward in Tomb Raider Legend. With screenshots showing the exact location of each collectable, it's also highly useful if you want to replay levels to find Rewards that you may have missed during your first playthrough.

You don't have to start your game all over again if you happen to miss a Reward. Instead, choose Load Level from the Main Menu,

then pick your most current save file. Now select the mission you wish to conduct your treasure hunt in, and select Continue to begin. Activate the PDA with <kbd>SELECT</kbd> to check how many Rewards you have yet to find. Once you've finished exploring and have found some missing Rewards, remember to use the Save Rewards option in the Pause menu to update your save file before you quit.

LEVEL 1: BOLIVIA — TIWANAKU

 1-A: Before you set off to jump the gap at the top of the ramp, follow the nearby wall on your left and run beneath the natural rock "arch" to find a Bronze Reward.

1-B: On your way to the small pool, examine the wall on your right. You will find a Bronze Reward inside a small recess.

 **1-C:** As soon as Lara hangs from the rope, turn to the left (approximately 90 degrees) until you see a cave entrance. Swing towards it and jump when you have sufficient speed to safely reach the ledge. Activate your Personal Light Source and run to the end of the dark passage to find a Silver Reward. You can safely drop from this ledge to reach the tunnel situated behind the waterfall here – there is no need to backtrack to the rope.

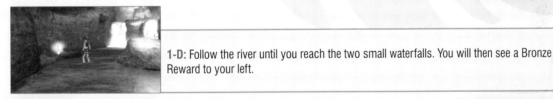 **1-D:** Follow the river until you reach the two small waterfalls. You will then see a Bronze Reward to your left.

1-E: Walk cautiously towards the left end of the narrow walkway behind the waterfall, and jump vertically to get to the ledge above. Pull yourself up to reach a small recess containing a Bronze Reward.

1-F: When you reach the other side of the gap, run forward a few meters. Once you reach the corner, look to your left and you'll see a Bronze Reward situated on a small ledge. Use the Magnetic Grapple to obtain it.

 **1-G:** After sliding down the slope, you can find a Bronze Reward in the small cul-de-sac directly ahead of you.

 1-H: Once you defeat all nearby soldiers, jump onto the ledge (it's the one where the soldiers appear) and run along the path to the right and underneath a small bridge to find a Bronze Reward.

1-I: Once the area at the foot of the temple is cleared of assailants, climb the ledges to the left of the steps until you reach a small alcove blocked with bricks. Shoot them to reveal a Silver Reward.

1-J: From the top of the small set of steps, turn left into the narrow corridor to find a Bronze Reward.

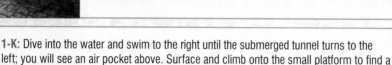

1-K: Dive into the water and swim to the right until the submerged tunnel turns to the left; you will see an air pocket above. Surface and climb onto the small platform to find a Bronze Reward.

1-L: From the entrance facing into the room, go to the right-hand corner of the upper level and climb into the far alcove to find a Bronze Reward.

1-M: To obtain this level's Gold Reward, you will need to reposition the barrier that previously blocked the exit. Pull the crate away from the central floor switch to close the exit barrier. Now remove a crate from one of the two adjacent floor switches. Return to the central switch, and return the crate to its former position on top of it; with one of the gears locked, it will not open. Now run over to the vacant floor switch and position Lara on top of it. Immediately face the exit barrier. Just before it is halfway open – the central "mouth" line will be on the same level as the uppermost horizontal lines (actually, ledges) on the pillars either side of it – immediately move Lara off the floor switch. Make your way over to the exit (consult the walkthrough for details), choose one of the pillars either side of the barrier, then jump up to the second ledge. With the mechanism making fruitless attempts to raise the barrier higher, climbing from here is slightly more difficult than it may initially seem – you'll need to time your jumps with a little care. Leap sideways to grab the ledge at the centre of the barrier (the "mouth"). Wait until the barrier begins to descend, then jump up; from this position, jump up once again when the barrier reaches its highest point. Now climb onto the platform and claim your hard-earned Gold Reward.

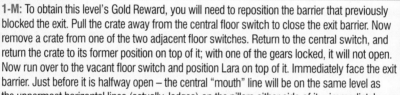

1-N: From the exit facing into the room, head left. Jump onto the ledge, and then move along it as far as you can. Jump up to the platform above. Now use the chain to reach the Silver Reward.

1-O: Beneath the entrance to this area you can find a small section of wall that is a different color to the surrounding stone. Push it forward to reveal a tunnel, and then run through it to find a Silver Reward. You may have noticed it shining on the ground below as Lara leapt for her life during the earlier Super Action...

1-P: Once you have jumped from left to right here, manually adjust the camera and align Lara with the horizontal pole behind her. Jump backwards to reach it, and the device will rotate by 90 degrees. Swing around the pole and jump to grab the wall ledge. Pull yourself up onto the platform above and retrieve the Silver Reward. You can now jump back onto the horizontal pole to return to your previous position.

LEVEL 2: PERU – RETURN TO PARAÍSO

2-A: From the village entrance, head to the back of the second house on your right, then climb onto its roof via the ledge behind it. Walk forward until the grapple symbol appears when you approach the edge of the roof – the entrance to the village should be to your left. Now use the Magnetic Grapple to swing over to the buildings opposite. Drop down into the back alley behind them, where you will find a Bronze Reward. Collect it, then grab the large crate and move it closer to the fence. You can now use it to return to the main street.

SECRETS

PREVIOUS
ADVENTURES

BEHIND THE
SCENES

CROFT MANOR

REWARDS

UNLOCKABLES

CAST

2-B: When you reach the balcony next to the flagpole, kick the nearby door open. There is a Silver Reward inside.

2-C: Drop down to the market square and climb the steps leading up to the church entrance. On the left you will notice that the railings are broken. Jump through the gap to land on top of the market stall. Hop from here to reach a roof. From there, use the two horizontal poles to swing over to the opposite roof. Collect the Bronze Reward. You can use the nearby cable to slide back to the ground.

2-D: Facing the church, run along the road to your right to find a Bronze Reward next to a fence.

2-E: Head left into the side alley to find a Bronze Reward.

2-F: There is a Bronze Reward situated in plain view on this platform.

2-G: Instead of going straight through the open door, first run to the right to find a Bronze Reward in a dark corner.

2-H: A Bronze Reward is hidden behind three boxes beside the sealed entrance to the excavation site.

2-I: Enter the ruined shack situated just in front of the pool to find a Bronze Reward.

2-J: After solving the underwater puzzle, you can collect a Silver Reward situated in front of an iron gate. From the exit facing into the room, it's just inside the opening on the far left.

2-K: Jump onto the hanging rope, turn slightly to the left to face the broken pillar. Climb further up the rope, and then begin swinging towards the ledge above it. When you have sufficient momentum, leap forward and grab it. Jump up to the ledge just above it, then move along to the left. Jump laterally across the gap and continue until you reach an opening. Pull yourself up, and head to your right to find a fourth boulder. Push it forward: it will roll down and destroy the wall below. Wait until it falls to the ground below, then drop down onto the pillar. Now jump over to the top of the statue, and make your way back to the ground. Grab the fourth boulder and push it onto the central floor switch, which will then bear the weight of two boulders simultaneously. This will cause the altar to rise, which enables you to collect the Gold Reward.

LEVEL 3: TOKYO – MEETING WITH TAKAMOTO

3-A: Jump onto the roof to the right of the skylight. Shoot the box there and collect the Bronze Reward.

3-B: Destroy the wooden box under the stairway: it contains a Bronze Reward.

3-C: There is a pile of boxes against the wall opposite the previous Bronze Reward. Pull them aside to reveal a wooden crate. Shoot it to reveal a Silver Reward.

3-D: Climb down the blocks behind Lara after the cutscene has finished, and run all the way to the end of the scaffolding – don't forget to jump over the gap! A Bronze Reward is hidden inside the crate at the end.

3-E: Go down the first set of stairs and fire at the wooden box to reveal a Bronze Reward.

3-F: Climb two more flights of stairs to reach the top of the stairway. Walk through the broken banister and onto the pipes. Jump onto the ledge on the left-hand wall, move along to the far right, and then jump backwards to land on the pipes. You can now retrieve a Silver Reward from the destructible wooden box. To return safely to the corridor below, jump back to the ledge. Release your grip to grab a second ledge beneath it, then drop down to the floor.

3-G: Facing the huge monitor screen, run to the cubicle at the far left of the room. Destroy the box to reveal a Bronze Reward.

3-H: Climb the stairs to access the upper area of the office. Run to the right, and kick the left-hand cabinet open to reveal a Silver Reward.

3-I: After the fight, go through the door next to the stairs in the gallery. Kick the second cupboard from the left to discover a Silver Reward.

3-J: Go up to the mezzanine above the gallery, shoot the wooden box and collect the Bronze Reward.

3-K: Facing the elevator, go to your right and enter Takamoto's office. Grab the black and red crate, drag it into the corridor, then push it through the broken window. It will smash as it hits the chest below, revealing a Gold Reward.

HOW TO PLAY

WALKTHROUGH

EXTRAS

SECRETS

PREVIOUS
ADVENTURES

BEHIND THE
SCENES

CROFT MANOR

REWARDS

UNLOCKABLES

CAST

4-A: From your position in the water after landing, face the direction of the raised bridge on the central islet. Now turn approximately 90 degrees to your left and dive down. There is a Bronze Reward to the right of (and just behind) a rock outcrop. The waterfall above means that the current is quite strong here, so you'll need to make Lara swim faster in order to get close enough.

4-B: Return to your previous position in front of the central islet, turn 90 degrees to the right, and then swim down and forward in that direction to find a Bronze Reward behind another rock outcrop. Again, the current is rather strong, so be sure to increase Lara's swimming speed to reach it.

4-C: After disabling the main waterfall, return to the front of the islet (where you first climbed up onto dry land) and jump back into the water. Turn around to face the direction of the bridge, dive straight down, and swim through a small tunnel to find a Silver Reward.

4-D: Facing into the room from your position on the upper platform, there is a Bronze Reward in plain view to your left.

4-E: There is a Bronze Reward just behind the raised stone platform – you should see it clearly as you walk down the steps.

4-F: As you drift into this area, leave the raft and swim over to the far left-hand corner of the water. There is a submerged (and barely visible) ledge here that enables Lara to climb up and collect a Silver Reward from the platform above.

4-G: There is a Bronze Reward behind the pillar to your left.

4-H: Once the boulder rolls over the ledge, climb down the ladder to your left. It leads to a platform where you can find a Silver Reward in plain view.

4-I: From your position on the ledge, jump over to your left then drop down onto the platform. Throw a grenade at the base of the wall segment – Lara's guns *will not* break it, so don't waste any time trying – then move to a safe distance before it explodes. Now collect the Silver Reward. If you don't have any grenades, there's a second (but rather more complex) way to get to it. Follow the main walkthrough until you reach the upper area where you face the group of mercenaries, then kick one of the explosive barrels into the small channel of the river that flows off to the right. The barrel will fall and explode by the barrier, shattering it. You can now make your way back down to collect the Reward.

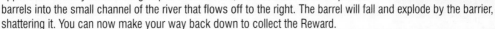

4-J: After treading on the floor switch that opens the level's final door, quickly run back down the stairs and duck underneath the descending barrier situated between the ruined staircase before it reaches the ground. If you make it on time, you will find a Gold Reward on top of a pedestal at the end of the passage.

LEVEL 5: KAZAKHSTAN – PROJECT CARBONEK

5-A: Jump to the upper part of the building (to Lara's right as she faces the turret). Walk to the end of the roof, face the flagpole and jump over to the horizontal bar. Swing around it, then jump and grab the ledge ahead. Pull yourself up onto the roof. If you haven't dropped down to ground level and encountered the second wave of soldiers yet, they will now appear below, so don't linger at the edge. Destroy the wooden box to discover a Bronze Reward.

5-B: Turn and run to your right as you enter the building and go into the storeroom to find a Bronze Reward tucked under a supply shelf.

5-C: After the battle, head towards the fenced-in area to the left of the medical building. You should see a Reward inside a wooden box. To access it, you can either shoot the fuel barrel to destroy the gate, or smash the wooden boxes piled between the two crates to reveal a big hole in the fence. Once you enter the fenced-in area, shoot the wooden box and collect the Silver Reward.

5-D: Facing the wall after dropping down from the sign, run to your left and drop to the ground. Shoot the box to find a Bronze Reward.

5-E: Drop down, turn around and destroy the wooden box to obtain a Bronze Reward. To reach the exit, climb onto the crate at the far end of the pit, jump forward and fire the Magnetic Grapple at the metallic object on the ceiling.

5-F: Facing the lab map, turn to your right and jump up to grab the lower of the two ventilators. Jump vertically, move to your left, then pull yourself up onto the platform. Use the Magnetic Grapple to pull open the cage door, then jump through it. Shoot the wooden box to reveal a Silver Reward.

5-G: A Bronze Reward is hidden to the right of the Tesla tower.

5-H: When you reach the upper platform, run over to the hanging cage. To open the door, stand at a safe distance and fire at the fuel barrel. Run inside to collect the Silver Reward.

5-I: Climb inside the magnetic gun and turn 90 degrees to your right. Above the grille there is a small section of wall that causes the weapon's reticle to turn red. These are actually metal blocks that can be pulled out. Dismount the magnetic gun and push the large crate on the nearby raised area over to the left of the platform, next to the newly-created ledge.

Remount the magnetic gun and move the hanging platform as far to the right as you can, then target a point just to the left of the very top of the metal device that connects it to the rail on the ceiling. Now begin to very rapidly tap the magnetic gun's "fire" button to push the platform along the rail and up the slope. Very carefully move the reticle to follow it as it moves forward, always being careful to maintain a position just to the left. This is very tricky – you may need more than a few attempts before you get it right – but you'll eventually manage to push the platform up to the upper section of the rail.

Leave the magnetic gun, jump on top of the crate you positioned earlier, then jump over to the small ledge. Hop up to the ledge above, move around the corner to your left, and then drop down to the small platform. Hop across to the hanging platform, and from there to the broken balcony. Now use the horizontal bar to reach the Gold Reward in the alcove.

LEVEL 6: ENGLAND – KING ARTHUR'S TOMB?

TOMB RAIDER
LEGEND

HOW TO PLAY

WALKTHROUGH

EXTRAS

SECRETS

PREVIOUS
ADVENTURES

BEHIND THE
SCENES

CROFT MANOR

REWARDS

UNLOCKABLES

CAST

6-A: A Bronze Reward is hidden inside the wooden box.

6-B: From the room entrance, head to your right to discover an opening in the wall. Jump over, crawl through and drop into the room to retrieve the Bronze Reward hidden inside the wooden box. To return to the main room, climb into the vent, hang from the ledge on the other side, and then spring backwards.

6-C: Crouch or roll through the small opening to the right of the exhibit after reaching this platform to find a Bronze Reward in a wooden box.

6-D: Pull down the vent cover situated high on the wall (from the entrance, it's to your right) with the Magnetic Grapple. You now need to create a makeshift staircase with the crates in this room. Move the first crate under the vent hole; put the second crate on top of the first one, and then a third crate next to them. Now jump up and climb through the vent. You will find a Silver Reward in the room beyond, where you will also witness a brief (and otherwise unavailable) plot-related conversation between Lara and Alister. If you have a hard time transporting the crates, remember that positioning the forks in a central position as you pick the crates up will make them more stable. Don't move too quickly: the more you accelerate (especially while turning), the more likely you are to drop the crate.

6-E: Smash into the sarcophagus with the forklift to destroy it and reveal a Silver Reward.

6-F: Turn to your right and fire the Magnetic Grapple at the Bronze Reward in the alcove, and then pull to obtain it.

6-G: Walk to the lower end of the steps and fire the Magnetic Grapple at the Bronze Reward in the far alcove, and then pull to collect it.

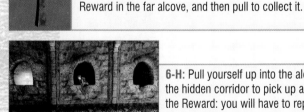

6-H: Pull yourself up into the alcove at the far right of the ledge, then run to the end of the hidden corridor to pick up a Bronze Reward. If you drop down, you cannot collect the Reward: you will have to replay the entire stage up until this point using the Load Level option.

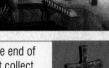

6-I: Push the crate into the middle of the blade trap to your left to halt its rotation. Walk through into the room beyond to collect a Silver Reward.

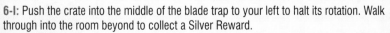

6-J: Look at the Bronze Reward behind the metal bars. Place Lara behind the chandelier so that she, the chandelier and the Bronze Reward are all in line. Pull the chandelier with the Magnetic Grapple to make it swing into the bars, dislodging them from their position in front of the alcove. Now collect the Reward with your grapple.

6-K: Swim through the opening beneath the platform you dropped down from. You will find a Bronze Reward below the surface of the water.

6-L: Having pulled the lever, climb on top of the casket and turn to face the direction in which it is floating in. Now turn Lara to the right. There is a lantern on the wall at the far right-hand side of the passageway. Quickly throw the Magnetic Grapple and pull yourself over to it. Now jump over to the alcove to collect the Silver Reward. You can use the lanterns to return to your previous position.

6-M: Run to the other side of the roof. A Silver Reward is hidden behind the group of stalagmites.

6-N: Drop down to the other side of the portcullis and collect the Bronze Reward. You can use the shields to return to the rope.

6-O: Move the crate blocking the propeller blades beneath the raised platform on the right, then push the second crate (it's in the centre of the room) beneath the raised platform on the left. Jump up onto the right-hand platform, then push the wall section bearing the Roman numeral "I" as far as it will go. Now climb onto the platform on the other side of the room and push the wall section marked with the Roman numeral "II" until it will go no further. Follow the main walkthrough until you reach the room with an elevator, then push the wall section marked with the Roman numeral "III". This will open a secret compartment to your right that contains this level's Gold Reward.

LEVEL 7: NEPAL – THE GHALALI KEY

7-A: Climb down the other side of the pillar, then drop down twice to discover a Bronze Reward in a small recess. You'll need to hang from the ledge either side of the opening in order to jump back up.

7-B: Instead of climbing onto the snowy platform, continue to your right. Pull yourself up onto the small ledge to collect a Silver Reward.

7-C: Turn around to face the horizontal pole, switch to Manual Aim mode and aim at the lighter section of the ice wall to your right. A couple of bullets will reveal a Silver Reward. Take a run-up and leap at the very last second to reach the recess.

7-D: When you land, turn to your left. A Bronze Reward can be found behind the wreckage.

7-E: Facing the fuselage, turn to your right and jump to the small platform above. Throw your grapple at the wreckage across the gap and pull to make it fall down. Now jump across the gap and collect the Silver Reward on the other side.

TOMB RAIDER
LEGEND

HOW TO PLAY

WALKTHROUGH

EXTRAS

SECRETS

PREVIOUS
ADVENTURES

BEHIND THE
SCENES

CROFT MANOR

REWARDS

UNLOCKABLES

CAST

7-F: Once you land, turn around and retrieve the Bronze Reward you can see across the gap with your grapple.

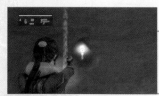

7-G: Jump over to the wall ledge, move to your right and pull yourself up onto the platform. Turn around, move against the wall on the right, switch to Manual Aim mode, and use the Magnetic Grapple to grab the Bronze Reward situated in the small recess behind the teetering ice platform.

7-H: Drop down and hang from the floor ledge on the other side of the platform. Move to your left, then drop down to the ledge below; move to your left again until you can't go any further; drop down twice to the bottom ledge; finally, move to your left one last time and pull yourself up onto the platform to obtain a Gold Reward.

7-I: From the entrance, run to the left end of the area. A Bronze Reward is hidden next to the small stream.

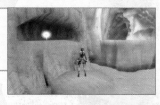

7-J: From the entrance, pull yourself up onto the small platform to your left. Switch to Manual Aim mode and destroy the ice wall above you. Jump over to the alcove to collect the Silver Reward.

7-K: There is a Bronze Reward in plain view on this platform.

7-L: You can find a Bronze Reward inside a small alcove on the left-hand wall.

7-M: As soon as you land on the other bank, turn around and you'll see a Silver Reward. Wait until several platforms float past at once, then jump from one to the other until you can reach the Reward. Be careful to avoid falling into the water!

7-N: Climb down the narrow stairway to your right. When you reach the lower level, turn to your right, switch to Manual Aim mode, and fire at the broken wall section to reveal a Silver Reward.

7-O: Facing the statue, climb the stairway to the left. Run to the other end of the passage to pick up a Bronze Reward.

7-P: Facing the statue, climb the stairway on the right. You will find a Bronze Reward on the balcony.

UNLOCKABLES

Tomb Raider Legend is absolutely bursting at the seams with bonus features. Over the next few pages we explain how, when, and where you can obtain them. You can view your total secrets haul to date by choosing the Extras option at the Main Menu. Select your current save file to study (and, in some instances, interact with) the features you have unlocked.

Table 1 reveals when you can expect to obtain bonus features if you follow the Walkthrough chapter to the letter and collect every Reward, leaving the Croft Manor level until last. Further rewards can be obtained by completing Time Trials.

Table 1

Achievement	Unlocks
Beat Bolivia, all Rewards	Cinematics (10/60), Character Profile (Lara Croft), Location Concepts (Bolivia), Outfits (Legend, Union Jack; Sport), Object Models (Bolivia), Time Trial (Bolivia)
Beat Peru, all Rewards	Cinematics (24/60), Character Profile (Zip), Location Concepts (Peru), Outfits (Legend, Blue; Classic), Object Models (Peru), Time Trial (Peru)
Beat Japan, all Rewards	Cinematics (31/60), Character Profile (Anaya Imanu), Location Concepts (Japan), Outfits (Evening, Ripped; Evening, Red; Catsuit), Object Models (Japan), Pistol Upgrade 1/3 (Increased Magazine Size), Time Trial (Japan)
Beat Ghana, all Rewards	Cinematics (38/60), Character Profiles (Toru Nishimura and Shogo Takamoto), Location Concepts (West Africa), Outfits (Legend, Pink; Classic, Gray), Object Models (West Africa), Time Trial (West Africa)
Beat Kazakhstan, all Rewards	Cinematics (47/60), Character Profile (James W. Rutland), Location Concepts (Kazakhstan), Outfits (Winter; Winter, No Coat; Winter, Orange No Coat; Special Forces), Object Models (Kazakhstan), Time Trial (Kazakhstan)
Beat England, all Rewards	Cinematics (52/60), Location Concepts (England), Outfits (Biker; Biker, Red Jacket; Biker, No Jacket; Special Forces, Urban), Object Models (England), Pistol Upgrade 2/3 (Increased Accuracy), Time Trial (England)
Beat Nepal, all Rewards	Cinematics (57/60), Character Profile (Amanda Evert), Location Concepts (Nepal), Outfits (Snowsuit; Winter, Orange), Object Models (Nepal), Time Trial (Nepal)
Beat Bolivia Redux	Cinematics (60/60), Special menu, Textureless Mode cheat code, Unfortunate Mishaps video, Object Models (Bolivia Redux), Time Trial (Bolivia Redux)
Beat Croft Manor, all Rewards	Character Profiles (Winston Smith, Alister Fletcher and Unknown Entity), Location Concepts (Special), Outfits (Legend, Black; Suit; Suit, Cream), Object Models (Croft Manor), Pistol Upgrade 3/3 (Increased Damage)

RAIDER LEGEND

HOW TO PLAY

WALKTHROUGH

EXTRAS

SECRETS

PREVIOUS
ADVENTURES

BEHIND THE
SCENES

CROFT MANOR

REWARDS

UNLOCKABLES

CAST

TIME TRIAL

Although the vast majority of Tomb Raider Legend's bonus features are unlocked by successfully completing levels and collecting Rewards in the main adventure, you'll also need to successfully complete every level on Time Trial mode to obtain every unlockable. The Time Trial option is made available when you complete the Bolivia stage for the first time. Further levels are then added for Time Trials as and when you complete them.

To play a level in Time Trial mode, select Load Level from the Main Menu, then choose your most current save file. Now pick the level you wish to take the Time Trial on from the list that appears. On the Mission Prep screen, select Difficulty and choose the Time Trial setting. You can also change Lara's outfit if you wish. Once satisfied with your choice, take a deep breath and select Continue to begin the level.

A countdown timer appears at the bottom right-hand corner of the screen once play begins. This is the time you have to reach the very end of the level. The time limit for each stage (and the unlockable features you can obtain when you beat it) can be found in Table 2. Completing Time Trials can be very challenging: you'll need a detailed knowledge of a level's layout and complete confidence in your ability to control Lara. The following tips may also be of help:

- Use the Skip Cinematics option in the Pause menu to bypass cutscenes in order to maintain your rhythm: you may find that breaks in play can lead to a loss of concentration.

- If Lara dies, you will be sent back to the last checkpoint. The clock will restart at the time reached at the point of death. You may be able to afford one, perhaps two, deaths on a stage, but no more. Be careful! If you're facing a particularly dangerous climbing sequence, it's better to be patient and methodical than risk losing dozens of vital seconds should Lara plunge to her doom.

- Time Trials are easier once you unlock all three Pistol Upgrades (see page 167). If you can happily use Lara's default weapons during battles, you'll save time that might otherwise have been spent collecting ammunition.

- Try to skip battles whenever possible. If you can't, be as aggressive as possible: don't waste a second hiding behind cover or performing elaborate close-quarters attacks. You should also note that Aerial Assaults slow down the clock, which can be very useful indeed.

- Don't forget to choose the Save Rewards option to record your achievement when you beat a level!

Table 2

Level	Time Limit (Min : Sec)	Unlocks
Bolivia	12:30	Special (Draw Enemy Health cheat), Outfit (Sport, Green)
Peru	21:30	Special (Infinite SMG Ammo cheat), Outfit (Winter, Pink No Coat)
Japan	12:15	Special (Infinite Assault Rifle Ammo cheat), Outfit (Goth, Lace Shirt)
Ghana	20:00	Special (Infinite Shotgun Ammo cheat), Outfit (Amanda)
Kazakhstan	27:10	Special (Infinite Grenade Launcher Ammo cheat), Outfit (Amanda, Winter)
England	27:00	Special (Bulletproof cheat), Outfit (Goth)
Nepal	13:40	Special (Wield Excalibur cheat), Outfit (Winter, Pink)
Bolivia Redux	04:15	Special (One Shot Kill cheat)
Complete all Time Trials	–	Outfit (Swimsuit)

CINEMATICS

All major cinematic interludes in Tomb Raider Legend are unlocked for viewing in the Extras menu once you complete the level they appear in. Table 3 contains a full list of all 60 cutscenes.

Table 3

Level	Cinematic Name	Level	Cinematic Name	Level	Cinematic Name
Bolivia	Nepal, Part 1	Bolivia	Nepal, Part 2	Peru	Wrecking Crew
Bolivia	Meet Tiwanaku	Bolivia	James Rutland Talks	Peru	Digging Up the Past
Bolivia	PDA Check	Bolivia	The Stone Dias	Peru	Demon of the Past
Bolivia	First Contact	Peru	Returning Home	Peru	Amanda Falls Behind
Bolivia	Second Contact	Peru	Unwelcome in Paraíso	Peru	Going Back In
Bolivia	Falling In Love Again	Peru	Rendezvous with Anaya	Peru	Amanda Survived
Bolivia	Death By Irony	Peru	Any Bike Will Do	Peru	The Queen's Story

Level	Cinematic Name
Peru	Viracocha's Staff
Peru	The Queen's Sword
Peru	Artifacts Recovered
Japan	Fashionably Late in Tokyo
Japan	Nishimura's Warning
Japan	Meeting with Takamoto
Japan	Heading for the Roof
Japan	Takamoto Found
Japan	Artifact Revealed
Japan	Recovery and Exit
Ghana	Hunting Rutland in Ghana
Ghana	The Postcard Business
Ghana	Grand Entrance

Level	Cinematic Name
Ghana	Dearest Amelia
Ghana	The Ghalali Key
Ghana	Two Shards
Ghana	Hasty Departure
Kazakhstan	Trouble in Kazakhstan
Kazakhstan	Allies Under Fire
Kazakhstan	Command Center
Kazakhstan	Runaway Train!
Kazakhstan	Reunion with Amanda
Kazakhstan	Headset Hijack
Kazakhstan	Shields and Maps
Kazakhstan	Amanda's Pet
Kazakhstan	Prize Obtained

Level	Cinematic Name
England	Destination: Cornwall
England	Myth Becomes Fact
England	Bedivere's Legacy
England	The Final Piece
England	Team Reunited
Nepal	Home Again
Nepal	Return to Nepal
Nepal	The Key Obtained
Nepal	Excalibur Reforged
Nepal	Chapter Closed
Bolivia Redux	Bolivia Redux
Bolivia Redux	Amanda Rises
Bolivia Redux	Answers Breed Questions

CHARACTER PROFILES

By collecting Bronze Rewards you can unlock ten character biographies. Table 4 shows the order in which these can be collected.

Table 4

Character Profile	Level	# Bronze
Lara Croft	ALL	10%
Zip	ALL	20%
Anaya Imanu	ALL	30%
Shogo Takamoto	ALL	40%
Toru Nishimura	ALL	40%
James W. Rutland	ALL	50%
Amanda Evert	ALL	70%
Winston Smith	ALL	80%
Alister Fletcher	ALL	90%
Unknown Entity	ALL	100%

LOCATION CONCEPTS

Collecting every Bronze Reward on each level unlocks a selection of beautiful concept sketches. The order in which these are obtained is shown in Table 5.

Table 5

Location Concepts	Level	# Bronze
Bolivia	Bolivia	ALL
Peru	Peru	ALL
Japan	Japan	ALL
Ghana	Ghana	ALL
Kazakhstan	Kazakhstan	ALL
England	England	ALL
Nepal	Nepal	ALL
Special	Croft Manor	ALL

OBJECT MODELS

Completing levels and collecting Silver Rewards enables you to view items encountered during the main adventure and inside Croft Manor with the Model Viewer in the Extras menu. See Table 6 for details.

Table 6

Object Model Set	# Silver	Notes
Bolivia (13/13)	Incremental	Each Silver unlocks % of models
Peru (15/15)	Incremental	Each Silver unlocks % of models
Japan (17/17)	Incremental	Each Silver unlocks % of models
West Africa (13/13)	Incremental	Each Silver unlocks % of models
Kazakhstan (9/9)	Incremental	Each Silver unlocks % of models

Object Model Set	# Silver	Notes
England (13/13)	Incremental	Each Silver unlocks % of models
Nepal (9/9)	Incremental	Each Silver unlocks % of models
Bolivia Redux (10/10)	Incremental	Models unlocked after level is completed
Croft Manor (10/10)	Incremental	Each Silver unlocks % of models

HOW TO PLAY

WALKTHROUGH

EXTRAS

SECRETS

PREVIOUS
ADVENTURES

BEHIND THE
SCENES

CROFT MANOR

REWARDS

UNLOCKABLES

CAST

PISTOL UPGRADES

Automatically applied once the Reward totals in Table 7 are reached, there are three Pistol Upgrades in total. These are active in all play modes: the main game, individual levels accessed via the Load Level option, and Time Trials.

Table 7

Upgrade Name	Level	# Bronze	# Silver	Notes
Increased Magazine Size	ALL	25%	25%	Ammo per pistol increased to 20, for total of 40 bullets per load
Increased Accuracy	ALL	50%	50%	Pistols can now shoot further
Increased Damage	ALL	75%	75%	Pistols do more damage

SPECIAL

The Special menu remains locked until you have completed Tomb Raider Legend's final stage, Bolivia Redux. It contains the Cheat Codes sub-menu, which provides instructions on how to activate the cheats detailed in Table 8, and the Unfortunate Mishaps video. The latter is an eye-watering, wince-inducing montage of Lara's potential deaths during the Super Action interactive cutscenes.

You cannot use cheat codes until you have completed the Bolivia Redux level. Furthermore, a cheat code cannot be activated until it has been unlocked. A distinct sound effect will inform you that the code was entered correctly.

Table 8

Cheat Code	Level	# Gold	How to Unlock	Code	Effect
Textureless Mode	-	-	Complete game	Press and hold L1, then press L2, ✕, ◎, ✕, ▲, R1	Removes textures; repeat code to restore them
Draw Enemy Health	Bolivia	-	Complete Time Trial, complete game	Press and hold L1, then press ◻, ◎, ✕, L2, R1, ▲	Enemy health levels are displayed on screen; repeat code to disable
Infinite SMG Ammo	Peru	-	Complete Time Trial, complete game	Press and hold L2, then press ◎, ▲, L1, R1, ✕, ◎	Provides submachine gun with infinite ammunition
Infinite Assault Rifle Ammo	Japan	-	Complete Time Trial, complete game	Press and hold L2, then press ✕, ◎, ✕, L1, ◻, ▲	Provides assault rifle with infinite ammunition
Infinite Shotgun Ammo	Ghana	-	Complete Time Trial, complete game	Press and hold L2, then press R1, ◎, ◻, L1, ◻, ✕	Provides shotgun with infinite ammunition
Infinite Grenade Launcher Ammo	Kazakhstan	-	Complete Time Trial, complete game	Press and hold L2, then press L1, ▲, R1, ◎, L1, ◻	Provides grenade launcher with infinite ammunition
Bulletproof	England	-	Complete Time Trial, complete game	Press and hold L1, then press ✕, R1, ▲, R1, ◻, L2	Lara is impervious to enemy weapons. She can still die in other ways, though. Repeat code to disable
Wield Excalibur	Nepal	-	Complete Time Trial, complete game	Press and hold L2, then press ▲, ✕, ◎, R1, ▲, L1	Lara is given Excalibur to use as her secondary weapon
One Shot Kill	Bolivia Redux	-	Complete Time Trial, complete game	Press and hold L1, then press ▲, ✕, ▲, ◻, L2, ◎	A single bullet is sufficient to kill enemies; repeat code to disable
Wield Soul Reaver	-	100%	Complete all Time Trials, complete game	Press and hold L2, then press ✕, R1, ◎, R1, L1, ◎	Lara is given the Soul Reaver, a sword making a cameo appearance from Crystal Dynamics' Legacy of Kain series

OUTFITS

The Outfits menu enables you to browse apparel unlocked by collecting Rewards and beating Time Trials. These can be manually chosen when playing via the Load Game option; you can also make Lara change clothes by visiting the Bedroom during the Croft Manor level. Table 9 explains the achievements required to unlock each Outfit.

Table 9

Outfit Name	Level Acquired	# Bronze	# Silver	# Gold	Other
Legend	N/A	-	-	-	Unlocked from game start
Legend, Union Jack	Bolivia	-	100%	-	-
Legend, Black	Croft Manor	-	100%	-	-
Legend, Blue	Peru	-	100%	-	-
Legend, Pink	Ghana	-	100%	-	-
Biker	England	-	-	-	Finish level
Biker, Red Jacket	England	-	100%	-	-
Biker, No Jacket	England	-	100%	100%	-
Evening, Ripped	Japan	-	-	-	Finish level
Evening, Red	Japan	-	100%	-	-
Classic	Peru	-	-	100%	-
Classic, Gray	Ghana	-	-	100%	-
Winter	Kazakhstan	-	-	-	Finish level
Winter, No Coat	Kazakhstan	-	-	-	Finish level
Winter, Orange	Nepal	-	100%	-	-

HOW TO PLAY

WALKTHROUGH

EXTRAS

SECRETS

PREVIOUS
ADVENTURES

BEHIND THE
SCENES

CROFT MANOR

REWARDS

UNLOCKABLES

CAST

Outfit Name	Level Acquired	# Bronze	# Silver	# Gold	Other
Winter, Orange No Coat	Kazakhstan	-	100%	-	-
Winter, Pink	Nepal	-	-	-	Complete Time Trial
Winter, Pink No Coat	Peru	-	-	-	Complete Time Trial
Catsuit	Japan	-	-	100%	-
Snowsuit	Nepal	-	-	100%	-
Suit	Croft Manor	-	-	100%	-
Suit, Cream	Croft Manor	-	100%	100%	-
Special Forces	Kazakhstan	-	-	100%	-
Special Forces, Urban	England	-	-	100%	-
Goth	England	-	-	-	Complete Time Trial
Goth, Lace Shirt	Japan	-	-	-	Complete Time Trial
Sport	Bolivia	-	-	100%	-
Sport, Green	Bolivia	-	-	-	Complete Time Trial
Amanda	Ghana	-	-	-	Complete Time Trial
Amanda, Winter	Kazakhstan	-	-	-	Complete Time Trial
Swimsuit (For use in Croft Manor only)	N/A	-	-	-	Complete game, beat all Time Trials
Swimsuit, Black (For use in Croft Manor only)	N/A	100%	100%	100%	Complete game, beat all Time Trials

169

XBOX 360 ACHIEVEMENTS

If you're curious as to how you can improve your Gamerscore with the Xbox 360 version of Tomb Raider Legend, Table 10 explains all 25 unlockable Achievements – and, of course, the Gamerscore value you can earn with each one.

Table 10

Achievement	Requirement	Gamerscore
01	Found 5 Bronze Rewards	10
02	Found 35 Bronze Rewards	15
03	Found all Bronze Rewards	20
04	Found 10 Silver Rewards	20
05	Found all Silver Rewards	25
06	Found 5 Gold Rewards	30
07	Found all Gold Rewards	35
08	Found all Rewards	50
09	Bolivia Level completed	50
10	Peru Level completed	50
11	Japan Level completed	50
12	Ghana Level completed	50
13	Kazakhstan Level completed	75
14	England Level completed	75
15	Nepal Level completed	75
16	Game completed on Explorer or Adventurer difficulty	125
17	Game completed on Tomb Raider difficulty	125
18	Bolivia Time Trial completed	10
19	Peru Time Trial completed	10
20	Japan Time Trial completed	10
21	Ghana Time Trial completed	10
22	Kazakhstan Time Trial completed	10
23	England Time Trial completed	10
24	Nepal Time Trial completed	10
25	All Time Trials completed	50
-	Total Gamerscore	1000

CAST

LARA CROFT

Lady Lara Croft is an 11th-generation Countess. The Croft family was granted the title and rights to Abbingdon, Surrey by King Edward VI in 1547. The Croft Estates comprise of three separate manor houses, one of which is home to Lady Croft. Lady Croft herself has suffered several personal tragedies, including the deaths of both parents on separate occasions before she came of age. Reputably an accredited genius and Olympic-standard gymnast, Lady Croft is the focus of wild speculation and intense debate in both the scientific and political communities in addition to the popular press. Idealized and vilified in equal measure, she is perhaps one of the most fascinating and enigmatic figures of our time.

PERSONAL HISTORY:

Lara Croft was born in Surrey's Parkside hospital to Lady Amelia Croft and the notorious archeologist Lord Richard Croft, the late Earl of Abbingdon. Between the ages of three and six, she attended the Abbingdon Girls School, where it quickly became clear that she was an exceptionally gifted child. At the age of nine she survived a plane crash in the Himalayas. In perhaps the first example of her prodigious indomitability, she somehow survived a solo ten-day trek across the Himalayan mountains, one of the most hostile environments on the planet. The story goes that when she arrived in Katmandu, she went to the nearest bar and made a polite telephone call to her father asking if it would be convenient for him to come and pick her up.

For six years following the plane crash, Lara rarely left her father's side, traveling around the world from one archeological dig site to another. During this period she was ostensibly given a standard education from private tutors, but it would probably be more accurate to say she was her father's full time apprentice.

When Lara was 15, her father went missing in Cambodia. Extensive searches by the authorities and Lara herself turned up human remains that could not definitively be identified. Since Lord Croft's body was not officially recovered, Lara could not directly inherit the Croft title and Lara was thrust into a bitter family feud over control of the Abbingdon estates with her uncle Lord Errol Croft. Lara eventually won the legal battle, and took possession of her inheritance but at the cost of a deep rift in the Croft family that left her estranged from her living relatives.

PROFESSIONAL HISTORY:

Lady Lara Croft has already eclipsed her father's career; as of this writing she is credited with the discovery of some 15 archeological sites of international significance. These sites are still yielding new and exciting insights to the past on an ongoing basis. No one can deny Lady Croft's incredible contribution into the field of archeology; however, she is not without her detractors.

Lara's methods have been frequently called into question by government officials and other practicing archeologists. She has been described variously as anything from cavalier to downright irresponsible. Some scholars have suggested that her notorious lack of documentation and brute force methodology

have contaminated countless sites and done more harm than good. There have even been (unsubstantiated) allegations that Lara actually takes items from these sites before informing the international community of their locations, and that she is nothing more than a glorified treasure hunter.

SUMMARY:

Despite the tabloid press infatuation with her, Lara Croft guards her privacy with complete determination. She has never granted an interview nor personally commented on to any of the rumors associated with her, preferring to express herself through brief formal statements given by the family solicitors, Hardgraves and Moore.

Predictably there have been a number of unofficial biographies printed about the young Countess that attribute wild and fantastic feats to her exploits, ranging from discovering living dinosaurs in the Congo to infiltrating the infamous Area 51 in Nevada. The official line from the Croft Estate on these works is simply that "... these books are utter rot: disgraceful, trashy works of total fiction."

Nevertheless if you even make a cursory search on the Internet for the Unexplained, the Mysterious and the Downright Unbelievable, time and again you will find Lara Croft's name appearing. She appears to be a hero to conspiracy theorists and alternate history aficionados alike.

It seems the further you dig into Lady Croft's life, the more bewildering and mysterious she becomes. Perhaps like the archeological sites she discovers, we have only scratched the surface of this incredible woman, and the complex and inscrutable secrets buried deep within her.

HOW TO PLAY

WALKTHROUGH

EXTRAS

SECRETS

PREVIOUS ADVENTURES

BEHIND THE SCENES

CROFT MANOR

REWARDS

UNLOCKABLES

CAST

WINSTON

Winston's family has been with the Crofts for generations, and he has been the family butler since he was honorably discharged from the military in his late twenties; just as his father before him. He moved into Croft Manor as the only live-in staff when his wife died, before Lara was born. He tends to all Lara's household needs, going far beyond the duties of a traditional butler, given Lara's unusual lifestyle and pursuits. He has never disappointed her. His loyalty to Lara, her parents, and Croft Manor is beyond question.

ZIP

Zip is Lara's right hand man and tech expert. Always in contact with Lara via her headset, he is able to instantly provide her with a wealth of information by accessing various electronic reference resources, and other online knowledge databases. In his spare time, he tinkers around with electronics, developing new technology that might prove useful to Ms. Croft in the field. In addition to being a savvy purveyor of all things "geeky", Zip is also a distinguished chef, and has worked in some of the best kitchens in Northern Europe.

ALISTER FLETCHER

Alister Fletcher is Lara's research assistant and a repository for a fantastic array of detailed historical information. He confines his research to libraries and museums, however, concentrating on understanding and explaining what has already been found, as opposed to Lara's search for new artifacts. He's a 15th-year doctoral student at Oxford and has yet to receive his doctorate: his belief that everything is connected to everything else makes it impossible for him to draw the boundaries required to finish his dissertation.

ANAYA IMANU

Anaya Imanu is a civil engineer working in impoverished areas of South America. She's a friend of Lara's dating back to their days at university, and she was with Lara during the tragedy near Paraíso, Peru. She has since led a distinguished career of her own, routinely crossing paths with Lara.

HOW TO PLAY

WALKTHROUGH

EXTRAS

SECRETS

PREVIOUS
ADVENTURES

BEHIND THE
SCENES

CROFT MANOR

REWARDS

UNLOCKABLES

CAST

TORU NISHIMURA

Toru Nishimura is a wealthy media magnate who owns a half a dozen television stations and newspapers throughout Southern Japan. His rise to this position was rapid, and he still enjoys acting like the journalist he once was, so his days aren't completely filled with corporate concerns. One investigation led to a corrupt cabinet minister, a priceless silver statuette, and a young archeologist who saved his life when the artifact turned out to be much more than it appeared. Lara Croft and he became friends after the incident, and they help each other whenever needed.

SHOGO TAKAMOTO

Shogo Takamoto was a rising star in the Japanese mob for years, and is now a Yakuza Kumicho (boss). He has a love of ancient weapons, and he has become a fixture in the upscale black market, frustrating collectors and adventurers alike with his mixing of forgeries with authentic rare items, hiding behind the might of the Yakuza to protect himself from cheated buyers. A confrontation with Lara Croft over some forged items, however, led to a loss of face so extreme that he was forced to withdraw from the antiquities underground. Why he did not kill her remains a mystery within the Yakuza, because the idea of him being unable to kill her is beyond belief.

AMANDA EVERT

Amanda Evert was one of Lara Croft's best friends at university. While she was a promising cultural anthropologist, she had a love of metaphysics and a fascination with mysticism that, in Lara's opinion, interfered with her ability to be an effective scientist. Amanda dreamed of rediscovering mystical knowledge from the past, knowledge that the scientific age not only lost sight of but also actively drove out of the world. She hoped to then teach these forgotten truths to others so they could gain spiritual enlightenment. But her career, wherever it was headed, was cut short by a terrible, unexplained event in Peru, where her body remains with a dozen others in a collapsed tomb.

JAMES W. RUTLAND

The Rutland name has been attached to politicians and CEOs for decades – an American aristocracy, if you will – so James William Rutland Jr. grew up in a bubble of enormous wealth and privilege. He went to West Point and managed to graduate on his own merits, albeit barely, which gave him a sense of self-discipline and strength that he finds useful now that he's free of the military. Except for his time at West Point, he has never known scarcity or refusal. He is an energetic man who plays hard and has never been lazy in that regard, working hard only in pursuit of his desires.

PREVIOUS ADVENTURES

To offer dedicated fans of the series an opportunity to a bout of misty-eyed reverie, and provide a chance for newcomers to the world of Tomb Raider to view Lara's evolution over the years, this section takes a look back at her six main adventures to date. We begin with an extended look at Lara's first adventure, now in its tenth anniversary year.

Despite its very obvious influences, Tomb Raider was a truly groundbreaking and unique videogame: technically accomplished, artfully crafted and, most importantly of all, utterly engrossing. Defined by its imaginative set pieces and puzzles, it is an enduring classic; a game packed with inventive touches that, almost a decade after its release, still have the power to entertain and amaze.

While creating Tomb Raider Legend, the development team at Crystal Dynamics looked, first and foremost, to the original Tomb Raider for inspiration. Over the following pages, we'll show you exactly why...

1996
1997
1998
1999
2000
2003

TOMB RAIDER FEATURING LARA CROFT (1996)

Formats: Saturn, PlayStation, PC, N-Gage

LARA'S HOME

Lara's mansion – then simply referred to as "Lara's Home" – was built over the space of a weekend by her creator, Toby Gard. With voice prompts explaining how to

perform her many moves, it acted as a gentle introduction to the art of controlling the agile Croft. Unlike its two subsequent sequels (and, of course, Tomb Raider Legend), Tomb Raider's comparatively spartan rendition of her abode did not contain any secret areas.

CAVES

Tomb Raider's opening level, "Caves", was a very short and simple stage, designed to ease players into the Tomb Raider world. With a handful of combat encounters – Lara

was attacked by bats, wolves and, if you chose to collect every secret, a bear – and with no puzzles bar the timed door switch pictured here, it could be completed in mere minutes.

SECRETS

Every level featured a handful of "secrets". These were collectable items placed in locations that were hard to find or reach, such as the health pick-up pictured here.

This is actually the very first hidden item in the Tomb Raider series, situated near the start of the Caves level. Due to an unfortunate bug in its final stage, Atlantis, Tomb Raider did not acknowledge the collection of its last secret – something that left hardcore completists aghast.

COMBAT

Tomb Raider's combat system was never its strongest feature, although its limitations were less apparent in the first adventure than in subsequent episodes. With Lara

automatically acquiring a lock-on to an enemy with a weapon drawn, winning battles was often a case of firing wildly while dodging – a far cry from the frantic and varied battles in Tomb Raider Legend. While the actual fights may have lacked sophistication, the placement of creatures could be ingenious. Some surprise attacks, such as the bear in the City of Vilcabamba level pictured here, were genuine jump-out-of-your-seat moments.

TRAPS

From collapsing floors and spike pits to rolling boulders, Tomb Raider was packed with traps that could lead to Lara's instant demise. This swinging blade, found

towards the end of the City of Vilcabamba level, was triggered when Lara reached a certain point in the corridor. An incautious player simply running through would be caught full-force by the first swing; the player who sensed danger and walked forward would survive.

THE LOST VALLEY

Tomb Raider's third level was home to one of its most memorable set pieces. As Lara ran along the valley floor, the screen shook in time to the crash of footsteps as an enormous T-Rex strode into view. Armed only with her default pistols – unless the player had taken the time to find the shotgun located elsewhere in the level – Lara had to slay this enormous beast. An additional surprise lay in store for players who made the mistake of pausing in front of the creature's head. With a sudden lunge, the T-Rex would grab Lara in its jaws and shake her brutally from side to side, before throwing her broken body to the ground.

BETRAYAL

Having retrieved a portion of the "Scion" artifact, as commissioned by Jacqueline Natla in the opening FMV sequence, Lara was attacked by Natla's henchman Larson: her first human adversary in the Tomb Raider games. This double-cross established Natla as the villain of the story. An excellent incidental touch in the Scion room was the presence of two mummies either side of Qualopec's remains. Foreshadowing her encounters with Natla's mutants later in the adventure, the head of the mummy on the right followed Lara as she moved around the room. While it did not attack, Lara could shoot it and cause it to fall to the floor, which would count towards her "Kills" total displayed at the end of the level.

CINEMATIC INTERLUDES

Broadly divided into four distinctive chapters – Peru, Greece, Egypt and Atlantis – Tomb Raider had FMV sequences that marked the transition between these sections. The cinematic interlude at the end of Lara's Peruvian expedition showed her breaking into Jacqueline Natla's company headquarters in spectacular fashion: by snapping an elevator cord and, in a virtual stunt that predated The Matrix, using the severed cable to reach the roof. Inside, she discovered the location of the second part of the Scion, and set off for one of Tomb Raider's most inventive and fondly-remembered levels: St Francis Folly…

VERTIGINOUS VIEWS

One of Tomb Raider's most impressive feats was its ability to communicate a genuine sense of scale. Although its engine's draw distance could not always match its level designer's ambition (far-off level architecture in open areas would often be replaced by inky blackness until Lara moved sufficiently close), there were certain sights that worked brilliantly. A classic example could be found in the final area of the St Francis Folly level. Emerging into a room several stories high, with a central structure providing a circuitous route to the ground below, Lara had to climb up and down to access four themed "challenge" rooms: Neptune, Thor, Damocles and Atlas. With the merest lapse in concentration being enough to send Lara plummeting to her death, the designer's placement of bats in this area – usually, the least dangerous of Lara's animal adversaries – was a clever touch.

ATHLETIC PROWESS

The PC and PlayStation versions of Tomb Raider featured an undocumented move. If players held the "walk" button before instructing Lara to climb up onto a ledge, she would perform a graceful handstand – something that many Tomb Raider devotees discovered entirely (and pleasingly) by accident.

Special mention should also be made of her "swan dive" move. Although you could simply jump or drop into water, there was always something unusually satisfying about performing a camera-friendly dive.

Tomb Raider fans may be curious to learn that Lara's many gasps and grunts of exertion were not performed by the original actress hired to provide her voice. They are a mixture of sounds provided by Core PR Manager Suzie Hamilton, level artist Heather Gibson, and even sound effects designer Martin Iveson – with, naturally, the latter's contributions adjusted to a higher pitch.

LARA'S RIVAL

Throughout the Greek levels, Lara was attacked by Pierre DuPont, a rival adventurer hired by Jacqueline Natla to retrieve the second section of the Scion. Pierre would appear suddenly, open fire at Lara, then retreat (and, quite literally, disappear into thin air) when players managed to inflict a set amount of damage. After five levels of his sniping, the showdown with him at the end of the Tomb of Tihocan stage was genuinely satisfying…

PAYING CLOSE ATTENTION

Not every trap and pitfall in Tomb Raider was harmful to Lara. Sometimes, with mischievous (and, on occasion, rather cruel) intent, its level designers would include a hazard that could force players to retrace their steps. In the screenshot from the Palace Midas stage pictured here, you can see a health pick-up beside three fragile floor sections. Players who failed to notice these would be punished for their lapse of concentration by being plunged, albeit safely, back to an earlier part of the level.

HOW TO PLAY

WALKTHROUGH

EXTRAS

SECRETS

PREVIOUS ADVENTURES

BEHIND THE SCENES

TR

TR II

TR III

TR IV

TR CHRONICLES

TR ANGEL OF DARKNESS

THE MIDAS TOUCH

Palace Midas was one of Tomb Raider's largest and most complicated levels. Midas, for those not au fait with the Greek legend, was a king of Phrygia given the power to turn everything he touched into gold by the god Dionysus; a power that, as he discovered to his horror when he attempted to eat, was more akin to a curse. In the Palace Midas stage, players had to find three gold bars to unlock the level exit. Having discovered three lead bars instead, the solution was to use the severed hand of a buried statue of Midas to perform a miraculous feat of mystical alchemy. In a stroke of genius, Tomb Raider's designers implemented a fantastic surprise for players who decided to jump onto the hand. As Lara's feet touched the palm, her feet became stuck to the stone. In the cutscene that ensued (and is pictured here), Lara's entire body was transformed into gold in one of the most memorable and unexpected "death" sequences in videogame history.

THE CISTERN

Not one of Tomb Raider's largest stages, the central feature of The Cistern was that players could adjust the water level. Specific keys that Lara had to find in order to progress could only be collected with the waters raised or lowered. Players who explored in a methodical manner and found the first keys before flicking the switch to flood the area – something that, technically, only needed to be performed once – were rewarded with an easy passage to the exit. For others, it was a puzzle that turned a relatively short and compact 20-minute level into a marathon that could last for hours.

TOMB OF TIHOCAN

At its time of release Tomb Raider was likened by some, rather erroneously, to Capcom's Resident Evil. One feature that both games definitely had in common, however, was their ability to make players jump out of their seats with clever set-piece events. One such moment was found at the end of the Tomb of Tihocan level. Approaching the tomb for the second time, players had no reason to expect any imminent surprise. Suddenly, though, the centaur statue on the left would shake off its stone exterior and attack, firing explosive blasts at Lara. The showdown with long-term antagonist Pierre that followed seemed almost prosaic by comparison…

PYRAMID

When Tomb Raider was first put forward as a potential game in 1993, creator Toby Gard was keen that it should involve pyramids. The Egyptian levels in the final game (and, later, the Atlantean pyramid) were obviously inspired by that initial idea. Lara's foes in Egypt were far more dangerous than the majority of those faced in previous stages. Facing fast-moving "mutant" mummies and weapon-toting centaurs, even adept players needed to start drawing heavily on reserves of ammunition and health packs acquired through diligent acquisition of "secret" collectables.

SANCTUARY OF THE SCION

Just as the waterfall in Ghana is an awe-inspiring vista in Tomb Raider Legend, the first sighting of the underground Sphinx in the original Tomb Raider was an impressive moment. Pictured here is the view from below (note how, again, Tomb Raider's original engine could not quite match its designers' vision in terms of draw distance), and a shot of Lara looking down at a convoluted sequence of platforms that she had to negotiate in order to reach a vital switch. Undoubtedly the best (and, for that matter, most challenging) of the three Egyptian levels, Sanctuary of the Scion ended with a long (and impressive) cutscene in which Lara had the three portions of the Scion wrestled from her by Jacqueline Natla and a trio of new henchmen. After making a daring escape, diving from a cliff into a river below, Lara hid inside Natla's boat to reach Tomb Raider's final location: a small island situated somewhere in the Atlantic…

NATLA'S MINES

One of Tomb Raider's more challenging levels, by turns engaging and frustrating, Natla's Mines began with a weaponless Lara seeking to reclaim her trademark dual pistols. Having achieved this, players then had to fight against Natla's henchmen: a Magnum-wielding cowboy, a skateboarder with Uzis (who, in a feature that seemed oddly out of place, actually rode his board) and, finally, a shotgun-toting assassin at the foot of the buried Atlantean pyramid. As Lara killed each in turn, she was able to reclaim the weapons they dropped.

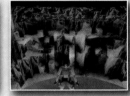

INSIDE THE PYRAMID

With their animated fleshlike textures and the perpetual percussion of a heart beating in the background, Tomb Raider's final two levels, Atlantis and The Great Pyramid, could be more than a little unsettling – especially if you reached them in the small hours of the morning. It was at this point in Lara's adventure that the difficulty level shot up into the stratosphere. From spike pits to lava, rolling boulders to chomping blade doors, almost every trap previously encountered could be found in a more fiendish form or arrangement. More pressingly, both levels were absolutely packed with Natla's vicious creations. The opening battle of the Atlantis level, pictured here, involved a desperate fight against numerous mutants as they hatched from their pods.

TOMB RAIDER LEGEND

HOW TO PLAY

WALKTHROUGH

EXTRAS

SECRETS

PREVIOUS ADVENTURES

BEHIND THE SCENES

TR

TR II

TR III

TR IV

TR CHRONICLES

TR ANGEL OF DARKNESS

LARA'S MUTANT DOUBLE

The Atlantis level featured one of Tomb Raider's best puzzles. Entering a new chamber, players encountered a fleshy creature that mirrored Lara's every movement: running, jumping, climbing, and even shooting. As Lara could not use her guns to kill this entity – it would reciprocate in kind – players had to find another way to dispatch it. The solution, when discovered, was pleasingly simple. Although the two halves of the chamber were decked in different textures, a symmetrical arrangement of pillars and platforms existed on either side of the room, leading to raised areas. One of these featured a switch that opened a trapdoor to a lava pit below. All players needed to do was to flick the switch, run and climb over to the opposite raised area, then walk over a precise spot to send the mutant into the pit. Easy to perform in principle, the presence of a time limit before the trapdoor slammed shut made this a surprisingly challenging task.

"BOSS" BATTLES

After a cutscene-based confrontation with Natla at the end of the Atlantis level, The Great Pyramid – Tomb Raider's final stage – began with an epic fight against a giant legless mutant. Towering above Lara, but slow and ponderous, this creature would inexorably pursue her around the chamber. Complicating matters no end, the platform that the battle took place on was surrounded on three sides by a dizzying (and deadly) drop. The mutant's standard attack was to swipe at Lara, causing damage and potentially knocking her over the edge. A far more gruesome death awaited her if she hesitated within grabbing distance. The mutant would reach out, snatch Lara in its claw, and then beat her against the ground. In an extremely macabre touch, it would then dangle Lara by a leg, shaking her for any sign of life in an inquisitive manner, and then casually toss her corpse aside…

THE FINAL SHOWDOWN

After destroying the assembled Scion, players had to fight Jacqueline Natla in a climatic battle. Now in possession of a large pair of wings, Natla swooped around the large chamber and fired explosive bolts at Lara. Like all notable evil masterminds, she had to be killed twice: once in her winged form, and again on foot. Once that feat was achieved, players had to use the pillars in the room, and adjoining corridors, to climb to the very top of the pyramid and escape.

THE END

Tomb Raider's all-too-brief final cutscene showed Lara racing away from the blazing pyramid, before setting sail in Natla's boat as the entire island exploded. Those left hungry for more Tomb Raider would not have long to wait…

TOMB RAIDER II STARRING LARA CROFT (1997)

Formats: PlayStation, PC

After the remarkable success of Tomb Raider, work began almost immediately on a sequel – though this was not announced until early 1997. Toby Gard left Core early in the project to establish his own development studio, Confounding Factor, and it's arguable that his departure had a profound effect on the design of Tomb Raider II. Gard had been reluctant to populate the original game with human assailants; in his absence, the number of combat encounters (especially against generic human "henchmen") was increased enormously. Despite being significantly more difficult than its forebear, with a razor-sharp learning curve, Tomb Raider II is actually Lara's most successful adventure to date.

With a greater emphasis on action and an ambitious choice of locales – particularly "real world" destinations such as Venice and the Maria Doria, the wreck of an ocean liner – it's important to remember just how impressive it was at the time. It may not have aged quite as well as its groundbreaking predecessor, but there are many Tomb Raider devotees that choose this as their favorite episode of Lara's early adventures.

Destinations: Beginning with a single level set on the Great Wall of China, Tomb Raider II took players to Venice, an offshore oil rig, a sunken wreck, Tibet and, finally, China once again.

New Features: Additional polygons gave Tomb Raider II's updated Lara a rather more "rounded" appearance, but this was merely one of numerous incidental improvements. Lara was also given the ability to wade in shallow water, climb ladders, use flares to light dark areas, drive vehicles (a speedboat and a snowmobile), use a harpoon gun during underwater combat, and various miscellaneous extra moves, such as being able to turn 180 degrees while jumping or swimming. Her mansion was also expanded to include a garden (featuring an assault course that players could race time trials on) and a secret treasure room.

Lara was tangibly more "rounded" in Tomb Raider II – her "cone" bra evidently discarded after her quest for the Scion…

Players could partake in time trials on Lara's assault course, which also acted as an introduction to her new moves

Tomb Raider II featured a revised secrets system. On every level, players had to collect a silver, jade and gold dragon to receive a cache of collectables

The Tibetan Foothills level was essentially an extended assault course for the snowmobile, though it was possible (albeit difficult) to complete it on foot

After the showdown with Tomb Raider II villain Bartoli, there was one final surprise: an assassination attempt at Lara's mansion

TOMB RAIDER III: ADVENTURES OF LARA CROFT (1998)

Formats: PlayStation, PC

Much more refined and attractive than its forebear, but still only an evolutionary step forward, Tomb Raider III was a large and sprawling adventure. Once again, it did not pull its punches: even dedicated players commented that its difficulty level was rather severe in places. Core's designers began to experiment with new concepts, such as multiple routes and "stealth" elements but, as critics were quick to point out, it rarely deviated from the format established by its predecessors.

Its legions of fans, however, viewed that observation from a rather different perspective. Demanding and yet oh-so-rewarding as a consequence, Tomb Raider III combined tried-and-tested mechanics with countless surprises. Few players will have forgotten the canoe ride through the rapids on a South Pacific island, the first encounters with the blade-wielding statues in India, or exploring the Natural History Museum in London.

Destinations: Tomb Raider III's first stages took place in an Indian jungle, followed by visits to a South Pacific island, London, and Area 51 in Nevada before its final chapter in Antarctica.

New Features: As well as an inevitable increase in abilities (Lara could now "monkey swing" on overhead bars, sprint for short periods, crouch and crawl, among other activities), Tomb Raider III also allowed players to choose their own route through its three central chapters. Additionally, the secrets system used by its predecessor was discarded in favor of Tomb Raider's original (and more equitable) distribution of collectables. Players who found every single secret were given a massive reward for their labors: All Hallows, an entirely new level set in London. Lara's mansion was expanded once again to include a secret quad bike racetrack.

For those that took the time to find the Racetrack Key, racing time trials on Lara's quad bike could be a curiously engaging diversion

The journey over rooftops during the Thames Wharf level was a demanding test of a player's ability to judge jumps and plan routes over difficult terrain

Lara riding the rapids (and narrowly avoiding a particularly cruel trap) in the Madubu Gorge stage of the South Pacific chapter

Core's designers paid homage to Indiana Jones and the Temple of Doom in a series of mine cart rides during the RX-Tech Mines level

For those dedicated enough to find every single secret, All Hallows appeared as a bonus stage once the final Antarctica level had been completed

TOMB RAIDER IV: THE LAST REVELATION (1999)

Formats: PlayStation, PC, Dreamcast

The most radical overhaul of the Tomb Raider format prior to Angel of Darkness, The Last Revelation dispensed with the classic "menu rings", discarded the training level set at Lara's home and, following its two tutorial missions at Angkor Wat, kept its action within a single country. Benefiting from a host of improvements to a game engine that was beginning to show its age in Tomb Raider III, it was faster and much more attractive than its predecessors. More importantly, though, it included a much wider range of different puzzles, and confronted players with less combat, but more varied assailants. It also had a much more approachable difficulty level, although the inclusion of multi-part levels (with Lara moving back and forth between areas) was something that some players found frustrating.

Destinations: A mandatory two-level trek through ruins at Angkor Wat in Cambodia replaced the traditional side-trip to Lara's house, followed by a grand tour of Egypt that included visits to the Valley of the Kings, Karnak, Alexandria, Cairo and Giza.

New Features: Lara was given the ability to swing on ropes, traverse around corners and "combine" objects within the new inventory system to solve puzzles; there was also the addition of a choice of manual or automatic targeting. The most notable change, however, was The Last Revelation's sheer variety of set pieces and puzzles. From combat on top of a moving train to playing ancient board game Senet against the spirit of a Pharoah, it relied far less on the staple flicking of switches and finding keys than previous outings.

By finding eight golden skulls in the first training level in Cambodia, players could open up an alternative (and more difficult) route for the subsequent footrace between Lara and tutor Werner von Croy

Double-crossed by her guide after The Last Revelation's opening levels, Lara pursued him in a frantic cross-country chase

It wasn't mandatory that players win – and, indeed, it was actually necessary to lose to collect every secret in The Last Revelation – but the game of Senet in Semerkhet's tomb was a memorable moment

Lara had to fight numerous assassins on top of a train en route to Alexandria in the Desert Railroad level, with a cringe-inducing death awaiting players who allowed Lara to fall to the tracks

Scaling the Great Pyramid prior to The Last Revelation's climatic battle was more akin to solving a puzzle than a test of joypad skills. Finding the correct path was the trickiest part...

HOW TO PLAY

WALKTHROUGH

EXTRAS

SECRETS

PREVIOUS ADVENTURES

BEHIND THE SCENES

TR

TR II

TR III

TR IV

TR CHRONICLES

TR ANGEL OF DARKNESS

TOMB RAIDER CHRONICLES (2000)

Formats: PlayStation, PC, Dreamcast

The shortest and, by common consensus, least impressive of Lara's five 32-bit adventures, Tomb Raider Chronicles took the form of four mini-adventures from Lara's past. With Core unwilling to resolve the issue of Lara's apparent demise at the end of The Last Revelation, these were related as "stories" told by a group of her associates meeting to reminisce at the Croft mansion.

Destinations: Lara visited Rome, a submarine just off the Russian coast, Ireland (as a young girl), and a high-tech office full of security devices.

New Features: Lara was given the ability to walk over tightropes and swing from horizontal poles. Each of the four mini-adventures had a specific theme and "feel". The Rome levels were redolent of the first Tomb Raider, while the stages set off the Russian coast were more akin to Tomb Raider II in style. Young Lara's escapade in Ireland was rather unique, though. With Lara denied the use of weapons, it was easily the most unusual set of levels in any Tomb Raider game. The final (and very difficult) stages put a strong emphasis on stealth, with Lara sneaking past guards and avoiding security devices. The PC version shipped with a long-awaited level editor.

The Rome levels featured cameo appearances by Larson and Pierre DuPont – two of Lara's adversaries from the original Tomb Raider

The Underwater Dive stage featured the Extreme Depth Suit, a device that enabled Lara to swim without worrying about finding an air source – until it suffered a puncture towards the end of the level, that is...

Young Lara was recalled after her brief role in The Last Revelation for a trek through Ireland in a Tomb Raider ghost story

Packed with security devices and other such hazards, and with Lara carrying a limited amount of ammunition, the final chapter focused on stealth and evasion

After five years of Tomb Raider games, Lara finally acquired the ability to... drum roll... search cupboards

TOMB RAIDER: THE ANGEL OF DARKNESS (2003)

Formats: PlayStation 2, PC

After a protracted gestation period, The Angel of Darkness was viewed by many fans as a crushing disappointment. Blighted by a cumbersome and unresponsive control system, weak combat and many bugs, the critical mauling it received put paid to Core Design's plan to create a trilogy of Tomb Raider games based on the upgraded engine. Development of future Tomb Raider games was switched to Crystal Dynamics – and the rest, as they say…

Destinations: Angel of Darkness took place in Paris and Prague, with a surprising amount of time spent on streets and inside buildings – although there were also trips to catacombs, tombs and, in a pleasing touch, a visit to a "true" archaeological dig site.

New Features: Although ostensibly very similar to past Tomb Raiders in terms of control and Lara's abilities, there were many new gameplay elements or alterations introduced in Angel of Darkness. The most major change was the introduction of RPG-style overtones. Players could interact with NPCs and choose from different conversational options and, in a curious (and ill-considered) move, Lara's strength and basic abilities could be improved by performing very specific actions, such as using a crowbar, or moving a particular chest of drawers. The addition of a "grip" meter used whenever Lara traversed along ledges added a sense of urgency (though some would argue "frustration") to bouts of climbing, and a new "stealth" movement mode enabled players to either sneak past would-be assailants, or to subdue them with non-fatal attacks.

Despite an obvious leap in visual fidelity and some nice ideas, control of Lara in Angel of Darkness was slow and cumbersome – something revealed during this opening training section

While using her new "stealth" movement mode, Lara could move silently, press up against walls, peer around corners, and disable enemies with silent attacks

The conversation system used during interactions with NPCs wasn't massively sophisticated, but it occasionally provided an easier way to obtain certain items or complete objectives

Later in the game, Kurtis Trent took centre stage for three levels. He's pictured here fighting "boss" monster Boaz in a battle that even adept players found to be hideously frustrating

Lara fighting Karel in the final battle of Angel of Darkness. When next called to draw a weapon in self-defense, Lara would have a few more tricks up her sleeve...

BEHIND THE SCENES

Last, but not least, we take a trip to Menlo Park, California: the home of Crystal Dynamics, creators of Tomb Raider Legend. In a series of honest and revealing interviews, members of the Legend development team explain how Lara's latest adventure took shape, and share some of the trials and triumphs they endured and enjoyed during their three years on the project. It should go without saying that this article contains numerous spoilers. Be sure to complete Tomb Raider Legend before you read any further!

Morgan Gray, Producer

"I can't think of a videogame character that has more recognition to gamers and non-gamers than Lara Croft," opines producer **Morgan Gray**. *"Mention Lara to non-gamers, and they'll say: 'Lara Croft? Oh, you mean Angelina Jolie?' and you're already having a conversation."*

Star of six previous outings on major games consoles and the PC, two movies, three handheld adventures, and typified by her startling success as a media and marketing icon, Lara Croft is arguably the most well-known gaming character ever created. At the end of July 2003, just over a month after the release of The Angel of Darkness, Tomb Raider publisher Eidos Interactive announced that Lara would be leaving Core Design – the original creator of the series, and the team behind the first six games – with immediate effect. Development responsibilities were transferred to the Eidos-owned Crystal Dynamics, author of successful franchises such as Gex and the acclaimed five-part Legacy of Kain series.

While Lara bidding farewell to her Derby birthplace (and the shores of England) was huge news in games industry circles, Crystal Dynamics maintained a surprisingly low profile in the months following the announcement. Quietly, with a minimum of fuss or fanfare, the company assembled a large team to begin initial design work on the game that would become Tomb Raider Legend.

Willow Place, Menlo Park: home to Crystal Dynamics and, since July 2003, Tomb Raider.

Some people at Crystal Dynamics claim to have been unfazed by the prospect of reinventing the defining franchise of the 32-bit era; for others, it took a little time to sink in. *"I think the first reaction was a naive one. It was just, like: 'Great!' I don't think the full weight of the responsibility set in right away,"* admits lead designer **Riley Cooper**. *"The first reaction was just excitement, and then it was like, this is a **huge** franchise. Coming from the Legacy of Kain series… even though it also has a hardcore fan base, and the fans care very much about every little choice you make, the*

Riley Cooper, Lead Designer

scale just didn't compare. With Tomb Raider, everybody is interested, everybody cares, and **everybody** has an opinion. [laughs]"*

The first task for the pre-production team at Crystal Dynamics was to

| RUNNING TO EDGE OF CLIFF | LAST STEP | JUMPING OFF CLIFF | TUCKING | EXTENDING TO SWAN POSE |

Lara's famous "swan dive" was a move that Crystal Dynamics were keen to retain.

analyze which features of previous Tomb Raider games they should keep, and which they should drop. Lara, obviously, was an ingredient that no one disputed for a second – few would be so foolish as to question the fact that she *is* Tomb Raider. Looking back at her early adventures, the Legend team sought to understand what made them so engaging and, for some, frustrating. *"At the time, she was an extremely mobile character, life-like in her animations and the way she moved, and in the different things she could do,"* says Riley Cooper. *"You really found that, even with something as simple as jumping a gap, you would kind of hold your breath a little bit. Actually, one of the things that we found while researching the games was that people have a two-sided relationship with Lara. On one hand, they want to go crazy and do the jumping and shooting, take risks – all the things you need her to do. On the other hand, they were very protective of her, and almost felt bad if they let her get hurt. It was more than just frustration at a setback."*

How many virtual deaths has Lara endured over the past decade in homes all over the world? With total game sales of over thirty million, and with Tomb Raider games typified by their unusually high difficulty level for such mainstream titles, it's not unreasonable to speculate that she has died over a billion times. You can attribute many of those demises to operator error, traps too numerous to mention, assailants ranging from prosaic thugs to famously anachronistic dinosaurs, and level design that has varied from cunning to downright cruel. The simple fact is, though, that Lara

HOW TO PLAY

WALKTHROUGH

EXTRAS

SECRETS

PREVIOUS
ADVENTURES

BEHIND THE
SCENES

Croft may have been a lithe, well-animated and iconic virtual star, but she was notoriously hard to master. Only veteran players ever felt truly comfortable with the control system used to guide her, and even they had long clamored for change. Less pressing in her 1996 debut, her recalcitrant nature was viewed as a greater handicap with each successive adventure.

For that reason, the dated grid-based movement and animation system – used in the first five Tomb Raider games, and later revised for Angel of Darkness – was naturally the first feature that Crystal Dynamics chose to discard. *"The biggest choice, the biggest imperative that came out of personal memories, discussions with editors, reading fan forums and talking to each other, was, number one, make Lara control the way people had wanted her to for a long time,"* explains Riley Cooper. *"We set the ambitious goal of trying to retake that crown of the most mobility, the most controllability, which she did have when she started, but quickly lost. That was number one."*

The second resolution that Crystal Dynamics made was to have Lara spend more time in the remote locales that made her first

adventure so eerily atmospheric. *"An equal number one I guess, maybe number two, was getting her back into the tombs,"* continues Cooper. *"For the first two hours in Angel of Darkness, you're on the abandoned streets of Paris. We felt strongly – again, during all the discussions that we had – that this wasn't where Lara should be. Lara should be in tombs: it is Tomb Raider, after all."*

With those two design pillars in place, another hurdle was to cherry-pick the most important features of previous games, and prune those deemed surplus to requirements. As long-term fans will recall with variable enthusiasm – it was a "love it or loathe it" aspect of the series – Core Design had a longstanding fascination with stealth-based gameplay, evident in the Nevada levels of Tomb Raider III and the final stages of Chronicles. Angel of Darkness went one silent step further, adding a dedicated "stealth" mode for Lara, and placing a much greater onus on evasion over aggression by limiting the player's access to munitions.

Stealth and design-imposed restraint were features that, after subjective reflection, the Tomb Raider Legend team was keen to move away from. *"You're not playing Lara Croft if you're counting your ammunition on your pistols: it becomes a different game,"* comments Morgan Gray. *"You start to slow down, you start to hide behind corners and try to conserve. Lara Croft to me is: you run into a room, you do cartwheels, you jump off a guy's head, and then you shoot him [laughs]. Unlimited ammo and dual pistols was a 'must keep'."*

Jason Bell,
Technical Director

FALLING   FALLING   DIVE POSITION   SPLASH   LOOP AROUND BACK TO SURFACE   SURFACING

Certain aspects of previous games were obviously brought forward with scant reflection or debate. From traversing along cliff ledges to swinging on ropes, challenging puzzles to evocative environs and vistas, few would dispute the power and potential of many classic Tomb Raider ingredients. *"We needed to retain her athletic moves, we needed to retain her guns because they're such an icon, it had to be a third-person action adventure game, there had to be swimming, and we wanted to use vehicles,"* summarizes technical director **Jason Bell**.

"The things that Lara is and does are great for videogames," says Riley Cooper. *"She's an acrobatic character: great. She's acrobatic in combat: great. She goes to these cool, mysterious places and overcomes traps and solves ancient puzzles. She's perfect for videogames, she's great [laughs]. The initial design by Core, and Toby Gard et al, was good stuff. We weren't going to lose the spirit of the game but, beyond that, it was kind of open season. We definitely wanted you to come to the game and go 'Okay, this is definitely Tomb Raider'. We didn't want you to have any doubts about that. She still has her backpack; she still does most of her adventuring in shorts. But most of it is new. Spiritually it's the same game – but functionally, it's very, very, very different."*

REINVENTING LARA

Developing and refining the appearance of a central protagonist is a challenge in any game viewed from a third-person perspective. Working with Lara, however, the Tomb Raider Legend team had the delicate and demanding task of updating one of the most recognizable videogame characters ever created. *"That was a tough one for us, because there were so many different ideas floating around on what to do with Lara, and there were so many people that wanted to chime in at any given point,"* says art director **Jacob "Jake" Wendler**. *"We knew we needed to modernize her, and we were looking at her to see what we could do. We used the Angel of Darkness model at the very beginning as a base model, and then we started adjusting her from that. We slimmed her down, tried to tweak her face, tried to take the harsh lines off her eyes (Fig. 1 and Fig. 2). It wasn't really until Toby Gard got on the project that he wanted to mix things up, which I was all for. Toby's a pretty outspoken guy in terms of what he wants."*

Jacob Wendler,
Art Director

[0 2]

Early Lara model a few
months after project start

[0 1]

Toby Gard, Lara's original creator, was brought over from England to work on the project, and would play a pivotal role in her redevelopment. *"His coming on board helped a huge amount because, as he actually created Lara in the first place, he wasn't afraid of her,"* says Jason Bell. *"He said 'She's my character, I'll do what I want'. He could just do it, and that helped a lot, because before he came along we were a bit confused about what we should be doing, and it was hard to get any decisions made about Lara. We could see that Lara is athletic, but we didn't have any real details: we were asking things like 'How does she walk?' which was kind of tricky. When Toby joined, he would say, 'She walks this way', and things would happen. That was probably one of the turning points of the project, I think. We would have got a game done without him, but I'm not sure how different Lara would be right now – and whether she'd be quite as good."*

Toby Gard,
Creative Consultant

"He really helped me make decisions," says Jake Wendler on Toby. *"At first we were kind of nitpicky in terms of 'Well, let's not change her that much'. When Toby came on board, we looked at the model that we were thinking about – and that's when all hell broke loose in terms of trying to figure out a different costume for her, doing something different with her hair, getting away from the braid, getting rid of the sunglasses, putting things on her. We sat down and he wanted to totally get a new costume (Fig. 3); he was very good at designing stuff as well. He wanted to radically change her figure. We just sat down and did a lot of crazy things to her. Sometimes, we went too far. I remember when we finally sat down and saw the costume that is on Lara today, though. It took eight months to really finalize the look of Lara, and then we had everybody sitting down and saying, 'this is it'. It was cool to see."*

Redesigning Lara wasn't merely a question of choosing a new costume and performing minor cosmetic surgery. As these images show, the team also considered a number of very different faces.

[0 3]

TOMB RAIDER
LEGEND

HOW TO PLAY

WALKTHROUGH

EXTRAS

SECRETS

PREVIOUS
ADVENTURES

BEHIND THE
SCENES

*Matthew Guzenda,
Senior Producer*

Redesigning Lara wasn't simply a matter of performing an aesthetic overhaul: there was the not inconsiderable matter of how she would move and interact with environments. *"A lot of work was already done on the engines,"* says senior producer **Matthew Guzenda**. *"She goes into pretty big environments. We had never really done very wide-open spaces, so we did some tests on that. But the main thing was that we had to go over the control system. We were concerned about the previous games: she looked very smooth, she looked very realistic, but she just wasn't very easy to move around."*

Deciding to create a more maneuverable, athletic and responsive Lara was one thing, but actually putting such ideas into practice was arguably the biggest obstacle the Tomb Raider Legend team had to face. It wasn't enough that players be able to control Lara with pinpoint precision: she also had to perform her moves with signature style and grace. *"With the Soul Reaver games, we had guys that were sort of human, but they had a lot of abilities,"* continues Guzenda. *"They could do very high jumps, they could move really quickly… the characters were very responsive and could do all kinds of things. But when we put Lara in and had her move around with our system, it looked too jerky. It took almost a full project to finalize, but we needed to find a balance between appearance and control. And this is always something you fight with: the artist wants her to look really good and be really smooth, and the designer always wants her to react quickly and be really maneuverable."*

Lara is completely hand-animated (Fig. 4). The way that her animations blend together so seamlessly is the end result of many months of demanding labor; countless thousands of hours to ensure that, for example, a leap from point A to point B is suitably responsive and visually convincing. In truth, there is never one solitary animation in progress as Legend-issue Lara moves. Instead, there can often be several working together at once, each one dealing with a specific part of her anatomy. From pointing her guns in one direction while moving in another, to the direction her head faces as she passes a point of interactivity, there are many subtleties that many players will entirely fail to appreciate on a conscious level.

"The hardest thing we had to work on, which is something that I think people are going to take for granted, is her movement system," explains Morgan Gray. *"It took a good four to six engineers the better part of over a year to develop the technology that allows Lara to be controlled fluidly, and to perform all of her animations. These are many little things that some people won't notice, but we wanted Lara to be as realistic as possible – and in motion as much as possible. Even the system where Lara jumps over something that's knee-high, where she bends her leg as*

she gets on, took lot of work to implement. Pushing up on the controller and having Lara's feet dangling, and having her do the look-over… there are so many small subtleties."

"We had a significant portion of our engineering department devoted to getting Lara to look right, to move correctly and to work well with the world," reveals Jason Bell. *"Probably a good third of our engineering effort went into that because it was the thing that everyone would notice: the game was so much about Lara that she was the most important thing to get right. I think she accounts for about 15-20 percent of the overall code size, which is quite a lot, and it has been the most challenging part."*

Updating Lara and creating an entirely new control system wasn't just a matter of imbuing her with greater flexibility and athletic prowess. The team also had to consider how their changes would affect how she would and could interact with environments. *"We knew that Lara was going to have to move a lot better,"* says Jake Wendler. *"We just didn't know the visual implications of it, especially early on in the project. We didn't know how hard that was going to be. What does a ledge look like that you have to ledge-grab? Soul Reaver and Legacy of Kain had very specific mechanics. But with Lara, you can do pretty much anything in her environment: jump on things, ledge-grab, and swing on poles throughout eight very distinct environments. Thinking about the visual language of getting through the levels was a challenge that we had to constantly go back and forth with, in terms of design and focus testing. We had to get people into the game and figure out what made visual sense."*

[04]

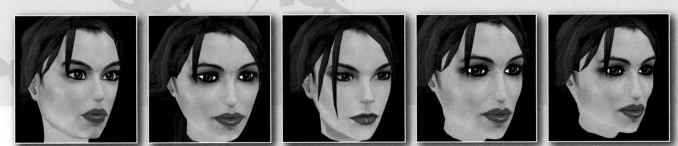

"Being able to come at walls at awkward angles and have her body attach and react appropriately took a lot of time," agrees Morgan Gray. But as much of a trial as rebuilding Lara was, her new abilities opened up a world of new opportunities in terms of level design. *"With previous games, you actually had a grid-based level design where things were very blocky, and the path that you could walk down was very much easier to spot, because there was a perfectly straight 90 degree line,"* Gray explains. *"Now, because*

her AI, her movement, is opened up, we have been able to make much more realistic environments. Obviously, the path you're supposed to follow still hints at you, 'Hey, go here!' but we're not a world of 90 degree angles. We have a lush and far more detailed environment; you really feel like you're exploring when you find that movement path and how you're supposed to get out of there. You feel smart, as opposed to being sort of force-fed. That's a big, big difference."

BACK TO THE TOMBS

With her passport bearing stamps from so many countries, choosing locales for Lara to visit wasn't a case of merely sticking pins in a map. *"We wanted them to be different, and we wanted them to be remote,"* says Riley Cooper. *"We wanted you to be going into ancient tombs with some plausibility for why they hadn't been discovered. There aren't too many huge temples sitting in the middle of the ground for any satellite photo to see – they're generally hidden away a little bit."*

"We wanted to make sure we globe-hopped as much as possible, and to make sure that we picked locations that would be different enough to make each level unique," says Morgan Gray. *"Each level had to work with our story goals, be somewhere unique, and enable*

These concept drawings show recognizable scenes from Tomb Raider Legend's Toyko level.

FOCUS ON: STREAMING SYSTEM

Tomb Raider Legend uses a "streaming" system, where every individual stage is separated into a series of "units". When Lara approaches the end of one unit, the Legend engine begins to load the next one from disc. This seamless process has enabled Crystal Dynamics to pack every level with an otherwise impossible level of detail, as Jason Bell explains.

"A lot of other games have streaming systems now, but we first developed ours back with Soul Reaver in 1998-1999," says Bell. "We've made various improvements over the years, but we've had a nice stable base and it's always been something we've been able to rely on. The streaming system has been massively important, because it allowed so much else to happen. It's kind of a way of partitioning the world so that nothing gets too overwhelming for the console. I think I did a rough estimate that one of the PS2 levels, if you had to load everything into memory, would take up about 150MB. The PlayStation 2 only has 32MB of memory. The stream system allows us to do big, giant levels that feature a lot of complex data. This is why we could get so much detail into the world, and it's something we just couldn't have done if it was just a single level game."

us to generate unique gameplay. Bolivia was picked because we thought it would be great to have the first level of the game with Lara climbing up cliffs en route to a tomb. Previous games in the franchise got away from the tomb explorations. We wanted to get to a tomb, and wanted to get there quickly."

Despite the team's steadfast belief in helping Lara return to her roots as the titular Tomb Raider, Legend has one level that takes place in a highly contemporary setting. *"Tokyo for us was a good one, because we had a 'No urban, no urban, no urban!' mantra when we first started,"* laughs Gray. *"We wanted nothing but tombs, nothing but being out in the wild… but then we started saying: 'What if you scaled a building like you scaled a cliff?' When we started to get our physics system integrated, we thought about having scaffolding, and pulling washing platforms, and things like that. We said: 'Okay – what's urban and could be cool? Tokyo!' As we got more of the story together, we found ourselves saying: 'The sword fragment – we could have this guy who's a Yakuza! Okay, we'll do **one** urban!' [laughs]"*

TOMB RAIDER
LEGEND

HOW TO PLAY

WALKTHROUGH

EXTRAS

SECRETS

PREVIOUS
ADVENTURES

BEHIND THE
SCENES

Tomb Raider Legend's most awe-inspiring moment is, arguably, the encounter with the massive waterfall at the beginning of the Ghana level. This powerful visual set piece was one of the first ideas to be discussed and, later, implemented. *"First we'd brainstorm about the locations themselves, so West Africa came up,"* reveals Jake Wendler. *"Then we would split off and we would take that location and see what we could do with it. What would be something new and exciting about West Africa? We said, 'Man, wouldn't it be cool if we had this big huge waterfall that nobody's ever been to, in West Africa? Wouldn't it be cool if that waterfall opened up by some crazy ancient mechanism?' It started off with initial ideas like that, and then we performed tests, 2D concepts of what it might look like. It kind of snowballed. It went from a vague idea, to creative brainstorming, to conceptual work, and even 3D testing, to thinking about technical limitations. We had to ask: is this achievable in our engine?"*

One of the more fascinating aspects of the Tomb Raider Legend development process is one of the techniques used to test and experiment with concepts and features. With an idea in place, designers and programmers would put together a

Early paintings showing one of Tomb Raider Legend's defining moments: the temple hidden behind the waterfall in Ghana.

"block mesh", a rudimentary, playable prototype of an area without 3D textures. This enabled the team to test the strength or plausibility of proposals before beginning the process of working on expensive, labor-intensive 3D art.

"What happens is that you come up with ideas, you come up with locations, and the design department headed by Riley isn't really thinking about architecture, they're thinking about gameplay," explains Jake Wendler. *"They would come up with the flow of the ideas, and early block mesh gameplay setups, and sometimes we would find that they wouldn't work with the architecture that we had. Most of the time, you have a room and, usually, you know what is going to be there – like Lara has to get from A to B, and she's going to be using certain mechanics to get to B. So they would do a test run in block mesh to try out how she got there. We would then take screenshots of the block mesh, and then we'd paint over them. When we were happy in terms of how it looked and played, we would go forward with production and get it into 3D. Painting over screenshots is actually a big way for us to visually communicate to the artists and everybody else."*

Naturally, vistas like the Amahlin waterfall sequence and the rolling boulder puzzle in Peru are hardly scenes that can be researched at a local library, but the Legend team drew inspiration for level design and art from a variety of sources. *"For every single level we would look for something as reference,"* says Riley Cooper. *"It depended on how real-life the thing was. In some cases, there would be*

no specific reference, so we couldn't, but in the Himalayas we researched Tibetan architecture for use in that space. We do have one city, Tokyo, and we certainly looked at pictures of Tokyo and city spaces for that. That was something that our artists spent a lot of time on."

The sheer visual variety in each of Tomb Raider Legend's seven main levels is an integral part of its appeal. It engenders a genuine feeling of progression, of exploration and, as Jake Wendler reveals, was entirely intentional. *"We had a formula that we developed at the very beginning of the project,"* says Wendler. *"In all the levels, we decided she was going to start in a place which was somehow familiar, like outside environments that you could really tell were grounded in reality. Later, you would reach the tomb, and you would understand: 'Okay, that's the tomb we're going to, and that's where we're going to be.' Once you got into the tomb, it was a free-for-all. We really tried to get a different feel, still using architectural pieces that made sense, but with a certain flair that felt exciting and different. I think that's why people like going into the tombs: because it's different, it's not something you see every day. So that was enjoyable, for us artists, that we got to do something really different. Tomb Raider was definitely cool to see at the very beginning of the PlayStation era. There were some key areas where you could look around and say, 'Wow, I'm in this big wide-open world, and I'm all by myself'. We've tried to capture a similar sense that the areas are sometimes bigger than they actually are, a sense of grandeur, at least two or three times per level."*

From early "block mesh", to painted screenshot, to final game, these three images show the evolution of the opening room of the "flashback" sequence in Peru.

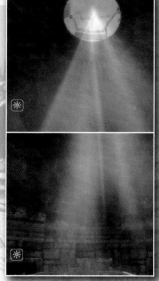

[05]

[06]

[07]

[08]

These screenshots show the full-screen "post filter" effects in action. Picture 5 shows a scene without a post filter applied; picture 6 is the same moment as it appears in the final game. Pictures 7 and 8 demonstrate how profoundly these effects can change the look and feel of an environment. Eagle-eyed readers will recognize the post filter used in picture 8 from Lara's flashback in Peru.

HOW TO PLAY

WALKTHROUGH

EXTRAS

SECRETS

PREVIOUS ADVENTURES

BEHIND THE SCENES

FOCUS ON: POST FILTERS

Part of Tomb Raider Legend's massive visual appeal is due to its clever use of full-screen "post filter" effects. *"Post filters blur the screen, and you can do anything you want with it,"* explains Jake Wendler. *"It's an art director's dream: you can de-saturate it, you can add higher contrast, you can add a little more green or red, or anything that you want. We start with a filter that we like for a level, and then we'll tune each unit differently depending on what we want to achieve. If the player's going into a tomb and it's hot, we tried to make it a little blurrier, to make it feel warmer; in some environments we touched up the blue a little bit, so that it would feel a little colder. You'll definitely notice something different when going from outside to inside. We went through the whole game, looked at all the full-screen effects, and tweaked them. It makes the game feel and look very cool."*

TELLING TALES

By neatly sidestepping previous Tomb Raider storylines and presenting a new interpretation of Lara as a character, Tomb Raider Legend is free to tell its own tale. It offers a much more involved and complicated story than any of its predecessors. Interestingly, this achievement can be partially attributed to the clever reintroduction of an obscure bit-part character from a previous adventure.

FOCUS ON: MUSIC & SOUND EFFECTS

Troels Brun Folmann is the in-house composer for Tomb Raider Legend, and is the mastermind behind its wonderfully varied and evocative soundtrack.

Troels Brun Folmann, Internal Composer

How many minutes of music are there in Tomb Raider Legend?

TBF: We probably have around 4.5 to 5 hours all in all, and we have got two hours of additional scores that did not make it in the game. Probably around 7.5 hours all in all, with five hours in the game. It is a lot, and it was done in ten months. I am creatively burned!

Tomb Raider Legend uses a lot of context-sensitive music. Can you tell us a little about that?

TBF: We have literally hundreds of different small scores. I developed a methodology that I call 'micro-scoring', or 'micro-scores', which is making small tracks and having them play at the same time. You have the normal generic in-game music in the background, but then you also have small complimentary tunes. When you play, you can shoot, you can do all those cool moves and you are the hero of the game. In order to get the music to compliment that, it needs to be more connected to what the player does and what happens in the game. That is where the micro-scores start working. The reason we wanted to break down the music into small components was to make the player feel empowered. Like: "Wow, the music is adapting to what I do – when I start shooting, more drums are added to the tune." But then again, composing is a secret, nobody notices it, but that feels kind of strange. If you are playing the game for several hours, the idea is not to get the music to stand out at all times. It should just compliment the experience.

Lara seems much less inclined to punctuate movements with grunts and groans than in previous Tomb Raider games. Why was this

decision made? What else can you tell us about the use of sound effects in Legend?

TBF: In general, we really went into constructing Lara's character. There was a new generation of sounds. Just Lara's character alone has, depending on the level, three to six hundred different sounds. In older games you would have footstep sounds. In this game, we have a sound of the heel going down, we have the sound of the foot touching the ground, and we have a sound when the foot detaches from the ground – and on many different surfaces. We have multiple versions so we can randomize it. I think what we wanted to do is try to get more complexity into the sound environment. When she moves around, you can hear her gear: when she has grenades, you can hear them. We bought grenades and banged them towards each other, so we know what it sounds like when she has them. But when she loses them in the game, that audio disappears. Every time the gun shoots a bullet, you will hear the case fall to the ground. It is a different sound every time it goes off.

And the reason for why we don't have so many grunts is that if you have been playing this game for X amount of hours and you are constantly listening to grunts it gets…nobody grunts that much. We did not consciously remove them, I think we did the amount that we wanted to have in the game. But we have been pretty careful about not having too many repeated sounds.

Which moments in Tomb Raider Legend are you most proud of, and why?

TBF: I think I am proud of the fluency; the way the music evolves in the game. There is not any specific moment where I can say, "here is my highlight" – quite the contrary, actually. If I had to be proud of anything, it would be that the micro-scores are very well connected, and seem to be working in the way that I designed them to be.

"Lara has pretty much killed every single enemy that she has ever met, so there was no strong character that could continue between the games," says Matthew Guzenda. "Even characters that she has interacted with have died. We brought Zip back in this game – he's in Chronicles briefly at one point – though we've changed him, so he's a different Zip to the one that players met before. But there weren't really any characters that we could carry over. With Batman you have, say, the Joker and Robin to work with, and they're part of your storyline. With Lara, there wasn't really anybody else."

The return of Zip and the introduction of Alister is a pivotal change to the Tomb Raider template. The fact that these sidekicks can communicate with Lara (and vice versa) as and when required is something that many players will hear, enjoy and find useful, but without necessarily recognizing the important role that such conversations play. First and foremost, this design device has enabled the Legend team to gradually drip-feed plot elements during the course of the game, removing the need to exclusively use dedicated cutscenes to develop the storyline. It's also a tool that facilitates necessary or subtle exposition: not only can it provide gameplay tips and guidance, it can also provide further context and detail to the many sights, sounds and experiences that players encounter. Tomb Raider Legend is a far richer narrative experience as a result.

Radio chatter between Lara, Zip and Alister is key to Crystal Dynamics' efforts to weave a layered, involving and cohesive tale. There are a handful of carefully interwoven plot strands: Lara's drive to understand her mother's death, her encounter with (and subsequent battle against) Rutland and his mercenaries, the events at Paraíso and Amanda's survival, and, finally, how all of these elements are bound together by the Arthurian legend. "In our universe, the sword that Arthur uses, Excalibur – there's the whole thing with recovering the sword shards throughout the game – is a relic from an ancient civilization that we're never going to name," reveals Morgan Gray. "We have a big back-story. It's through Lara tracking down Amanda, and then trying to figure out what she's up to, that she discovers how Arthur ties in. If you've read Joseph Campbell, he talks about 'monomyths': that every civilization generates myths that are pretty similar. For example, everyone has the farm boy being taken from his home to become a hero by the old wise guy. That farm boy could be young King Arthur, or Luke Skywalker, or Superman. We use the monomyth concept in reference to King Arthur and the sword of power, and then connect it to the things we find in Peru and in Japan. It's through researching what Amanda's up to that Lara makes the King Arthur connection, and ultimately, as players know, ends up getting to see where the once and future King waits for England's time of greatest need – and borrows a little something."

Facial expressions and finely tuned editing lend many Tomb Raider Legend cinematics a dramatic weight that few other videogames can rival. Speaking to the team, it's clear to see that they're enormously proud of their achievements in this area. "There's a Lara and Amanda scene at the end, where Lara has Amanda on her knees with a gun to her head, execution style," explains Gray. "We're a T-rated game in the United States, so I'm sure no one thinks Lara's going to shoot this woman through the head, but Lara's also pretty serious at points in our game, so you're not entirely certain. There's a moment which I think is probably one of the most violent things I've seen in a game where

[09]

Lara gives a yell and fires her gun next to Amanda's head (Fig. 9). For me, that's the scene. There's power in that scene. It's not gratuitous; it takes a mature step forward for me. I get a chill every time I see that sequence."

DELETED SCENES

HOW TO PLAY

WALKTHROUGH

EXTRAS

SECRETS

PREVIOUS
ADVENTURES

BEHIND THE
SCENES

With a project the size of Tomb Raider Legend, there will always be features or functions that fail to make the final cut. With deadlines to meet, and standards to maintain, decisions must be made, and once-promising ideas removed with barely a backward glance. As a player, someone that has just spent hour after hour exploring every last inch of a virtual world, it's always interesting to learn how elements of a game changed during development. This isn't something that you often get to hear about, though – and for good reason. Many development teams are understandably (though, as a gamer, frustratingly) reticent to discuss such changes, preferring to have players focus on the features that their game actually has.

Plans to have Lara fire while climbing ladders and swinging on ropes were discarded. The abilities certainly looked good, but contributed little to Tomb Raider Legend's gameplay.

"It's so painful to tell people things we removed," admits Morgan Gray. *"Some people may be upset, thinking that we had something and we just decided not to do it, but when we say 'removed some things', they weren't really in the game that well [laughs]. We removed the wall jump ability [see "Wall Jumping"] because it was something that she could do, but it didn't fit with really any of our level layout goals. It was sort of superfluous, because it didn't fit into any of the movement lines that we had put into our levels. It just seemed like it wasn't adding anything. And then, the worst aspect, as we kept going on, it actually started bringing up issues where you could bypass some gameplay. So that was an easy walk away."*

"A ton of things come up in the course of development that you just decide to leave out because they just don't fit," contributes Riley Cooper. *"We had a sniper rifle on the table, way, way long ago, sticky grenades, Molotov cocktails, and dust clouds – little cloud bombs so you could hide yourself and move somewhere else. With the wall jump, though, we didn't want her doing the Prince of Persia thing. Wall runs obviously came up as a topic of discussion, but we didn't want to be that cartoony with her mechanics. We wanted her to be more real, more grounded. Our design philosophy with her was 'Human Plus' – just a little bit of a stretch on what we get to do."*

"One of the big things, the big surprises… well, originally we intended to have a whole highway vehicular chase scene, leaving the Arthur's Grave level after recovering the shard from Arthur, with Zip and Alister being held hostage by some of Rutland and Amanda's bad guys," explains Morgan Gray. *"They were actually going to be kidnapped and there was going to be a whole chase on the bike, and that's a big thing that we had to walk away from due to scheduling concerns. We used to have a lot more grandiose plans for animal features, but we started to notice that they weren't really fitting in with what we wanted to do. Unfortunately,*

even with the ambient animals, we started quickly running up against memory concerns. We actually built a good two-dozen animals – we even built a platypus! [laughs]."*

"One of the more difficult things in development, certainly for me, is knowing when you're at a crossroads where you make a decision to walk away from something," Gray laments. *"It might work, but you're kind of thinking it won't, or you just go the other way and hope against hope. Generally though, I find that when your soul's telling you that something's probably not going to work, it's rare that it ever actually does [laughs]. Especially when the instincts of a collective group of people are telling them so. We're all collectively smarter than we are individually. If we all think something's bad, then as opposed to hiding it under the bed it's better to confront it immediately. It generally helps."*

THE "WALL JUMP"

For those unfamiliar with the concept, the "wall jump" once enabled Lara to spring from walls to reach higher platforms. In the sequence pictured here – one of a mere handful where the move was of any real utility – we can see Lara using it to take a shortcut to Peru's first Bronze Reward.

REFINING AND POLISHING

It would be wrong to view features removed as "lost" content. Discarding ideas has merely been a part of the continual process of tweaking and polishing that has made Tomb Raider Legend so notably refined. Many of the most interesting changes to have been implemented, from a player's perspective, are those to existing characters, levels and gameplay. Rutland, for example, was once a much more stereotypical "macho" bad guy, but then evolved to become the intelligent, egocentric individual we first encounter at the

MANY OVERLAPING ELEMENTS IN CHEEK/ JAW AREA

SPINES CAN LAY FLAT OR SPIKE UP.

NECK POUCH EXPANDS AND CONTRACTS

SEA-SERPENT

ARTHUR'S TOMB

end of the Bolivia level. Some scenes changed several times before Tomb Raider Legend's code was finalized. One example is the fight against the sea serpent outside King Arthur's final resting place. *"That went through a number of revisions,"* says Morgan Gray. *"It was going to be a dragon at one point, then we went with the snake. There was going to be a network of caves that you would fight it in. Round after round, we tried to figure out what we wanted to do with it. For us it was blurring the line. Is this a boss encounter? Is this a puzzle with an opponent in it? How do we label this in terms of what we want to do with it?"*

Every moment in Tomb Raider Legend was subjected to a painstaking critical examination by not merely the Crystal Dynamics team, but by external playtesters and focus groups. *"The last step, which is something we did more on this project than on any other I've been on, and I think it made all the difference, is that we got*

people who had never seen the game before to play," says Riley Cooper. *"Invariably, what we found is that people got stuck in the same places. Some 'stucks' are okay. You come into a room and there's a puzzle you have to solve, and you have to look around and figure it out. That's great. But when players have no idea what to do next, that's not fun, that's why they put the controller down. We had to think of something that we could do to fix that problem, and then run people back through. That's a hugely important part. It made a huge contribution to the quality levels in the final game."*

With Lara being so maneuverable, one of the greatest challenges was to ensure that the game world made sense to players, and that the path forward could always be found without too much frustration. The visual language of any given Legend level could not be too ambiguous. For example, having a scenic detail that could be interpreted as a safe ledge, an apparent point of interactivity that Lara would annoyingly refuse to grab, was something that Crystal Dynamics was keen to avoid. *"That was the biggest problem for us, in terms of gameplay,"* says Jake Wendler. *"We had all these areas that we tried to make visually interesting, but the gameplay had to stand out more. We had to tone back things that looked like ledges, try to slope off things that you couldn't get to, because we tried to make the areas as lush as possible, and as detailed as possible. That was definitely a challenge for us."*

"Based on watching people play on our game, we've probably made in the order of 300 changes, all of them important," reveals Riley Cooper. *"In code, we have 'A' bugs. They're official, because it's obvious to everybody that there's a point in the game where people can't proceed. So you call out a playthrough, stop where all the alarm bells go off, and everybody knows what they have to do to get rid of it. Games ship with the equivalent of that in their level layout, in their art, and these are effectively 'A' bugs. For the most part, testers find code issues. They don't as often find layout issues. Focus testing is what we call it when we bring people in who haven't played before. They find layout issues, they find design issues. You just have to watch them, and it becomes obvious really quickly."*

Addressing actual problems and performing delicate gameplay balance adjustments, the team nonetheless found that some of Legend's most satisfying moments are, of course, those where the player solves a difficult puzzle. It was a crucial ingredient in the original Tomb Raider, and it's just as important in Legend. One classic example is the room featuring the "teetering platform" late in the opening Bolivia level, where players have to activate three floor switches to raise the barrier covering the exit. *"It was our first real physics puzzle,"* says Riley Cooper, who cites it as one of the features that he is most proud of. *"It's one of those puzzles that people in the focus tests said was the most frustrating part, which wasn't great. Sometimes, though, they said that the hardest part was that puzzle, and the same person would then say that the **best** part was that puzzle, because of the feeling of achievement they had when they figured it out. Usually, when they saw that block sail through the air, they had a giddy smile and a bit of a laugh."*

FOCUS ON: COMBAT

HOW TO PLAY

WALKTHROUGH

EXTRAS

SECRETS

PREVIOUS
ADVENTURES

BEHIND THE
SCENES

on one that most people enjoyed, one that satisfied skilled players and non-skilled players alike."

"Really, the guiding philosophy was that Lara's not a stealth assassin and she's not Rambo, so what is she? We started from there," explains Riley Cooper. "We know that she's very acrobatic, so we introduced acrobatics into combat. And there's a degree of puzzle solving, too. Puzzle is probably a little bit of a strong word, but the targets of opportunity that we have mean that you can often use the environment to your advantage. Even though we wanted to make sure that combat had depth for those people who like it, the fact is that a lot of people don't love combat in Tomb Raider games. It's not why they come to a Tomb Raider game. Fictionally, Lara's goal in life is not to kill enemies; Lara's goal is to acquire artifacts that help her unravel mysteries. She fights because she has to, so we wanted to make sure we got the proper balance."

Combat in Tomb Raider Legend is a vast improvement over previous games in the series, but it took an enormous amount of effort to perfect, from initial design to final adjustments late in the project. "We went through a lot of different control methods, like two-stick targeting and automatic targeting," reveals Jason Bell. "Eventually, we settled

SLIDING KICK

RUNNING

GRABBING GUNS & STARTING SLIDE

SLIDING WITH GUNS DRAWN

KICKING WITH HAND PLANT

PUSHING UP WITH A TURN

SHOOT HIM WHILE HE'S DOWN

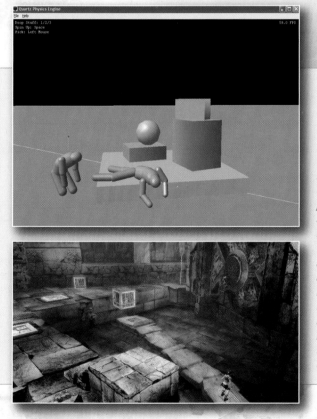

FOCUS ON: PHYSICS

Bucking the trend followed by many major developers of buying off-the-shelf "middleware" physics engines from external teams, the Tomb Raider Legend staff instead chose to build their own. The influence of this code can be found everywhere, from puzzles (such as the moving platforms in Japan, and the crate catapulting in Bolivia), to using the Magnetic Grapple to swing across deadly drops. "One huge difference in the engine right now is that we have an actual physics engine that is capable of doing a lot of stuff," explains Jason Bell. "In Soul Reaver, we just had really basic physics where you could throw things, and that was about it. One of our programmers did some prototype work on knocking up physics code, and that worked out really well. It pointed to the fact that we **could** do physics, that it was possible to just get a programmer to do it, and we wouldn't have to worry about using middleware. Later on, we hired a programmer called Erin Catto to specifically write the physics system. He actually had a background in molecular biology; I think he was doing simulations on protein folding, or something weird like that. He's a very smart guy. He built the physics system that we use in Tomb Raider Legend. It's pretty much one guy's work, and I think we've ended up with a system that is equal to any of the others out there. It worked out really well, and it's one of the big success stories of this project."

A screen grab of a programmer working with Quartz, Crystal Dynamic's proprietary physics engine, and a scene of it in action during Lara's trip to Bolivia.

THE LONG WAIT BEGINS...

Having enjoyed this and other equally polished moments, our thoughts turn to what the future may hold for Lara. Over three years in development, Tomb Raider Legend marks a triumphant return for the world's most famous digital heroine. But what feats might Crystal Dynamics have in store for her next adventure? When might it be released? The question on everyone's lips must be that, given Tomb Raider Legend's cliffhanger ending, can we safely assume that another episode is already being planned? *"I would think there's a certain amount of safety to assume,"* is Morgan Gray's enigmatic response.

But can he give any clues as to what players can expect? *"This is where Eidos gets mad at me!"* laughs Gray. *"The hint that I would give is that we would never do a cliffhanger ending if we didn't intend to resolve it..."*

It could be a year before Lara returns; it could be three, or five. But having explored and enjoyed every square centimeter of Tomb Raider Legend, some players might ruefully acknowledge – if only to themselves – that it already feels like an eternity...

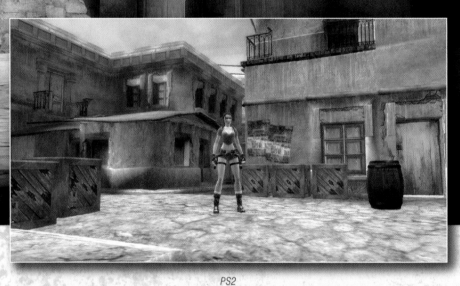

PS2

LEGEND ON XBOX 360

It's beautiful on every format, but groundbreaking work by a dedicated art, programming and production crew has made the Xbox 360 version of Tomb Raider Legend truly astonishing to behold.

Visit **www.piggybackinteractive.com** to read exclusive interviews with members of the Xbox 360 development team, including lead artist **Drew Medina**, senior programmer **Rob Pavey**, and senior producer **Matthew Guzenda**.

XBOX 360

INDEX

Term	Page
Advanced Hold (Lock Mode)	11
Advanced Toggle (Lock Mode)	11
Alister Fletcher	172, [188]
Amanda Evert	173, [188]
Anaya Imanu	172
Assault Rifle	39
Basic Moves	14 - 15
Behind the Scenes	180 - 192
Binoculars	20, [37]
Binoculars (Croft Manor)	151
Bolivia (Level 1)	44 - 61
Bolivia Rewards (Level 1)	155 - 156
Bolivia – The Looking Glass (Level 8)	142 - 143
Brightness	11
Button Configuration	7 - 10
Calibration	11
Camera	25, [14]
Cast	171 - 173
Change Weapon	19
Character Profiles	166
Cheat Codes	167
Checkpoints	29
Cinematics	165
Combat	18 - 20, [191]
Combat Modes	11
Contrast	11
Controlling Lara	14 - 24
Croft Manor	146 - 154, [10]
Destructible Objects	19
Difficulty Level	6
Display	11
Dual Pistols	38
Enemy Behavior	31
England (Level 6)	116 - 129
England Rewards (Level 6)	161 - 162
Equipment	36 - 39
Excalibur	141, [188]
Extras	144 - 192, [12]
Extras Menu	164 - 169
Flares	38
Gear	36 - 38
Ghana (Level 4)	88 - 101, [185]
Ghana Rewards (Level 4)	159
Grenades	39, [20]
Grenade Launcher	39
Handstand	21
Health Pack	38, [15]
Horizontal Pole Moves	23
Interactive Cutscenes	25
James Rutland	101, 173, 190
Japan	See "Tokyo"
Kazakhstan (Level 5)	102 - 115
Kazakhstan Rewards (Level 5)	160
Lara Croft	171
Lara's Home	146 - 154, [10]
Load	7
Lock-On	18
Magnetic Grapple	17 - 19, [36]
Magnetic Grapple (Croft Manor)	147
Main Menu	10 - 12
Manual Aim Mode	19
Moveable Objects	33 - 35
Nepal (Level 7)	130 - 141
Nepal Rewards (Level 7)	162 - 163
New Game	10
Objectives (PDA)	26

Term	Page
Onscreen Display	12 - 13
Options Menu	11
Outfits	168 - 169
Pause Menu	25
PDA Menu	26
Personal Light Source	37, [14]
Personal Light Source (Croft Manor)	148
Peru (Level 2)	62 - 75
Peru Rewards (Level 2)	156 - 157
Pistol Upgrades	167
Pistols (Croft Manor)	148
Previous Adventures	174 - 179
Progressive Scan	11
Quit	25
Quick Time Events	see "Super Actions"
R.A.D. Mode	20
Reward 1-A	47, 155
Reward 1-B	47, 155
Reward 1-C	47, 155
Reward 1-D	51, 155
Reward 1-E	53, 155
Reward 1-F	53, 155
Reward 1-G	55, 155
Reward 1-H	55, 155
Reward 1-I	55, 156
Reward 1-J	57, 156
Reward 1-K	57, 156
Reward 1-L	59, 156
Reward 1-M	59, 156
Reward 1-N	59, 156
Reward 1-O	61, 156
Reward 1-P	61, 156
Reward 2-A	65, 157
Reward 2-B	65, 157
Reward 2-C	65, 157
Reward 2-D	65, 157
Reward 2-E	65, 157
Reward 2-F	67, 157
Reward 2-G	69, 157
Reward 2-H	71, 157
Reward 2-I	71, 157
Reward 2-J	71, 157
Reward 2-K	73, 157
Reward 3-A	79, 158
Reward 3-B	79, 158
Reward 3-C	79, 158
Reward 3-D	81, 158
Reward 3-E	83, 158
Reward 3-F	83, 158
Reward 3-G	83, 158
Reward 3-H	83, 158
Reward 3-I	85, 158
Reward 3-J	85, 158
Reward 3-K	87, 158
Reward 4-A	91, 159
Reward 4-B	91, 159
Reward 4-C	91, 159
Reward 4-D	93, 159
Reward 4-E	95, 159
Reward 4-F	95, 159
Reward 4-G	95, 159
Reward 4-H	99, 159
Reward 4-I	101, 159
Reward 4-J	101, 159
Reward 5-A	105, 160
Reward 5-B	105, 160
Reward 5-C	105, 160
Reward 5-D	107, 160
Reward 5-E	109, 160
Reward 5-F	109, 160
Reward 5-G	111, 160
Reward 5-H	111, 160
Reward 5-I	113, 160
Reward 6-A	119, 161
Reward 6-B	121, 161
Reward 6-C	121, 161
Reward 6-D	121, 161

Term	Page
Reward 6-E	121, 161
Reward 6-F	121, 161
Reward 6-G	121, 161
Reward 6-H	121, 161
Reward 6-I	123, 161
Reward 6-J	123, 161
Reward 6-K	125, 162
Reward 6-L	125, 162
Reward 6-M	125, 162
Reward 6-N	129, 162
Reward 6-O	129, 162
Reward 7-A	133, 162
Reward 7-B	133, 162
Reward 7-C	133, 162
Reward 7-D	135, 162
Reward 7-E	135, 162
Reward 7-F	135, 163
Reward 7-G	135, 163
Reward 7-H	135, 163
Reward 7-I	137, 163
Reward 7-J	137, 163
Reward 7-K	137, 163
Reward 7-L	137, 163
Reward 7-M	139, 163
Reward 7-N	139, 163
Reward 7-O	139, 163
Reward 7-P	139, 163
Rewards	146 - 163
Riot Shield	111
Save	7
Saving Grab	15
Secrets	146 - 173
Shogo Takamoto	173
Shotgun	38
Skip Cinematic	25
Special Menu	167
Standard Lock Mode	11
Start Game	6, 10
Submachine Gun	38
Subtitles	11
Super Actions	25
Swan Dive	16
Swimming	16 - 17, [71]
Swinging Moves	22 - 23
Targeting	30
Time Trial	165
Tokyo (Level 3)	76 - 87, 184
Tokyo Rewards (Level 3)	158
Tomb Raider I	175 - 177
Tomb Raider II	177
Tomb Raider III	178
Tomb Raider: The Last Revelation	178
Tomb Raider Chronicles	179
Tomb Raider: The Angel of Darkness	179
Toru Nishimura	173
Traps	33 - 35
Unfortunate Mishaps Video	167
Unlockables	164 - 170
Vehicle Controls	24
Wardrobe	148
Weapons	38 - 39
West Africa	see "Ghana"
Widescreen	11
Winning Tactics	26 - 35
Winston	172
Xbox 360 Achievements	170
Zip	172, [188]

Red (Secrets) = Strong Spoiler Warning
Green (Walkthrough) = Light Spoiler Warning
Secondary references are presented in brackets []

LIMITED EDITIONS

Since 1998, we at Piggyback have published four game guides each year. We see each new guide as an opportunity to produce the ultimate gaming companion for you. Creating an ultimate guide means we must spend at least six months in the development of each title. And if we want to spend six months on one guide then we must limit ourselves to a select number of gaming titles each year. Limiting our editions, so to speak. Here is some background on what we spend these six months doing:

1. *Build up and enhance advanced strategies*

2. *Refine tried-and-tested techniques over thousands of hours of dedicated play*

3. *Create quality maps with icons and diagrams to enable you to visualize all strategies.*

4. *Work closely with the game developers to secure exclusive materials such as superior game secrets and behind the scenes details*

5. *Design each page to reflect the excellence and atmosphere of the game for the true discerning fan*

6. *Develop navigational aids such as the back cover foldout or the three-level tab system that enhance the use of the guide*

7. *Quality control, detail control and logic control our guide content so that you know you can rely on Piggyback*

Here are some examples of the guides we have published since 1998:

Feel free to download sample pages of each guide at our website: WWW.PIGGYBACKINTERACTIVE.COM

*This title is available in PAL territories only